ADAMSVILLE-COLLIER HEIGHTS

e-Loyalty

e-Loyalty

HOW TO KEEP CUSTOMERS COMING BACK TO YOUR WEBSITE

ELLEN REID SMITH

 HarperBusiness
An Imprint of HarperCollins*Publishers*

Grateful acknowledgment is made to the following copyright holders for permission to reprint excerpts of their works:

Rick Levine, Mancala Inc., from "The Cluetrain Manifesto"

Vincent Flanders, www.WebPagesThatSuck.com, from *www.WebPagesThatSuck.com*

Michael Quint, MicroStrategy, from MicroStrategy print advertisement

Jay Perlman, The Motley Fool Inc., from "The Motley Fool Privacy Statement" © Copyright 2000, The Motley Fool, All rights reserved.

FIRST EDITION

Designed by Joy O'Meara

Library of Congress Cataloging-in-Publication Data

Smith, Ellen Reid.
    e-loyalty : how to keep customers coming back to your website / Ellen Reid Smith.— 1st ed.
        p.   cm.
    Includes index.
    ISBN 0-06-662070-8 (alk. paper)
    1. Customer loyalty.   2. Electronic commerce.   I. Title.

  HF5415.5.S59 2000
  658.8'12—dc21   00-040955

96 97 98 99 00   ❖/RRD 10 9 8 7 6 5 4 3 2 1

This book is dedicated to my parents

Lots of people say I'm lucky, but the only part of my success I would classify as luck was being born to such supportive parents, who gave me the foundation that made it all possible. The rest was intuition and hard work, also inspired by my parents.

Contents

Preface

was riding to the airport with a man who had just heard me speak on e-loyalty, and he asked, "What should I do on my website to make my customers more loyal?" I get asked this question all the time. The question is complex and impossible to answer in a short conversation. The problem is that most folks don't realize the magnitude of the question, much less the complexity of the answer. I turned to my new friend in the taxi and asked, "Do you want the ten-minute, two-day or one-week answer?" He chuckled, realized the ride to the airport was short, and said he would settle for the ten-minute answer.

Here's my ten-minute answer. First you must understand the importance of knowing who your best customers are, what they want most, and what they expect of you. Then develop your Web strategy as well as your Web design to meet the specific needs of your best customers. Developing a site to match your average customers will do just that: attract average customers. I admit that defining your best customer is easier said than done, and it typically involves looking at customers' lifetime value, potential value and value as an advocate of your products or services. Once you have tackled the best customer strategy, you'll need to have brilliant copy and provide immediate value to persuade your best customers to want a relationship with you. This will involve the skillfull collection of customer data and using that data to have intelligent conversations. If you're successful and manage to start a relationship, you'll then need to reward these best customers by giving them what they want most. This doesn't necessarily mean points, discounts or free items. It may simply be the most up-to-date content possible, formatted how and when they want it. Regardless of the type of reward used, the goal is to make the reward create an opportunity cost for defecting from your site. And, by all means, you better provide these best customers with services that demonstrate your appreciation of their loyalty. Provide the best service you can afford, and if you can't provide the best service for all customers, provide the best for your most valuable customers. Lastly, you'll want to maximize the profitability of all this hard work by generating incremental revenues from these best customers and convincing them to get their friends to try your website. Of course, you'll want to reward your best customers for their loyalty, and you'll need to use marketing partners to do that economically. But the true test of e-loyalty will be achieving all of this with a positive return on the resources dedicated to your e-loyalty initiatives. You see, it's just too much for a ten-minute answer.

In these days of Web mania, every website would have loyal customers if mastering e-loyalty were simple enough to teach in a ten-minute taxi ride. Many Web leaders are now realizing that keeping customers—not just acquiring them—is the key to profitable websites that stand the test of time. The problem is that achieving customer loyalty is tough work, and keeping customers loyal can be even tougher. Every day I see websites that throw together some e-loyalty "tactics," with no clue as to how to actually engender loyalty from their customers. It seems the "e" of our industry has gotten in the way of the "L"—loyalty. It boggles the mind to estimate the money that is wasted on poorly executed chat rooms, harassing email, forty question profiles and, worst of all, point programs so rich they inevitably bankrupt the site. These wet-behind-the-ears marketers (that's what my father always called them) strut their stuff, spending venture capital on expensive Web applications only to find they have alienated more customers than they had hoped would become loyal. I frequently hear these marketers say, "Email newsletters? Oh, we tried that and they don't work." Of course they don't work when you haven't asked for permission, haven't built value into the newsletter, didn't bother to personalize the content with relevant information, and failed to time its arrival to meet customers' needs!

The proliferation of poorly executed loyalty tactics is the result of overzealous Web application salespeople, preying on cash-laden website executives, who are hungry for the next big killer application. Selling e-loyalty tactics without strategy has become the norm. Amazon implemented product recommendation services not because it was the new rage but because its product category lends itself to relevant recommendations. Books can be more easily recommended than, say, clothes because of the similarity of topics and proliferation by single authors. The second reason Amazon's recommendations work is that we respect its knowledge of books. As Amazon branches out into toys, music and other product categories, it will be difficult for the site to convince us of its expertise, and its recommendations may carry less weight, not because its Web application is any better or worse but because we don't put credit in the company as a recommender of baby entertainment or training wheels.

When eBay amazed us with customer auctions, every site had to have one. It works for eBay because of the community it inspires and the power and independence the site instills in its customers. The auction idea is successful because of the "products" sold and community strategy that supports the auction application. It wouldn't work well for sites without an interactive community of similar interests and it wouldn't work well for perishable goods, clothes, or other products that are readily available at discount prices. The point is, it's not about the tactic, it's about the strategy. It's about the skill of eBay's marketers, who creatively used Web applications and tactics to simultaneously engender e-loyalty and create an opportunity cost for defecting. There are so many e-loyalty tools on the market that to assimilate them all into a toolbox would confuse even an experienced marketer. Sites like Amazon and eBay have carefully built a relationship with customers and selectively use the "right" tools for the "right" customers.

I once worked for a great loyalty marketer named Hal Brierley, CEO of Brierley & Partners, who taught me some great fundamentals of relationship marketing (yes, e-loyalty is all about relationship marketing, as I explain in part 1). Hal always professed that creating and sustaining customer relationships was both an art *and* a science. I cannot emphasize enough how true this is. For years I've watched frequency program service bureaus implement all the right loyalty tools without regard for the trust, respect, and honesty required to earn a customer's relationship. That's why e-loyalty is an art form. I've also seen companies with great customer relationship-building skills lose customers in droves when they had to dismantle a reward program for which they hadn't accurately forecast reward costs. That's why e-loyalty is a science. And the mistakes aren't just made by "the little guys." Industry leaders and Web gurus can also make the same mistakes. With enough money, any website can implement e-loyalty tools, but it is a true art to manipulate these tools into a relationship-building program, and it's a true science to generate incremental revenues by optimizing and rewarding these long-term relationships. The bottom line is: if you didn't build a relationship, you don't have loyalty, and if you can't prove your program-generated incremental revenues in excess of your program costs, the e-loyalty strategy was a failure. You can see why e-loyalty is a tough art and science to master.

This book is about humanizing digital loyalty by mastering both the art and the science of e-loyalty. It's about determining which customers you want to be loyal, learning the principles of developing e-loyalty strategy, selecting the best e-loyalty programs for your business, and ensuring your implementation plan is viable. Part 1 of this book answers some of the marketing riddles surrounding loyalty, retention and relationship marketing, and why you should care as a Web marketer. Part 2 outlines the seven steps I think are most critical in developing a successful e-loyalty strategy. Part 3 provides a road map for implementing an e-loyalty program and identifies the four biggest hurdles I find marketers overlook most often. Part 4 is intended for readers who are too impatient to get the strategy down first, or who believe they have a bulletproof strategy. This section covers what I have found to be the ten critical website design concepts for e-loyalty marketers and provides examples of a few websites that have mastered these concepts and some that still need coaching. (You can use these ten critical concepts as a test of your own e-loyalty strategy.) Finally, part 5 provides some e-loyalty resources intended to save you time and money. Here I also summarize what I believe will be the most critical changes companies need to make to keep their e-loyalty programs on the cutting edge and why e-loyalty will make or break the profusion of dot com start ups.

In an effort to demonstrate the e-loyalty strategies that I recommend, I have included numerous examples and case studies throughout this book. However, the major risk in including these examples and resources is the unbelievable speed with which the Internet changes and the excruciatingly slow process of getting a book published, printed and on the bookshelves. (I know, e-books will change all of this.) Inevitably, after this book has been published, a few of my examples of successful websites may not prove so successful due to failures in other parts of the dot com business. I can only hope that most of the websites I cite for not having successful e-loyalty strategies will have realized the error of their ways and rectified the problem. Let's hope they all prove me wrong.

I can't tell you how long I have waited for the Web to optimize loyalty marketing. I was a loyalty marketer before loyalty marketing was fashionable or even a familiar term. I was developing loyalty strategy when it was only acceptable to call it direct marketing. And I proudly held the title of director of relationship marketing when others thought it meant I marketed a dating service. During the past sixteen years, I've been on all sides of loyalty program strategy and implementation. I began my career trying to make soldiers loyal to government recreation facilities when the excitement of Europe enticed them to stray, and I convinced communities to love an army base despite the inherent problems a city encounters while coexisting with army base operations. Like most of the best loyalty marketers in the world, I cut my teeth on a frequent-flier program. Working first as an analyst on the largest loyalty program in the world, American Airlines' AAdvantage Program, I toiled away in an attempt to determine the loyalty and ultimate financial impact of multimillion-dollar program enhancements and partner forecasts. After working at American Airlines as a project manager, overhauling the largest point program computer system and database in the world, there isn't a point system or database architecture project that could challenge me more. And there isn't an industry or loyalty program type I haven't seen after years as a consultant for dozens of Fortune 500 corporations in every major industry. I've even solved my share of cultural marketing problems while developing international strategies for foreign airlines and hotels in the far corners of the globe—until I learned that international travel is *not* glamorous. I know the rigors and fast pace of developing e-loyalty business models and writing copy for dot com start-ups because I've pulled my share of all-nighters with their executives, who are out to maintain that all-important first-strike advantage. Now I own a successful loyalty marketing consulting practice, Reid Smith & Associates, and my clients count on me to develop e-loyalty strategy and programs that withstand the competition and the test of time. Because of my experience, I help my Web clients increase their chances of survival through customer retention and avoid implementation mistakes that I've seen others make.

This book covers the same steps and strategies that I walk my own clients through with each new e-loyalty design. And because my experience has taught me that there are no perfect organizations, much of this book deals with overcoming the limitations of your customer database, your unyielding organizational structure and your diminishing resources. This book is not an academic view of strategy but a tried-and-true account of what I know works and what I've seen fail over the past sixteen years. While I am able to cover most of the strategic points of designing e-loyalty programs, there is still much to learn and do. So, if after reading this book you find that you're ready for more of the hard sciences and humanizing factors of e-loyalty marketing, I invite you to visit this book's website at www.e-loyalty.com. There you will find budgeting, forecasting and point system models; ideas for building a business case for your loyalty program; as well as detailed implementation plans. And if you're searching for a list of companies that provide the applications you'll need to implement your e-loyalty program, you'll find the site particularly helpful.

Best of luck in all your e-loyalty ventures!

Acknowledgments

ur thoughts and achievements are shaped by those around us, and I have been fortunate to have been surrounded by some of the most intelligent people I've met in the business world. It would be difficult to mention everyone who contributed to my education in loyalty marketing. However, there are some individuals who deserve special mention. Diane Hope, one of the greatest professors, taught me the importance of combining psychology, sociology, rhetoric and marketing to truly understand how customers think and how we should communicate with them. Don Schmitt and my many other buddies at American Airlines helped me forge loyalty marketing strategies and measurement tools in a time when other companies couldn't even define their target audience. Susan Nelson, Richard Metzner, Howard Schneider, Hal Brierley and many other great minds at Brierley & Partners helped me hone my loyalty marketing skills. Lastly, thanks to Judith Remondi, who helped me "jump off the cliff" in order to start my own business, and to John Carter, who helped soften the landing by advising me during the transition.

This book really wouldn't have made it to press without the help of my publishing friends. Thanks to Jennifer Basye Sander and Peter Sander for making me get out of the grandstands and into the race by encouraging me to write this book. Without their help and insistence, you wouldn't be reading this now. And many thanks to my dear friend Chris Bailey, whose tireless editing and personal attention to my book was unbelievably helpful.

Many authors thank their spouses, and I'm sure most readers probably think it's merely an obligatory thanks. The truth is spouses take the brunt of the sacrifice involved in writing a book by putting up with late nights, months of antisocial schedules and urgent requests for the right word, creative thought or inspired editing. Many thanks to my husband for putting up with me, supporting me and encouraging me, but most of all for his inspirational pearls of wisdom scattered throughout this book, which can only come from a truly brilliant person. My admiration of his intellect grows with every year of our marriage.

PART

e-Loyalty
What It Is and Isn't

Where e-Loyalty Marketing Got Its Start

L oyalty marketing has become a worldwide trend in some industries. The reason for this trend is simple: intense competition for a larger share of an industry's best customers and the realization that share-of-market strategies based on advertising-driven acquisition programs do not maximize profits over the long haul. It has been a difficult lesson for offline marketers to learn. With leading dot com companies spending unreasonable proportions of their marketing dollars on advertising, and very little on loyalty marketing to build share-of-customer, it appears to be an equally hard lesson for online marketers to learn.

I'm sure you've heard it before but it's true, loyalty marketing all started with airline frequent-flier programs. But have you heard the rest of the story? Robert Crandall, CEO of American Airlines when the AAdvantage program was born, said he would discontinue the AAdvantage program if it were only possible. You see, once the other airlines matched the program, there was little loyalty advantage in just the miles. It was merely an additional cost of doing business. So, Mr. Crandall, being the smart man he is, had his marketing staff differentiate the program by adding elite tiers, which were unfortunately also matched by its competitors. Then customer services were layered onto these best customer tiers, and these, too, were matched. To make matters worse, American Airlines' competitors invited AAdvantage gold and platinum members to instantly become an upper tier member in their own programs. The one-upmanship was maddening. The frequent-flier wars continued to escalate with point promotions, redemption specials and additional member benefits. American Airlines, once known for developing the greatest competitive pricing software in the industry, had to develop the same rigor for monitoring their competitors' frequent-flier programs. What was the flaw in this strategy?

The programs were too easily matched by competitors. Are they effective today? Due to the high cost of launching a program, they are extremely effective in keeping new airlines from entering the market. But their real effectiveness is providing a reason for customers to be tracked so the airlines can target these customers with special benefits.

With accurate customer data the airlines are able to make better marketing decisions, improve forecasting and, most important, build relationships with their best customers to increase share-of-customer. Additionally, loyalty strategies that were developed to support the frequent-flier programs have been adopted by many industries. In fact, many of the best direct marketing techniques we use today—targeted marketing, personalized marketing and relationship marketing—were perfected by the airlines. That's why many of the Web marketing terms we use today, such as permission marketing and viral marketing, are tactics the airlines have employed for years, but have called "membership marketing" and "member-get-member marketing." But it wasn't just the science of loyalty marketing that the airlines perfected; they also perfected the art of building a lasting relationship.

Airline marketers are also leaders in some of the most profitable database mining techniques: database design and analysis, profile-driven communications and collaborative filtering. Because the airlines had some of the largest customer databases, airline marketers learned to "slice and dice" their databases, maximizing each direct marketing campaign. And to support these expensive direct marketing campaigns, the airlines turned their customer information, database skills and relationship-building tools into gold. There were years when the AAdvantage program was more profitable than airline operations due to the partner revenues and incremental revenue generated.

So it shouldn't be surprising to find that the leaders in loyalty marketing, database marketing and now Web marketing came from the airline industry. But before readers who work in the hotel, car rental and credit-card industries get too upset, I want to add that these industries—often working closely with the airlines—have also helped to perfect many of the loyalty marketing tools we use today.

Call It What You Like, but It's All About Loyalty

I t hasn't helped my profession that e-marketers use e-loyalty terms like we were all speaking a different language. I hear terms such as targeted marketing, relationship marketing, retention marketing, frequency marketing, loyalty marketing, database marketing and many others used interchangeably and inappropriately in documents written by marketing professionals and marketing novices alike. These terms are essentially tools and tactics under a big umbrella of loyalty marketing. But to ensure added confusion, new "webified" marketing terms like permission marketing, viral marketing, opt-in and personalization have been added to the e-loyalty marketing genre. At their core, all of these terms are marketing techniques, and all are used in loyalty marketing strategies to keep customers longer and increase share-of-customer. So why couldn't we just stick with the conventional "e" system that was working so well? The answer is that e-business, e-marketing and e-support have meaning for us. That's precisely why I propose we keep life simple and stick with what we know: e-loyalty. Once all the world is one e-marketplace, we can drop the unnecessary "e" and go back to normal.

However, before I "e-ify" everything, I want to get us all on the same sheet of music when it comes to using the time-honored terms of loyalty marketing. At the risk of becoming a lightning rod for controversy, I'm going to try to define the nuances of these marketing terms.

Targeted Marketing. Uses mass and direct marketing mediums to target different customer segments of the population using different communication messages. Unfortunately, this term has been rendered almost useless because old-school advertisers now use the term to mean buying targeted media rather than developing unique messages for targeted customer segments.

Database Marketing. Uses automation of customer and prospect information to generate the highest response rate possible through the constant closed loop process of trial, measurement and revision. While database marketing is at the core of most personalization and customization applications used on the Web today, it has an undeserved reputation for having been used only as an acquisition tool.

Frequency Marketing. Uses awards and benefits to reward customers who purchase frequently. The downside of this tactic can be that it rewards frequent customers who are not high-value customers, and does not build a relationship with the customer.

Retention Marketing. Uses advertising and public relations to remind customers to use a given product/service and explains why they should value continued use of this product/service. For companies that understand the value of metrics, this tactic typically focuses on churn rates. While retention marketing has the goal of growing the customer base by retaining customers, not just acquiring customers, it frequently doesn't include relationships or long-term reward programs. Instead it relies on advertising, PR and promotions to achieve "top-of-mind" placement in a customer's buying process. This strategy works well for product categories like cities ("Las Vegas: Entertainment Capital of the World" keeps this city top-of-mind when choosing a vacation destination) or food products ("Got milk?") where relationship marketing would be difficult given that there isn't a clear company brand with which to have a relationship. It's strength is in reminding customers of the product, making it top-of-mind in their buying process. It drives incremental demand and in some cases increases share-of-wallet by offering new ways to use the product. But it is not particularly cost-effective for branded products where the company knows the customer and building a relationship with the brand makes sense to the customer. For example, building a relationship with Heinz Ketchup really seems trivial to most customers, so retention marketing and brand marketing work well for these types of nonemotional product. This is why retention marketing is frequently used in tandem with brand marketing, and the two frequently overlap.

Brand Marketing. Uses advertising to build value and image into a product, service or company image that customers want to be a part of, want to belong to or, in marketing terms, want to be loyal to. Successful branding helps customers identify with a brand, want to be associated with the brand and ultimately become advocates for the brand (Polo, Tommy Hilfiger, Mercedes, Coach and Harley-Davidson all do this well by making customers proud to display the brand as a statement of who they are). The real goal of branding should be to build an experience around a brand (recently termed "experiential branding"). Mountain Dew is a great example of experiential branding, in that its commercials build a young, active, even daredevil experience into drinking Mountain Dew. You hear very little about taste in these ads.

One-to-One Marketing. Made famous by Martha Rogers and Don Peppers, one-to-one marketing proposes that instead of selling one product at a time to as many customers as possible in a particular sales period, you use customer databases and interactive communications to sell one customer at a time as many products and services as possible, with the objective of growing share-of-customer, rather than solely market share. For some companies, making true one-to-one marketing is too much, too soon, so they segment a market into very small groups, then tailor the marketing communications to those groups. Rather than trashing this adaptation of one-to-one marketing, I would applaud these companies for moving in the right direction. From my experience in mammoth corporations, being a change maker is hard work, and it's not always possible to take giant steps. What I do know is that the incremental profits driven from one-to-one strategies are so dramatic that encouraging management to invest in true one-to-one marketing, which builds unique relationships with each individual, becomes a much easier sell. One-to-one marketing is a great tactic for building relationships and, where profitable, should be included in all loyalty marketing strategies. However, I strongly recommend moving to a pure relationship marketing strategy, because companies that can make customers feel as though they "belong" to a program, exclusive customer group or merely a group they're proud to be identified with will reap the benefits of long-term loyalty. In my experience, telling customers that they will always be treated as individuals, that products will be customized to their needs and that all communications will be just for them, can easily backfire. It's a mighty tall order to fill consistently. A one-to-one company that falters because of a database glitch loses customers. On the other hand, customers who feels they "belong" to a desirable program/group are far more likely to be forgiving of infrequent database mistakes, because they *want* to belong, they *want* to be loyal and the opportunity cost of defecting is too great. (See the relationship marketing/loyalty marketing descriptions below for more on this concept.) As a matter of fact, a successful resolution of a problem has been proven to make these loyal customers even more loyal, because customers admire companies that will faithfully "right the wrongdoing."

Relationship Marketing, or Customer Relationship Marketing and Loyalty Marketing. Relationship marketing is as close to loyalty marketing as any other term I know. Like loyalty marketing, relationship marketing uses a formalized program to build customer relationships that can be cultivated to generate incremental revenues through a larger share-of-wallet. This formalized relationship could be a club, a reward program, a community-driven program or access to VIP services or benefits. A formalized program is important because customers want to be acknowledged and they want to belong. Additionally, because you can't have a relationship with customers if they don't want to have one, membership leaves no uncertainty as to whether or not there is a relationship. To attain this mutual consent typically requires a formalized program to join or in which a customer belongs. The act of joining, registering, and so on, is what consummates the relationship. Simply profiling on a website could be considered a relationship if the customer understands that by profiling, a relationship has begun (I'll talk much more about this in Steps 3 and 6 of designing an e-loyalty strategy). This is. what I believe to be the important difference between direct marketing (merely personalized communications) and a relationship. Where loyalty and relationship marketing differ is that loyalty marketing aims to take the relationship to a level where the customer is so loyal that he or she doesn't even want to consider competitors. The relationship is so strong and the loyalty so intense that the customer becomes an advocate for the brand and believes the competition can't be better, so they don't even consider competing brands. Few brands achieve this kind of loyalty. There are only a few brands which epitomize great loyalty marketing. Harley-Davidson,

with it's tattooed customers, tops the loyalty marketing list. Hertz maintains its best loyalty marketer status because even though it continues to charge more for the same service as its competitors, it clearly demonstrates the value of a membership program that customers believe is exclusive.

Customer Relationship Management. This term grew from customer relationship marketing, and was adopted by so many technology firms that it often represents only the "science" of managing customer interfaces and the management of the customer information generated by these interactions. Some companies use it to refer to database marketing that doesn't include relationship marketing programs. Most customer service companies define their companies with this term, but frequently their work is more about customer satisfaction than about building relationships. Other companies use the term to refer to the internal organizational changes necessary to make a company become customer focused. While all three uses include important fundamentals of loyalty marketing, they lack effectiveness without a loyalty strategy. On the positive side, some companies have used the term to refer to managing customers based on their value and the desired relationship with these customers— an extremely important part of loyalty marketing. But this, too, is the "science" part of the equation. With so much focus on the technical aspects of customer relationship marketing, very few creative agencies purport to specialize in customer relationship management, which is a shame, because it is the art of loyalty marketing that is the critical missing link in most customer relationship management plans. So while tactics of customer relationship management are important elements of a successful loyalty program, I'm afraid the term has been bastardized into a catch-all phrase.

Implementing e-Loyalty Applications Does Not Constitute e-Loyalty

n the beginning of Web marketing, e-loyalty was thought to be equal to bulletin boards and chat rooms, and the last time I perused my *Industry Standard* there were still companies advertising this promise. And for those sites led by Web art directors, the theory was that the cooler their website's animation (what I call "dancing baloney"), the more likely they were to have e-loyalty. The Web world thought e-loyalty was just a science because they failed to see the value of the "art" of e-loyalty. Shortly thereafter custom registration and email were the new hot tactics for loyalty. "Sign them up and deluge them with email" soon became the trend in 1998. So I wasn't the least bit surprised when the evangelists of trust and permission marketing became the e-loyalty gurus of 1999. Web users' distaste for spamming reminded marketers that just because you think you have a relationship with your customer, it doesn't mean the customer wants to have a relationship with you. In 2000 the rage seems to be point programs implemented with no loyalty strategy. Don't get me wrong. I have designed my share of point programs. So I endorse these e-loyalty tools when married with the right strategy. My problem lies with marketers' incessant focus on the tools and not the customer relationship—they focus on the science, not the art, of building relationships. This is the number one reason that many Web marketers miss their objective when it comes to making Web customers loyal.

Most successful online companies are pursuing relationships online, but are they really relationships? Just because you receive permission from your customers to send an email when a requested product is in stock, it doesn't mean you have a relationship. Just because I paid to subscribe to your e-zine last week doesn't mean we have a relationship. If it were that easy, you wouldn't be reading this book.

Building e-loyalty through relationship marketing is tough because it takes two consenting people to create a relationship. And all the wishful

thinking by your website marketing staff won't make up for an absolute lack of interest by a customer. The truth is that customers typically aren't that desperate to form an emotional bond with a database on a server. Sure, customers are willing to have relationships with a brand, a company and even a community, but they do so selectively, and only after trust and respect have been proven.

This book explores ways in which you can engender e-loyalty by creating relationships with your prospects and customers online. And by now you've guessed that I think relationship marketing is an extremely important element of e-loyalty, but e-loyalty isn't solely about relationship marketing, and the focus isn't limited to smart marketing concepts like permission marketing or one-to-one marketing. E-loyalty is about that wonderful moment when one human being reaches out and touches another at a level that actually means something. It's about humanizing digital loyalty. To achieve this is no smaller feat than painting that famous human touch on the ceiling of the Sistine Chapel. First of all, before you can even begin an e-loyalty strategy, you must first perfect your product, your Web execution and your distribution system. A bad first experience on your site can kill the millions you spent on e-loyalty. Several years back I was working for a Fortune 500 company to develop a customer loyalty program for a chain of eating establishments. We developed several program concepts and went out to research the ideas with customers. To our surprise we found that customers thought the retail locations were "dark, dirty and dingy" and the product unreliable. Their quarterly "satisfaction" studies hadn't picked up on this, because they hadn't discussed what would make customers loyal. Customers of chain restaurants want consistency. We told the client that before it instituted a loyalty program to fend off the competition's incessant couponing, it had to improve the environment and the product. The same is true for several unnavigable websites for which I have been asked to develop loyalty programs. The best e-loyalty program in the world won't overcome a bad website design, poor product quality or unreliable distribution.

You may think I'm making this e-loyalty concept into a much bigger deal than it is. You boast that you have 1 million registered visitors, and growth proves you have e-loyalty. But ask yourself these questions: "What's the churn rate?" "How often have they returned?" "How much time did they spend with you?" Better yet, "How much did they spend with you or your advertisers?" You don't have a relationship if customers don't return to your site or don't transact business when they do. Creating real relationships with prospects and customers online is the Holy Grail of e-commerce. And the reason is clear: real customer relationships that build e-loyalty insulate e-businesses from the competition because customers don't think they need to consider the competition's offers. In fact, they don't even want to. Loyal customers not only want to return to your website, they want to be associated with your website, and tell others about it. E-loyalty increases retention and boosts revenue per customer, which means getting a much bigger piece of each customer's lifetime value. The last time I checked, that all boiled down to increased profits and higher stock prices. Could this be why e-loyalty is all the rage?

The Youthfulness of e-Marketing Terms Inspires and Misleads

ne of my favorite things about the Web is the youthfulness that drives it. The rise of e-marketing has knocked stogy marketing terms out of the ballpark. However, taking their place are fun terms that are no less confusing than the original marketing tactics behind these newfangled terms. The following list defines the e-marketing terms most relevant to e-loyalty. If you are familiar with them skip on to the next section, but my guess is that many e-marketers would have trouble clearly defining these terms.

STICKINESS. Here's a term that causes real controversy. Does stickiness define number of pages viewed on a website, time spent on a website or frequency of visits to a website? I'll admit it, I'm stumped! To say a customer frequents Yahoo! just because each time his browser starts up it displays the home page for Yahoo! isn't really accurate. For most people, it doesn't constitute loyalty, in fact it often constitutes laziness—too lazy to change the default browser page. Or take my own viewing habits. I recently visited Pokemon.com and read all the associated pages on the entire site. It doesn't mean I'm loyal to the website, it means I am loyal to the brand, got my information and split, never to return again. A research study by Forrester Research, Inc., found that it is the amount of time spent on a site that constitutes loyalty. So does stickiness mean volume, frequency or duration? If stickiness doesn't involve a relationship, I propose it doesn't mean e-loyalty, and therefore is merely a part of our measuring system.

VIRAL MARKETING. This is my favorite. Leave it to youth to take one of the best loyalty marketing concepts ever invented (the member-get-member tactic started by the airlines) and slap on a phrase with the most negative connotation possible. I love it! This is a great new Web term for "advocacy marketing" or, as I like to call it, turning loyal customers into "brand evangelists." With viral marketing, you convince customers to recommend your site to their friends, and often reward them for doing so. The concept is old, but the tools of email marketing with embedded URLs have brought this concept new life and more profitable returns. I've even seen websites offer customers the choice of two or three email messages they can send as their own.

PERMISSION MARKETING. I can't tell you how important this concept is in starting a relationship. I know you're sick of hearing it, but the airlines started this concept by requiring customers to sign up for the frequent-flier programs. This was how the airlines got "permission" to track customers' travel and communicate with them about their personal travel habits. An important benefit of permission marketing is that you don't waste resources marketing to customers who don't want a relationship with you. In the "old days" we called permission marketing "the self-selecting principle," and others referred to it as "the hand-raising principle" because customers who wanted a relationship would "raise their hand" to be selected for membership or to receive communications.

CUSTOMIZATION. This is the new interactive targeted marketing. Customers self-select the targeted segments that appeal to them, and the communications associated with the selected segment are served to the customer. The messages aren't personalized on a one-to-one basis, but rather messages are customized based on target segments, of which the customer has selected one or more. Customization is a very simple technique that is frequently underrated in this age of technology one-upmanship. In simpler applications, customization can be just as effective as personalization in making content and e-commerce more relevant. What makes customization and personalization different is that in customization, the customer decides to be treated as others are in a group. In personalization, the content truly is personalized by the individual's preferences. A great example is that on Yahoo! you can customize your MyYahoo! page by selecting which categories of content you want. Then you can personalize your MyYahoo! page by indicating which specific news topics or sports games/teams you want to appear in the customized topic areas.

PERSONALIZATION. This is high-value, old-fashioned direct marketing accelerated into warp speed. Personalization is probably one of the best interactive uses of the Web, and will be the basis for more and more Web services that we grow to rely on. Customers can register and profile their preferences on the website, or in some instances simply select a topic or product. Based on this profile or selection, communications (content, advertising, suggested links, email, etc.) are tailored to their needs. Their responses to these communications are measured, and through continual testing of communications and the associated responses the predictability of customers' needs increases and communications become more and more targeted or more relevant. Typically this is done with collaborative filtering where all customers' responses are tracked and the aggregated data is analyzed to predict the next best communication. When collaborative filtering is combined with rules-based marketing, the individual's data is combined with the aggregate data to make communications even more personalized—and frequently more profitable.

I believe that if e-marketers understand exactly what e-loyalty tactics mean and where e-loyalty marketing tactics originated, they can learn, from history, the effective and ineffective uses of each of these marketing tactics. While I firmly agree that the interactivity of the Web and the new rules of customer engagement on the Web must change the way businesses interact with their customers, the rules of loyalty marketing don't change significantly—just the manner in which we implement them. This is why the Web industry is creating an enormous demand for skilled loyalty marketing professionals. Website executives now realize that the old rules of loyalty marketing do apply to the Web, and us old dogs can learn new tricks.

It's equally important that e-marketers understand the difference between tactics and strategy. Just as the clothes don't maketh the man, the chat application doesn't maketh the e-loyalty. As stand-alone concepts, these terms are not strategy. Frankly, I'm sick and tired of reading advice like "use a community to build customer loyalty," which oversimplifies the task of building relationships. Repeat after me, "Implementing e-loyalty applications does not constitute e-loyalty." Making your customers loyal to your website begins with a successful strategy that is implemented using a liberal dose of both the science (the right applications) and the art (the right content or offering) of e-loyalty marketing. It requires skills that can humanize digital loyalty. In fact, that's what the rest of this book will tackle: the appropriate mix of e-loyalty science and art.

Why e-Loyalty Is the Rage

e were all really excited when the wonders of the Web became real. The Web was going to allow e-businesses to provide customers with increasingly accurate, timely and inexpensive information. Unfortunately, this also meant that customers could immediately compare prices, bidding suppliers down to the lowest margins. The result: companies with a goal of simply selling as much volume as possible will be forced to do so at the lowest industry margins. To be successful, volume-based e-companies will always have to beat the lowest price of its most aggressive competitor—unless they insulate themselves with a customer relationship program that generates e-loyalty. That's the harsh reality of e-technology: all the tools that make the Web so great also make it hard to retain customers and be profitable.

The second harsh reality is that venture capitalists won't be satisfied with negative profits forever. E-retailers and content portals are now facing the true test of their business savvy: can they rein in their customer-acquisition costs and keep customers coming back for more, or will customers click over to the latest site that offers a good deal? Will their customer retention strategy work? If the answer is "no," these businesses are destined to hit the dot com scrap heap when the VC dollars dry up. A purely customer acquisition marketing model can't survive. And this is why e-loyalty is all the rage—you gotta have it!

While we look at all this technology as driving the next business revolution, the principles behind making customers loyal is not too different from when our parents were trodding down similar revolutionary paths forty years ago. Take the gas station wars in my family's neighborhood back then. It all started with one gas station and a friendly owner named Sam. The gas was average, the service dependable, but, more important, he remembered you and your children's names, and every now and then a piece of bubble gum would appear through the window to put a smile on your child's face. The relationship was friendly, reliable, thoughtful and rewarding, even when it didn't have to be. My father wouldn't consider buying gas anywhere else. Then the competition came to vie with Sam's gas station. First, a station across the intersection was put in. Then two more gas stations popped up on the other two corners. But we didn't pay much attention, because like lots of other customers, we had a relationship with Sam and we would be embarrassed if he caught us buying from one of those new out-of-towners. But then the price wars started, and finally our relationship with Sam reached its economic limit; we bought from one of those out-of-towners because the price differential was too great. There wasn't a piece of gum for me, but Dad saved money, so he bought a piece of gum when he paid for the gas. You guessed it, the out-of-towners drove Sam's gas margins to unprofitable levels. But there is an upside to this story. Sure the neighborhood and other neighborhoods started buying gas from these new gas stations running the price wars, but Sam benefited from this new traffic. You see, due to his relationship with his customers, they might be willing to buy gas from these out-of-towners, but when it came to service, they only trusted Sam to do the work. His loyalty marketing paid off. Because of the traffic generated by the new gas stations, Sam had more repair work than before and that's where the bulk of Sam's profits came from. The new gas stations continued their price wars, making smaller and smaller margins. They even tried reward programs: a free Dallas Cowboys glass with every fill-up. Wow! Dad could get a set of those useless glasses in a month or two; who cared if Mom hated them. But all these rewards were just short-term bribery because there was no relationship like with Sam.

This scenario is no different today. There are drugstores on every corner of the Web using price wars and point systems to get my business — but do they have my e-loyalty? Not if we don't have a relationship. Several drugstores, including Mothernature.com, PlanetRx and eNutrition, have won my short-term business with their sales and free shipping. But for health and vitamin information, About.com is where my long-term relationship is, because they have honest, unbiased and extensive information on a number of products I am interested in, as well as well-populated communities. Now, if only About.com would sell me my vitamins, or if one of these drugstores could harness the content found on About.com . . . You see, all these drugstores haven't made it progressively more valuable for me to return to their sites by building a relationship that includes an opportunity cost for switching to the low-cost providers. Likewise, none of these drugstores has ventured to ask me how much I spend at online drugstores each month; if they did, they would target me for share-of-wallet. But these companies aren't retention focused yet. They are still acquisition focused. And when the acquisition ad dollars run out, they will be forced to focus on me, the customer, to determine if they want to spend the time and effort to retain me. At this point, these drugstores will use their research, databases and Web technology to identify high-value customers like me, determine what my individual needs are and build a unique relationship with me through relevant, targeted content. Then they will thank me for my loyalty with targeted rewards that generate incremental spending in their online store. Yep, these drugstores are going to have to provide mass customized services, but if all their competitors also implement one-to-one marketing, then what? What's the opportunity cost of defection? It will have to be the relationship, and which drugstore won my relationship first. The drugstore that masters this technique won't feel the need to match every competing discount.

Here's the bottom line: e-loyalty is all the rage because it is the only viable way to ensure a long-term profit for e-commerce initiatives. And I emphasize *long-term profit* because, as we have seen, start-up pricing promotions can make a website's customer base soar, but if continual price reductions are required to keep customers, long-term profit is not easily attainable. The stronger the opportunity cost for defecting, and thus loyalty, the more margin protection a company will have.

The Really Scary Part

And now for the really scary part: it doesn't require a lot of resources to build a relationship program on the Web. Therefore, your smallest competitors are not only establishing relationship marketing programs, they frequently build better relationships because they are closer to the customer—just like Sam at my neighborhood gas station. The small guys know your customers and focus on what is most important to your customers.

Jaclyn Easton, author of *Striking It Rich.com: Profiles of 23 Incredibly Successful Web Sites . . . That You've Probably Never Heard Of*, identified a number of small Web players who were building relationships with customers with "small-time" sites but "big-time" strategies. It's not surprising that many of the websites outlined in her book are now in the big leagues, giving their once "bigger" competitors a run for their money. Take, for example, FragranceNet.com. The site almost thrives on its "small-time" look and feel. But the value proposition is big, the navigation easy, the customer service spectacular and customer loyalty is growing. The site was ranked number five in Patricia Seybold's "Top 10 Customers.com 1998 Holiday E-tailers" report, and has won kudos for customer service by leading business magazines. They do one thing, and they do it very, very well. The e-loyalty strategy was best value proposition (beat any price by 5 percent) and the best customer service. The strategy has paid off as the site moves from one of Easton's twenty-three sites most people had never heard of to the largest fragrance site online, with revenues growing at a pace that makes its department store and drugstore competitors wake up.

So you might need to stop looking to your biggest competitors for benchmarking your next marketing move, because it's frequently the "little guys" who really understand the relationships required for e-loyalty.

What Generates e-Loyalty?

THERE'S NO SINGLE ANSWER

Obviously, there is no easy answer to what generates e-loyalty. If there were, my publisher would just stop at this introduction, and we'd save some trees. It's different in each industry and for each targeted set of customers. E-marketers generate e-loyalty by painstakingly sticking to the tenuous process of developing loyalty strategy that builds a relationship with their customers. And most important, these successful e-marketers who have attained e-loyalty must tenaciously defend their customers internally as well as externally, because the push and pull of budgets and operational obstacles will inevitably cause their organizations to steer off the e-loyalty course by not keeping the customer relationship in the forefront of decision making. This book will walk you through the seven steps in defining e-loyalty strategy and then take you through some critical success factors as well as guidelines for developing and acting on an implementation plan.

But it should be noted that before you can begin the e-loyalty journey described in this book, there is a minimum entry to e-loyalty that is required of every website, regardless of business model or industry. This minimum entry starts by requiring that your website operate efficiently, that your service be dependable, that using the site be easy and intuitive. Though it sounds easy, not adhering to these three core principles has been the death of many great Web businesses with the first-strike advantage. When they failed on first launch, their competitors cleaned up. But given the limitations of this book, we'll assume you've hired the talent to ensure these beginning principles are in place. Now you will need to baptize these technological wonder kids in your customers' wants, needs and preferences. This group, as well as your whole organization, will need to think like your customers and defend the interests of these customers.

If there was one answer to the question "What generates e-loyalty?" it would lie in psychology and sociology, because the same values that make us loyal to another human being make us loyal to a brand, product or website. These values include:

- ▨ We want to be liked, recognized or valued.
- ▨ We like the way we feel when we are around that person.
- ▨ We believe the relationship will enrich our lives.
- ▨ We think the relationship reflects who we are.
- ▨ We trust the other person.
- ▨ We feel respected.

The first key to making this sociopsychology philosophy work on the Web is to understand that your customer is a human. Yes, you might have a business-to-business website but, underneath it all, humans are calling the shots. That's why I belabor the point that e-loyalty is about humanizing digital loyalty. Because the fact is, loyalty is loyalty, on or off the Web—it's about making people feel liked, enriched, smarter, respected, and so on. What the Web does for e-loyalty is make building relationships easier, faster and cheaper.

The second key to understanding this sociopsychological approach is that we all build personal relationships a little differently. First of all, the timing is different for different types of people—some rush in where only fools tread, others take it slow with seven-year engagements. The same is true for different types of Web customers. Gamers are quick to jump into a new game channel, but a bit slower to pick a news portal. A Web novice selecting a financial site for stock trades will likely take a significant amount of time testing and exploring to select a stock trading website. The timing is based on the type of product and the associated need for trust and the Web savvy exhibited by your targeted customer groups. Websites and customers require different levels of trust and therefore different timetables to earn that trust—you'll agree that's not so different from human relationships. The same variance is true for building different *types* of relationships—they require different intensities. Take, for example, the difference in intensity between professional, personal and sexual relationships. These aren't too different from the relationships we have with our dry cleaner, our dentist and our financial adviser offline and our bookseller, our health community and our stock portfolio and trading site online. The point is that we don't bear our soul unless the relationship requires it, and website relationships work the same way.

It all comes back to the infamous "dating" example I've used in every loyalty speech I've ever given. Scene one: A man and a woman meet in a bar. The man immediately asks if the woman would like to have sex. She calls him a pervert, and walks away—too much, too soon, and there's no relationship. Let's take that same example again at a different bar. Scene two: A man and a woman meet in a bar. The man immediately asks if the woman would like to have sex. The woman asks if the man has AIDS. He says, "No," and she says, "Sure." Yes, there was an "intelligent" conversation based on an exchange of information. Sure enough, what happened later that night had intensity, but whether the individuals had a meaningful relationship that could lead to loyalty is not likely. My point is that what generates loyalty in one bar or website is different for another bar or website. There is no panacea for humanizing digital loyalty. And if you take the aggressive approach suggested in the bar scene above, you'll not only have short-lived relationships but more likely you'll scare away your customers.

DETERMINING THE DRIVERS OF YOUR CUSTOMERS' E-LOYALTY

To determine what generates e-loyalty for your website requires research on the loyalty drivers common to your industry, specific to your product/website and valued by your targeted customer segments. E-loyalty drivers include tangible product attributes (price and quality), intangible attributes like style and experience and emotional beliefs like the "coolness" or prestige associated with your website or whether your website cares about the customer. Determining what the loyalty drivers are for your product or website can be accomplished best through qualitative research using moderators trained in loyalty marketing, and in some cases through quantitative research using loyalty models. In researching e-loyalty drivers you need to answer several questions to identify drivers.

1. *What website/product features make your customer revisit, repurchase or recommend your website/product?* First, be sure you know what e-loyalty is. E-loyalty must be defined in terms of positive behaviors such as revisits, repurchase, recommendations or active participation in a customer program; it's not just about satisfaction. One of the biggest mistakes I've seen is companies measuring loyalty in terms of satisfaction—many a satisfied customer defected to the competition. Once you've defined e-loyalty in terms of behavior you can start helping researchees determine what is driving those e-loyalty behaviors.

2. *What is the decision/buying process behind reselecting the product in question?* In other words, what factors, attributes, personal situ-

ations, and the like come into play when deciding to revisit, repurchase or recommend?

3. *What makes a customer consider or not consider another brand or buy your product despite it's higher price?* The best research subjects for this topic are your most loyal customers. Ask these customers why they don't consider other websites/brands, or if considered, why they continue to be loyal to your website.

4. *How do your customers feel about your website management or your company?* Do they think you are a leader or are the best in the industry? Do they want to be associated with your website because it makes them look or feel better? Do they think you care about your customers and are responsive to customers? To engender e-loyalty, customers must believe your website cares about them, and getting to the bottom of how they know you do care, how they know you don't care or why you're perceived to be the best is critical.

Qualitative research using well-trained loyalty researchers is the best way to determine these drivers. E-loyalty is a very "human" thing that isn't easily ferreted out of most customers using a laundry list of questions. Developing loyalty toward a website is typically a process, not a yes/no scenario. Most customers cannot clearly tell you why they are loyal; therefore, defining e-loyalty drivers is typically best accomplished through a combination of narrowing down the most important buying factors and exploring the emotions behind each. While I recommend qualitative research to identify important e-loyalty drivers, using quantitative research to prioritize these drivers can work well in most cases. One of the best quantitative tools I've seen for predicting the drivers of loyalty is used by IntelliQuest, a technology research firm now owned by Millward Brown. IntelliQuest's loyalty analysis uses customer research to build a model for each type of product or even multiple products within an industry. As an example, Intelliquest's initial qualititative research found that the three most common loyalty drivers in personal technology products were product and service quality (perceived or real), price (reasonable price as well as any opportunity costs for switching brands) and image (is the company a leader and do they care about their customers?). IntelliQuest then performed qualitative research on the many attributes identified for these four loyalty drivers in order to rank specific attributes that made up these three drivers, as well as the four main drivers (see diagram).

From my own experience in researching loyalty drivers in many different industries, I can attest that these four components of PC loyalty— product offering, quality, price and image—apply to many other industries, and certainly apply to websites and Web entities. However, before you think finding these four key loyalty drivers is the answer to your e-loyalty strategy, I want to remind you that your focus needs to be on discovering the unique attributes behind these drivers for your most valuable customer segments. Obviously these attributes vary for a given product class, but even within product categories you should find differences. For example, these e-loyalty attributes will vary based on your target

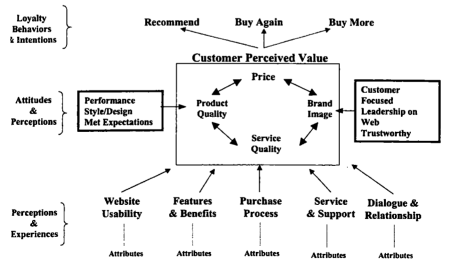

Source: Based on IntelliQuest's *"Customer Satisfaction and Loyalty Management Research"* April 1999

audiences, your brand image, your business model and your competitors' marketing programs.

I'm reminded of a consulting project I completed several years ago for an auto manufacturer that made high-end luxury cars. This company wanted a customer loyalty program designed around its most valuable customers, who they defined as affluent, executive males living in urban areas who valued technology and speed. When we went out to interview current loyal customers, we found that these most valuable customers were not only *not* male, they were middle-income females who weren't executives living in suburbia. And guess what? They cared most about style and accessories—mostly the makeup mirror lights. We scrapped our program concepts and started over because what we assumed to be the correct loyalty drivers wouldn't have increased loyalty at all. It was a valuable lesson in confirming target customers and loyalty drivers before designing e-loyalty strategy.

HOW TO MASTER THE ART AND THE SCIENCE OF MAKING CUSTOMERS LOYAL

But before I get this book and your loyalty strategy too out of sequence, I have to return to what I believe is the most reliable method for determining who should be loyal and how to generate e-loyalty. Develop your e-loyalty strategy by following the seven steps I outline in the next section of this book:

Step 1: Clearly Establish Your Goals and Objectives
Step 2: Identify the Customers You Want to Be Loyal
Step 3: Develop Your Website around an Intelligent Dialogue
Step 4: Design Your Website for Your Most Valuable Customers, Not Your Average Customers
Step 5: Formalize an e-Loyalty Program for Your Most Valuable Customers

Step 6: Persuade Your Customers to Want a Relationship

Step 7: Constantly Improve e-Loyalty by Listening and Measuring

After following these seven steps and having your strategy developed, use the second half of part III of this section to develop a viable implementation plan. In this section I discuss implementation plans for start-ups as well as established companies. And because any great loyalty strategy can get killed in an executive meeting, I outline what I have found to be the four biggest challenges to gaining the support needed to get your e-loyalty program off the ground:

Challenge #1: Integrating e-Loyalty and Adopting It as a Business Goal

Challenge #2: Gaining Consensus and Garnering Support

Challenge #3: Maintaining a Customer Lifetime Value Focus

Challenge #4: Appropriating the Funding and Resources Required

Finally, use part IV to test your e-loyalty strategy against the ten most critical e-loyalty design concepts to master:

Design Factor #1: Make Your First Impression Count

Design Factor #2: Make It Simple to Solve Problems

Design Factor #3: Design for Your Best Customers

Design Factor #4: Create Value and Engender Trust

Design Factor #5: Include Features That Start and Continue the Dialogue

Design Factor #6: Seize Every Opportunity to Build Community

Design Factor #7: Deliver All Parts of the Sales Cycle or Subject Covered

Design Factor #8: Provide the Best Service You Can Afford

Design Factor #9: Make It Easy to Recommend Your Site

Design Factor #10: Create an Opportunity Cost for Defection

From the process outlined in this book, you'll come to understand why e-loyalty is about humanizing digital loyalty by mastering both the art and science of building relationships online. And if you apply the advice laid out in the following chapters, you'll understand why e-loyalty is not a tactic, it's a way of doing business.

PART

Humanizing Digital Loyalty in an -Crazed World

ALL THE COOL INTERACTIVE WIZARDRY, DATA WAREHOUSES,
AND CUSTOMER LIFETIME VALUE CALCULATIONS IN THE WORLD
WON'T GUARANTEE CUTTING-EDGE LOYALTY . . .
IT'S UP TO YOUR STRATEGIC SKILLS AS AN E-MARKETER.

Buying into the Loyalty Mantra

Through years of consulting, I have learned that starting a loyalty strategy assignment before a company's executive staff believes in e-loyalty can be futile unless the program is projected to drive instant profitability. Many corporate organizations focus too much on short-term quarterly results and not long-term profitability driven by the economics of loyal customers. How many times have you heard, "Revenues are down, so we are cutting all marketing budgets"? It happens because the marketing department can't prove the return on their expenditures and, more important, because senior management doesn't believe that loyal customers produce incremental revenue and lower acquisition and operational costs.

Before a company can develop, much less implement, an e-loyalty strategy, management and all employees have to believe in what I call the basic mantra of loyalty marketing. This is why I start each client project by testing their marketing faith. I do this by covering the following relationship marketing principles.

It is more cost-effective to retain than acquire customers. Simple enough? Companies will not only spend far more acquiring new customers than retaining best customers, they also run the risk of depleting what can be a finite number of best customers in the marketplace.

All customers are not equal, and shouldn't be rewarded equally. This statement usually leaves half the marketing staff with dropped jaws and gaping mouths. Inevitably someone blurts out, "But, that's not fair!" Tough love worked on me as a kid, so I always respond with my mother's favorite comeback, "Life is not fair!" Let's pretend you're standing in a twenty-person line at the airport and one of those forever whining "gold" members gets into a separate line with no more than two people waiting—I know you've been there. Do you shout out, "That's not fair"? Of course you don't, because you know that gold members fly more, spend more and get better treatment because of their loyalty to the airline. You know the system works because as you're standing in that twenty-person line, you start scheming on how to concentrate all your travel on one airline so that you, too, will have gold member perks and get out of that blasted line.

Loyal customers are more profitable. Sure, lower acquisition costs mean cost savings, but companies with a focus on keeping their most valuable customers loyal also experience savings in customer service, customer research, product development, distribution and customer rewards because resources are spent only on customers with the greatest return. Savings and increased profitability are by-products of an entire company focused on loyalty as a driving business metric. And revenues typically are higher, too, because loyal customers spend more than average customers. This means companies enjoy a larger share-of-wallet per customer. Lastly, on a broader perspective, companies that focus on loyal customers find that when employees begin focusing on best customers, their operations become more efficient.

It takes two-way communications to build a relationship. I have heard some e-marketers profess that you cannot create a meaningful and lasting relationship without a conversation with a real person. I will admit that letting customers connect with a human being at your company will improve your customer relationships, but keeping these conversations to a minimum and ensuring that they always drive incremental revenues can be tough. If yours is like most companies, margins and limited resources prevent this human touch by phone. But it is possible to create lasting relationships with a website, a brand or a company without constant human intervention. Using intelligent agents, personalization techniques and cost saving e-support, an intelligent dialogue can be created and e-loyalty generated. The key is to demonstrate that you value customers' input by using their data to create an intelligent dialogue. An intelligent dialogue means that when a customer supplies information, you respond with more personalized service, products and dialogue. I'll talk a lot more about this in Step 3, "Develop Your Website around an Intelligent Dialogue."

Loyalty exists when there is an opportunity cost for defecting. This simply means that your customers must feel that they have to give up something in order to defect to the competition. Now most people immediately think the most powerful opportunity cost is generated by a point program because that is the loyalty tactic they are most familiar with. But in fact, high-value airline customers believe the opportunity cost for defecting is losing premier tier benefits—the miles are merely a measurement to achieve premier status. The strongest opportunity costs are customer relationships built on providing superior content, service and selection, and demonstrating trust that the company will always follow through and support the customer. The bottom line is that an opportunity cost is about what the competition doesn't have, so having an opportunity cost that is tough for your competition to match is imperative.

Short-term loyalty can be bought; long-term loyalty must be earned. Short-term loyalty is typically bought through discounts and extras like free shipping for a limited period of time. Long-term loyalty takes time because companies have to earn trust by proving value, dependability and respect. This process typically takes time because relationships require an intelligent dialogue with several exchanges of information or transactions. Naturally, the instant interactivity made possible by Web applications has increased the speed at which we can create relationships, but it has also increased the speed at which we can screw those relationships up. Customers may be quick to give you their trust, but even quicker at taking it away. It's not that free shipping for ninety days is a bad tactic—it frequently drives trials of long-term loyalty features—but it should be used as an acquisition tool and not as a loyalty tool. Besides, free shipping is too easily matched and not sustainable as a opportunity cost for defecting.

If you believe these loyalty marketing statements to be true, then you're ready to begin creating your e-loyalty strategy by working through the seven e-loyalty design steps I have outlined on the following pages. These are the same seven steps that I walk my clients through to develop an e-loyalty program. While seven steps sounds easy enough, I've seen companies get hung up on one or two steps for months. The reason this strategy can be so laborious is that it requires companies to clearly identify priorities in every aspect of their business. Companies that have a clear and unified understanding of their goals, their metrics and their customers have an easier time with the strategy. So while I have tried to simplify the instructions, take heart in the fact that most companies don't find this process simple at all.

The Seven Steps to Designing an e-Loyalty Strategy

STEP 1: CLEARLY ESTABLISH YOUR GOALS AND OBJECTIVES

When I start working with a client to develop a loyalty strategy, I always start by reviewing the website and marketing goals and objectives. I am continually surprised at how frequently executives can't clearly define their goals and objectives in having a relationship with their customers. Sure they know the revenue targets for the next four quarters and budget constraints by heart, but they don't empirically know what the relationship with their customer is all about. And this lack of focus stems from not having a company-wide understanding of what the *specific* business strategy is, beyond "make X amount of revenue" or "attain X percentage of market share." Although I am purposefully called in to develop an e-loyalty strategy, 50 percent of my assignments include clarifying the Web business strategy. Clarifying goals and defining the measurements of success are critical in determining which type of e-loyalty strategy will generate success. After all, how could I possibly pick an e-loyalty strategy of best customer service, or best content or best rewards, if I don't know whether the strategy is to create the best buying experience, become the respected knowledge expert in the field, or one-up a competitor's reward program? That's why I devoted Step 1 to nailing down this issue that most seem to avoid.

Clearly defining your goals and objectives for your e-loyalty strategy is usually easier said than done. I've facilitated strategy meetings where the client thought that scheduling sixty minutes for establishing goals and objectives for e-loyalty would be adequate—it never is. The debates that ensue from executives who thought they all agreed on the strategy are healthy dialogues, because they clearly identify a difference in each executive's interpretation of the corporate and marketing goals. So don't shy away from this exercise. Give it the time it deserves.

Frequently, this multi-interpretation of the business goals stems from a lack of detail within their business goals. Companies that still believe a mission statement on the wall of every conference room will keep employees focused are filled with hardworking employees that frankly work too hard trying to get consensus around vague business strategies. Generalized goals such as "retain customers" or "grow online customer base" don't provide the direction for a unified effort and just as important, don't allow employees to know if they are successful.

In 1999 *InformationWeek* completed a survey of corporate clients to determine if they had Web objectives and what they were. The answers were telling of a marketplace that is divided into two Web camps: companies with a "me too" approach to Web strategy and companies focused on the bottom line. Here are the survey result (percentage of companies with Web objective):

■ Create or maintain a competitive edge (90 percent)
■ Improve customer satisfaction (88 percent)

▦ Brand awareness (79 percent)
▦ Reduce operating costs (78 percent)
▦ New market channels (70 percent)
▦ Improve time to market (58 percent)

Based on these answers, where are all those companies that claim they are focused on customer relationship management (CRM)? How about the companies trying to become customer centric? I'm not sure where these companies are going with "customer satisfaction" as their objective because it doesn't equal CRM, and it certainly doesn't equal e-loyalty. For that matter, how come there aren't any customer retention or e-loyalty goals? And was everyone too afraid to list "sell more products and services" as their goal? What's this new Web contraption for, anyway? Not only do many Web initiatives fail to master the specifics, they have completely missed the biggest opportunities the Web makes possible.

The problem with the objectives in this survey, as well as most marketing objectives from which I am asked to create strategy, is that they don't really identify specific goals and objectives. Using the two examples below, I demonstrate how companies need to bring specificity to their goals and objectives before an e-loyalty strategy can be developed. As an added bonus, this exercise will also help focus employees and resources by making the definition of success clearer.

EXAMPLE 1: THE E-COMMERCE IMPERATIVE

Company goal: "Retain Web customers"
Why this goal isn't adequate: What does "retain" mean? Revisit the site, stay on the site longer or repurchase? More important, what quantity of revisit, surf time or repurchase will be considered retention success? Lastly, which customers should we retain? To retain *all* customers you must be all things to all customers, resulting in a dilution of your brand, product offering and communications.

Revised goal: Retain Web customers as measured in repurchases and increase share-of-wallet

Specific objectives:

- ▣ Increase second purchases by an average of 10 percent (by 25 percent from high-value customers).
- ▣ Increase number of products reviewed by an average of 10 percent (by 20 percent for potential high-value customers).
- ▣ Since the average customer spends X dollars per quarter in our product category, we want to capture 75 percent of this amount for at least 50 percent of our customers.

How these objectives might translate into initial e-loyalty goals:

- ▣ Go beyond the expected service level on the first transaction to create a positive impression and demonstrate value and reliability.
- ▣ Incent customers who have not repurchased within the average reorder time frame, and scale these incentives based on customer value.
- ▣ Ensure that all second-time visitors receive content personalized to meet their needs and that this content is embedded with relevant product recommendations.
- ▣ Because our research shows that our high-value customers generate a larger percentage of our overall revenues (e.g., a 20/80 rule where 20 percent of customers generate 80 percent of the revenue), develop an exclusive, formalized customer program to refocus retention efforts on lifetime high-value customers. Use this program as an incentive for customers with the potential to have high lifetime value to spend more on our website.

The second example below surprises many marketers because it is categorized as an e-loyalty effort, even though it appears to have an acquisition focus. The fact is, an e-loyalty program that creates a successful opportunity cost for defection typically also creates a great differentiator that can be used as an acquisition message. And since customers won't usually be acquired (i.e., register or profile) without an incentive to do so, a formalized e-loyalty program should be introduced at the time of registration to incent sign-up and subsequent sign-ins upon revisiting the website. Last, one of the most overlooked benefits of loyal customers is their ability to attract other customers like themselves. So building viral marketing or member-get-member strategies into an e-loyalty program can be one of the most cost-effective ways to attract prospective customers.

EXAMPLE 2: THE ADVERTISING REVENUE IMPERATIVE

The original goal: "Grow online customer base to support ad revenues"

Why this goal isn't adequate: To focus on total growth doesn't maximize resources and doesn't optimize revenue per expenditure. Chasing all the customers all the time results in average customers getting average—not customized—experiences. To communicate this point, I frequently twist President Lincoln's famous saying into a marketing imperative: "You can please all of the people some of the time and some of the people all of the time, but you can't please all of the people all of the time." Business models and e-loyalty programs that are based on this concept are successful because they have targeted their most profitable customers and have tailored their products, services and Web experience to please their best customers all of the time.

Revised goal: Increase the number of high-value customers who register and return to our site so that ad revenues can be increased 20 percent per CPM (click through per thousand)

Specific objectives:

▦ Develop advertising to target the values and needs of our high-value customers.

▦ Ensure 80 percent of our advertising is seen by customers who are likely to be high value.

▦ Increase site registration to 75 percent of visitors in order to identify high-value customers.

▦ Incent high-value customers to return to our website.

How these objectives might translate into initial e-loyalty goals:

▦ Develop a value proposition for registering that has immediate value.

▦ Develop a lifetime value model to determine key predictors of lifetime high-value.

▦ Differentiate website/brand and target high-value customers by developing a content/knowledge leadership position in the three subjects most valued by high-value customers. Ensure that this content is presented/organized in a manner most familiar/helpful to high-value customers.

▦ Stimulate return visits by high-value and potential high-value customers by developing a formalized communications program that focuses resources based on customer value (e.g., for subjects of most interest to high-value customers, spend more resources to personalize email content; but for subjects that are less likely to be of interest to high-value customers, limit resources to a more affordable customization email program).

▦ Develop a series of member-get-member promotions that reward customers proportionate to the value of their referred friends.

There are plenty of other common corporate goals that must be improved before an e-loyalty strategy can be developed. Here are just a few.

Inadequate e-Loyalty Goal ▦	Problem ▦	Improved e-Loyalty Goal ▦
Improve customer satisfaction	Satisfied customers defect websites every day. It takes more than satisfaction to retain customers.	Make service the differentiating feature that makes customers loyal or Make "100 percent satisfaction guaranteed" our promise to build an image and relationship that customers trust.
Immplement a point program to match our competition	Merely matching a competitor's point program won't engender loyalty; it will only level the playing field.	Develop a point program that offers unique rewards that will be difficult to copy (e.g., personalized reward charts that the customer builds; unique experiential rewards).
Develop an e-Loyalty program to create a new revenue stream from partners/affiliates	Without a strong customer value component driving this strategy, customers will view it as a come-on, and partners will drop out due to customer disinterest.	Develop an e-loyalty program that is self-funding by optimizing opportunities for partner-provided benefits.

e-Loyalty goals should be based on specific marketing goals and objectives. More important, when these goals are delineated into specific objectives, they need to be measured in incremental terms. For example, if overall revenues increase by 20 percent, but you don't know what amount of the increase should be attributed to e-loyalty efforts, then you could be spending money on an e-loyalty effort that doesn't have a positive return on investment. Therefore, if corporate goals are to increase revenues by 20 percent, then the loyalty program should be responsible for a designated portion of that increase. While I have seen e-loyalty programs treated as a completely separate, incremental target that is regarded as "gravy," I don't advocate this approach because it tends to keep the e-loyalty strategy from being completely integrated into the business. So whether the goal is to increase incremental customers, registrations, sales or advertising click throughs, you need to measure what percent of that increase was generated by your e-loyalty initiatives. Obviously the same is true for expenses; you need to understand what expenses are fixed, and which incremental expenses are directly attributable to the e-loyalty initiatives.

So far I have emphasized the reasons why business and marketing goals/objectives need to drive e-loyalty goals and objectives. In Step 5, "Formalize an e-Loyalty Program for Your Most Valuable Customers," I will explain why clarifying goals and objectives is also paramount in selecting the most effective loyalty program and Web applications. But before moving to specific program decisions, you need to know which customers you want to be loyal.

STEP 2: IDENTIFY THE CUSTOMERS YOU WANT TO BE LOYAL

Why the Old Ways of Segmenting Customers Doesn't Work
on the Web
Most companies can't figure out why, with each new change of management, the segmentation process changes. Generally, the process starts with a segmentation that matches the corporate organization. The old-school computer companies have been notorious for this. They manufacture a different sub-brand of PC for home and for work but sell them in the same retail store, as if customers of each segment are supposed to

know which PC is designated for home or for office. And customers aren't about to build a relationship with a PC company that keeps sending them office-related information for their home PC, and vice versa for their office PC. It's no surprise why the single-branded Dell PC is leading the industry. The old-school PC companies can't treat customers by needs, regardless of product purchased, because they haven't organized around the customer. They continue to organize their company based on retail versus reseller or preassigned home versus business products, even though the "business" brand is used in many homes and the "home" PC is used in many businesses. For this reason they create customer content based on which PC sub-brand the customer purchased, not his or her real PC needs. Banks and other industries can be just as guilty of old-school segmentation by not treating multiproduct users differently, or not recognizing loyal customers who have home and business accounts. Case in point: my bank still hasn't acknowledged, much less rewarded me, for having both my personal and business accounts with them.

In an effort to minimize channel conflict, some companies are dividing the marketplace and their customers into retail versus Web-direct sales. This might be tolerable as a temporary approach for companies that don't want to receive the brunt of disgruntled retailers by being the first manufacturer to turn coat by selling direct to the customer. However, it won't hold up as a long-term strategy. It's not a long-term strategy because it doesn't address issues or questions from offline sales, and it doesn't relate to customers with one consistent relationship. This is one reason a first-strike advantage by a pure-play, dot com start-up can be so powerful — they can master a consistent sales approach, speak with one voice and foster an all-inclusive relationship with customers.

Another primitive and usually ineffective Web segmentation approach is to view the world in geographical segments. Due to operational differences in PCs, IBM segmented its home PC market into worldwide geographical segments with autonomous subsegmentation within each country. While this foolish approach addressed engineering issues, the Web made it unworkable. Retailers and even customers from one country complained that it should get the same components, services or value adds that other countries received. Not only did it lead to disgruntled retailers and customers, it completely diluted and confused the brand message to have different brand positions in each country. The Web makes the world a very small place and won't be tolerant of websites that treat retailers and customers in various countries radically different.

A similarly disappointing approach is to assume that all customers who fit nicely into one of several given demographic segments will all want the same things. Ha! Rarely is this the case. It's even more preposterous to believe that strict demographic segments can be targeted segments for loyalty programs because it's our psychographics or emotional differences that drive loyalty, just like our emotions select and determine our personal relationships. Now some of you may want to argue that teen websites and seniors websites should obviously segment by age demographics. As an initial filter, I would agree with an age-based segmentation. But ask ThirdAge.com if all its seniors are alike, or ask Snowball.com if all their teen customers are alike. I know they will firmly disagree because their success is based on an understanding that all teens and all seniors are not alike. And not only are these teens and seniors websites offering different things in an online relationship, they have different financial values given their different website business models. Thirdage.com and Snowball.com choose e-loyalty tactics based on the needs and interests of their customers with the highest lifetime value.

Progressive companies that are trying to become customer focused often take a stab at usage-based segmentation where segments are created based on how customers intend to use the product or service. This strategy can actually work well on the Web as a quick navigation tool to find the right product to solve a given problem or to find relevant information about a product that was purchased. In fact, I always begin a navigational strategy by asking, "What problems are customers trying to solve and how can we solve them most efficiently?" So I would agree that there are real benefits in segmenting content and e-commerce offerings by intended use or the solution required. But to optimize profit, you must take this segmentation one step further and ask, "Which user group is most profitable?" Case in point: It comes as no surprise that the largest segment of online gamers is teenage boys. But despite its enormous size, it still doesn't always generate the most value, simply because this demographic segment doesn't have control of the VISA card. They may influence game purchases but their parents are making those purchases offline. Therefore, an older online gamer tends to spend more online, simply due to credit card availability. I think this will change as more and more kids get online "allowances" and more parents rely on e-commerce to simplify their lives, but currently the segmentation of teenage boys isn't the most profitable. That's why the optimum e-loyalty segmentation prioritizes customer segments by lifetime value, and while this may ultimately match one of the user-based segmentations, the critical difference is value—as in profit, not revenue. What follows in Step 2 is an in-depth discussion of this critical process of determining lifetime value segments as well as identifying in which value segment a new customer belongs.

But before you take this or any segmentation concept at face value, remember that you need to factor in your specific brand, product and corporate abilities. Case in point: When I first arrived at IBM's consumer PC division, the first customer segmentation filter was based on PC usage, but the fatal flaw was that they analyzed the most valuable customer by size of market, not by IBM's profitability per customer in that user group. Going with size of market led IBM to focus on a family and educational target audience and brand positioning. The problem was that IBM's brand didn't stretch that far in the minds of consumers—IBM was seen as a business tool, not an educational tool. Apple owned educational loyalty. Consequently the following year resulted in a loss of market share and diluted the overall IBM brand. At that time Abby Kohnstam, chief marketing officer at IBM, was running a brilliant Internet branding campaign for IBM, and the Consumer Division's decision to ignore this wave of successful branding was a fatal mistake. My point is that you should consider your own strengths and limitations when evaluating the value of customer segments.

Defining Customer Lifetime Value

To define what "best customer" means, you'll need to identify the difference in value between good, better and best. To determine this customer differential will require building a financial model of customer lifetime value. But the terms "lifetime" and "value" frequently stump many marketers because they have different meanings, based on your product and customer category.

CUSTOMER LIFETIME. Lifetime is relative to the product cycle. The lifetime for customers who buy diapers is initially assumed to be the years their child is in diapers. But to ensure you target future babies, it might be more profitable to assume the lifetime is the woman's childbearing years. Looking at single events like one child can distort this lifetime definition. The same is true for multiple PC households or corporations with more than one "start-up" operation. Your definition of customer lifetime should be based on product cycle as well as family or business cycle.

CUSTOMER VALUE. Base a customer's value in terms of profitability, *not* revenue. Basing customer value on revenue instead of profit is probably the biggest mistake I see in lifetime value analysis. Basing customer value on profit, you'll need to look at profit from three categories of revenue:

- Current value (should include all previous transactions)
- Future value (calculate future value based on current rate of purchase and on potential value if up-sold and cross-sold other products)
- Referral purchases (some customers have a greater ability than others to influence other potential customers. In some industries, a nonbuyer may still have high value because of the influence that customer/company has on others)

Creating a Customer Lifetime Value Model

Customer lifetime value (CLV) models are used to assign each customer a CLV index. This customer value index might be as simple as identifying high, medium and low value or, for more delineation, creating a percentile index using 10 percent increments (deciles). To be statistically significant, CLV models are built using a customer sample that is large enough and representative of customer types. Customers are then surveyed to determine lifetime value and identifying characteristics. These characteristics are then analyzed to determine which of the latter are most indicative of high value. If the model is accurate enough, the characteristics of old and new customers can be analyzed by the model to forecast their probable lifetime value. The complete process is described in the following section.

Step 1. Begin by conducting qualitative research to identify loyalty drivers for customers, and how those drivers differ by product usage or customer type. Based on the discussion of e-loyalty drivers in part I, remember that offering, price, image, service and quality are the four categories of e-loyalty drivers. The objective of this research is to determine which product/service attributes affect each of these four e-loyalty drivers and which of the four are most important. By identifying and ranking each attribute it will become clear which of the four categories are most influential in driving e-loyalty.

Step 2. Identify a statistically significant customer sample to be used in analyzing customer's value. Ensure you have adequate customer data on each customer in the sample. If the amount of customer data you currently own is limited, then you will need to buy and append customer data. Remember that the initial sample size should be large enough so that after a data append match rate of 50 percent or less, the sample is still large enough to be statistically significant in predicting customer behavior. This sample will be used to identify predictors of high CLV.

Step 3. Analyze transaction data for each customer in the sample developed in Step 2 to determine the value of each customer's purchase behaviors (e.g., past, present and future purchases and purchase amounts, frequency of current purchasing and potential frequency in the future). If you don't have transaction data, you'll need to make self-reported purchase data part of your quantitative survey in Steps 5 and 6. The purchase information will be used to place a lifetime value on each customer. To correctly define value, you'll need to assign a *profit* value (not revenue) for each product and service. If an exact profit cannot be assigned, then rank the products/services by profitability and assign a profitability value level to each. These product values can then be added as if they were actual profit figures for each product purchased. Customers can then be ranked by this profitability factoring much like above with actual profit data. After the customers are ranked by value, you can then index the customers into value indices. The only caveat to this value identification process is that some products have customers who don't rank as a high-value customers based on purchases, but who are extremely high value given their ability to influence others. So developing a profit value into your analysis that captures the level of influence a customer has on others' purchases is important.

Step 4. Next you'll want to develop customer value indices. Using your list of customers ranked by lifetime profitability from Step 3, look for obvious breaks or changes in levels of profitability. Indices can be as simple as good, better and best, or a more rigorous index can be created by partitioning the customers evenly over 10 deciles. By examining the significant variances in customer value distributions you should be able to determine the appropriate number of lifetime value indices to use, as well as the cutoff points for each value category.

Step 5. Use a regression analysis or neural network modeling tool to profile the customers. If you don't have complete demographic and psychographic data on your customers, you'll need to conduct quantitative research with each customer in the sample to determine factors driving purchase frequency. For example, frequency or size of purchase could be driven by demographics such as number of children, age of children and geography or by firmographics like number of employees, UIC code, etc. Psychographics or behavior could also have relationships to spending (e.g., lifestyle, changing jobs, how the customer uses the product, etc.). Once you have the customer profiles, look for common characteristics by value segment, or a pattern that increases with value. You need to use your modeling tool to quantify the importance of each characteristic and loyalty driver. The objective is to narrow down the characteristics and loyalty drivers to those that are differentiating, and which can be further analyzed through predictive models in Step 6.

Step 6. Using the shortened list of CLV characteristics/loyalty drivers identified in the descriptive model, develop a predictive model that identifies usage, demographic, psychographic and loyalty drivers that are indicative of high-value customers. The goal is to develop a list of data which can be collected from each customer and used to predict CLV value. Once the model is developed, it is tested against known CLV values in the research sample to determine the model accuracy level for predicting lifetime value. The biggest benefit of this predictive model is that it can help identify high CLVs without transaction data, and it can identify the most important data you should collect on your website to identify potential customers with high CLV. You will want to develop a second predictive model to identify the "triggers" for moving from medium value to high value. These high-value triggers may be obvious for some products, but others may be more illusive, and a predictive analysis of customer data which changes in relation to value can be very insightful.

Step 7. Once the predictive model is tested and put in place, it can be used to analyze each existing customer's data to forecast CLV. New customers would also be run through the model as they are acquired.

Step 8. Last, you'll want to analyze the loyalty drivers by CLV segment to determine what product/service attributes are most important to your most valuable customers. Once you have a list of the loyalty drivers that attract and retain high-value customers, you should use these attributes to drive site design, navigation, promotional copy, new content or features added and, most of all, which new products and services to develop.

This CLV analysis and model construction was once a very expensive and time-consuming task. However, with more data management companies qualified to perform these techniques and greater availability of inexpensive modeling software, these services are easier to find and now cost a fraction of the price charged five years ago. For resources on CLV modeling, check our website at www.e-loyalty.com.

The Four W's of Getting to Know Your Customers

Many times, marketers are quick to lump data collection into the "science" bucket of e-loyalty. With so much computer programming, relational database architecture and quantitative reporting required, perfecting data collection does require a good deal of "science." But the true "art" to collecting data comes from using creative techniques to identify the targeted customers and persuading these customers to provide data about themselves. Because some Web marketers have abused the privilege of hosting customer data by selling or giving it to partners, persuading customers to profile on a website has become even harder. The art of data collection also includes analyzing your Web data to determine what customers are thinking now and what they will do next.

To make this discussion easier, I have grouped the many techniques you'll need to use in collecting customer data into four basic areas. I developed these four categories because these are the four principle planning decisions you'll need to make before developing a customer data collection strategy that supports your customer lifetime value modeling and targeting efforts. The four principle planning decisions include:

- Who should you collect data from?
- Where will you find the right customers?
- When do you ask for data?
- What data should you collect?

I call these four principles "the four W's for getting to know your customers." The reason I include the four "W's" of data collecting techniques in this section is that in order to identify the customers you want to be loyal, you will need to collect the right data from them.

The first W: Who should you collect data from?

It might surprise you that I have to continually point out to e-marketers that "you can't have a relationship if you don't know who your customers are." Most companies underestimate the amount of resources needed to identify which customers they want to be loyal. And to truly understand your customers requires primary research. So don't let the quick-fix appeal of industry reports suck you into believing that numbers can tell you all you need to know about your customers.

Remember the example I used in part 1 where the luxury automaker almost based an entire loyalty program design on the wrong target customers? The auto manufacturer wanted a customer loyalty program designed around its most valuable customers, which they defined as affluent, executive males living in urban areas who valued technology and speed. Only our own research found the loyalists to be middle-income females, who weren't executives living in suburbia at all. Our ill-defined target customer segments would not only have targeted the wrong audience, we would have missed these women's loyalty drivers of style and accessories. If you use published reports of aggregated demographic data on Web users to drive your selection and understanding of your target audience, you won't be much better off than the aforementioned car manufacturer.

You will need to collect a minimal amount of data from every visitor to your website to determine if that visitor could be a potential customer, and more important a high-value customer. This list of minimal data that must be collected will be determined by your predictive CLV model (described above). The model will identify the customer data that is most predictive of high value. The only drawback is that a visitor will be turned off or discouraged if you ask for too much information (for more on this see *when* and *where* below). Therefore, you need to determine the "first filter" in your predictive model that can separate the potential customers from those with no potential. For example, assume your website sells baby clothes and toys. You will want to know from visitors what their connection with babies is: whether they have a baby, are about to have a baby, or are grandparents or caregivers. Then you might decide to reward the potential high-value visitors with a baby gift for completing a more lengthy profile (the gift also acts as a screener of value) in order to collect the data needed to identify actual or potential high CLV.

The second W: Where will you find the right customers?

We all know that "build it and they will come" doesn't always work on the Web. So you will need to drive customers to your website. The question is: "Where are your high-value customers?" And just as important: "How do you get them to your website?"

If you are a direct marketer, you may already know your customers; that is, have an address for them. Or you may run enough sweepstakes that you have a fair number of customer addresses on file. For customers with known addresses (mail or email), contact them directly and give them an incentive to visit your Web site.

If your product is sold through retailers/resellers or your product is new, and you don't know who your customers are, you will first need to do a customer lifetime value analysis. You will need demographic and psychographic data on your high-value customers to ensure that whatever type of advertising or marketing tactics you use to attract customers to your website, you have selected communication vehicles that accurately target a large share of your high-value customers in a cost-effective manner. Though the research to analyze which types of customer will become your best customers is expensive, using mass advertising to blanket a universe of potential and nonpotential customers is even more expensive. Nevertheless, the cost of identifying existing or potential customers through polling may be high for obscure products, so keep the scope of this analysis to the smallest sample necessary to be statistically significant. Once you know the characteristics of your high-value customers, you will need to use multiple communication tactics for making customers aware of your website.

MASS ADVERTISING. This costs a bundle, and for the most part is not cost-effective. Being a direct marketer by trade, I tend to advocate the use of mass advertising, but only in a targeted manner. That is, only advertise via communication vehicles—magazines, newspapers sections, television shows, and the like—that are targeted to your best customers and which they are known to frequently see, read or use.

BANNER ADS. The value of banner ads is highly debatable. But on several points most Web advertisers agree: that a banner should appear only on websites your customers frequent, that the banner should be targeted on the website by locating it next to content that your target audience is most interested in, and that the banner message itself needs to be targeted to your customers—not just product specific. The tighter the focus of the website on which your banner appears and the tighter the message on your banner, the higher the likelihood of your target audience clicking on the banner. Promotions and sweepstakes used in conjunction with a banner advertisement can increase the click-through rate, but only if your target audience is attracted by these types of promotions and only if the prize/reward is very targeted to the interests of your target groups. If your target audience is multifaceted, with differing interests, it might pay to run multiple targeted promotions rather than one big generic promotion. The exception to this rule is the "bonanza" prize scenario where the prize is so great it appeals to all customer segments.

LINKS ON RELATED PRODUCT SITES. Embedded links from a related product site is one of the best ways to target your potential customers. For example, if your product is software, a link from a PC e-commerce or self-help page has a higher response rate per thousand than a generic portal. The tightness of the product-content relationship, the visibility of the content within the embedded link and the value of the content containing the embedded link are all important factors in increasing response rates.

PRODUCT PACKAGING. Including a website URL on all product packaging and marketing materials is a "no brainer" for most of us, but I consistently find product packaging and marketing that forgot to include the website URL.

The third W: When do you ask for data?

While designing websites driven by customer profiles is getting easier, persuading customers to profile is getting more difficult. Collecting too much information creates distrust. Asking for personal data too soon is a turnoff. For starters, here are some fundamental factors that should help answer the big question of *when* you should ask for data:

▦ After you have demonstrated the value of providing the information
▦ After you have stated how the information is to be used

- ▦ After you have made your privacy policy easily accessible and easy to read
- ▦ After you have established trust
- ▦ After you have maximized data collection points

Demonstrate Value. There are many ways to demonstrate the value of registering on a site or providing personal information. Take, for example, the websites with a well-known reputation for content like the *New York Times*. The *New York Times* could easily require a sign-in prior to trial of the site because it doesn't need to demonstrate the value of its content. However, the site currently doesn't require me to sign-in until I want to interact with the site, such as posting a comment to a forum. The site waits for me to see something of value that I want, then requires registration to get it. On the other hand, there are many less-popular e-zines (Web-based magazines) that require registration prior to accessing content, which usually results in me bypassing the website because I'm not sure what value there is in taking time to profile myself. These lesser-known content sites must demonstrate value by showing the topics covered, listing articles, advertising the caliber of their writers, providing sample content and so on before asking for registration.

The value of supplying the information is normally a two-tier process. Value is initially communicated by the general value proposition for the entire site; for example, the biggest selection, the coolest, the best service, the cheapest prices, the most authoritative. The second-tier value proposition includes specifically outlining the value of providing information. A registration value proposition might be the ability to customize the look and feel, personalize content, receive free stuff or receive notifications, etc. However, the registration value proposition must be clear before you will convince visitors to link to the registration page. For example, a major pet supply website recently had a boxed phrase prominently located on the top of their vertical navigation column on the home page that read, "Join Today! Membership is free and easy. Join today and take full advantage of member benefits!" That was all it said! There was no "club" name like "Frequent Buyer Club" or any benefit mentioned that might give me an indication of what this whole membership thing was about. Why would I bother to click on an invitation to join, when I haven't the foggiest idea what I was joining, much less what the value would be to me? Upon clicking to the sign-up page for this pet site, I wasn't given any more details except that I would enjoy the club's "benefits." The point is that the value proposition for joining or simply registering needs to be blatant to be successful. MyPoints.com does a good job of this by placing the following copy in ad boxes that link from client sites to the MyPoints.com registration page:

> *Let the Internet Reward You!*
> *With MyPoints®, you earn Points for great rewards simply by reading email, shopping online, touring web sites and more. And it's free!*

Many websites have increased registration volume by giving free products for registering, but the customers typically join for the wrong reasons. These websites generate many visitor registrations that will never materialize into customers because the visitor is simply looking for the next free offer. The reason for this lies in my proposition that the Web is merely a tool for digitizing loyalty, but regardless of the tool, loyalty is about a human relationship. So just like any other human-to-human relationship, Web bribery sometimes works to start a relationship, but beginning a relationship with a bribe doesn't bode well for the longevity of the relationship and typically lowers expectations for trust and mutual respect. It goes back to my bar example to demonstrate e-loyalty relationships as being no different from starting relationships in a bar: some women or men will take money for starting a relationship, but is it really a true relationship or just a onetime sale? When a website pays a visitor to register, the value proposition is not that of the website in general. If a website value proposition is "largest selection," then the value proposition for registering should be a personalized list of books on the customer's favorite book topic that is larger than any other website. There are a couple of exceptions to this rule. One is when a site like iWin.com has a value proposition of giving away free money. In this case giving cash for registering fits the value proposition and attracts the targeted customer. Another exception is when a site's value proposition *is* earning a currency, such as points for transactions. For point-oriented websites, giving points for registering can be very effective because the act of opening a point account and earning your first points gives customers a taste of the relationship being offered. But I want to point out that this doesn't work when a website gives an unrelated currency like MyPoints for registering, but doesn't offer MyPoints for transactions.

State How Information Is to Be Used and the Privacy Policy. To engender trust, websites should be up front about how the registration information is to be used. This means putting information intent at the top of the registration form rather than at the bottom. The statement should include tracking intentions as well as your intentions for customization and personalization of content. When crafted by skilled writers, this statement should be positively viewed by the customer because it also explains how the customer will benefit from the improved online experience available only with customer data. Being honest and forthcoming about how information will be used typically leads to better information capture—that is, unless the intended use is somewhat suspect. Obviously being honest and up front about selling customer data will lead to fewer registrations being completed.

Stating how customer information will be used is slightly different than a privacy policy. A privacy policy typically contains a promise that the website will not sell or give away customer data without permission from the customer. The statement of how information is to be used only addresses internal uses of the data. Like information usage statements, privacy policies should be easy to find and, more important, easy to understand. Three pages of legal jargon will only serve to make customers more skeptical. One of the best privacy and information usage statements I've read is on Motley Fool (www.fool.com). It is prominently listed on the registration page and encourages visitors to read it by stating, "Concerned about your privacy? So are we! Click here to read our Privacy Statement." The Privacy Statement is easy to read, friendly and persuasive but at the same time covers the legal bases to protect the Motley Fool website. As usual, the Motley Fools are no fools at all, because they are explicit on how they use data, giving examples that even webophobics can understand and trust. (See the following sample from the Motley Fool privacy statement.)

Will The Motley Fool Disclose Any of Your Personal Information?

The Motley Fool will not disclose any information about individual users, except as described in this Privacy Statement, or to comply with applicable laws or valid legal process, or to protect the rights or property of The Motley Fool. We do not give, rent, lend, or sell individual information to our advertisers, only aggregate information. For example, we might tell advertisers that there are 120,000 Registered Fools in Metropolis, but we won't tell them that Superman is one of them, and we won't tell them that his email address is ckent@dailyplanet.com. We may also use this aggregated information to help the advertisers reach the kind of audience they want. Advertisers may give us an ad and tell us the type of audience they want to reach (for example, males in the 22314 zip code). The Motley Fool would then take the ad and display it to users who've told us they meet those criteria. In this process, the advertiser never has access to individual account information. Only The Motley Fool has access to individuals' accounts.

We may also disclose aggregate information (for example, 35 million of our readers clicked on a message board advertisement last month) in order to describe our services to prospective partners, advertisers, and other third parties, and for other lawful purposes.

> If you use our recommendation service to email one of our arti-
> cles to a friend, The Motley Fool will automatically send this per-
> son a one-time email, attaching the recommended article. Your
> email address will appear on the "From" line of this email,
> thereby disclosing this information to whoever opens and reads
> the email.
>
> We may disclose personal information in some limited circum-
> stances, but we will specifically describe them to you when we
> collect the information, such as in the rules of a sweepstakes or
> some new service. For example, if we're going to give personal
> information to the sponsor of a contest, we'll tell you that before
> you sign up for the contest, so that you can decide whether or not
> to enter.

Establish Trust. Much like the *New York Times* brand brings an immediate value proposition to its online presence, Fidelity.com enjoys an
immediate level of trust on its website. However, even though the
Fidelity brand has some degree of instant trust, Fidelity works to build
trust on its website through assurances for its trading and account tools as
well as its privacy policies. For websites without a well-trusted brand, a
great first step in establishing trust is to use a privacy policy review service
like Trust-e. But the Trust-e logo alone will not engender the degree of
trust needed to form a trustworthy relationship that leads to e-loyalty. The
e-commerce and application safety measures as well as the overall tone
must demonstrate that the website cares about each individual customer.
The trust factor is an important attribute of the e-loyalty driver "image."
Your company must earn the image of trust to engender e-loyalty based
on image. Being a proactive leader in online privacy is a proof point for
customers that you respect their rights and will in turn engender trust—a
critical element in building a relationship. This can be particularly
important for children's sites where collecting information from children
without parental consent is not allowed. Hasbro's Tiger Toy Federation

(tiger.com) and Hasbro Interactive's website does a good job of building trust by sensibly addressing children's privacy.

One of the best websites to study for engendering trust is eBay. eBay built a number of features into its site that it collectively calls the "SafeHarbor." Building security and reliability into online trades with total strangers that a customer will never meet eyeball-to-eyeball is the linchpin of eBay's success. One of its SafeHarbor tools is to keep track of all trade transactions by user name, and provide an opportunity for buyers to post feedback against a seller's user name. The site's customers now highly value positive feedback because it increases their ability to sell in the future. Thus the trust building tool becomes a loyalty tool because sellers don't want to switch to another site if they have numerous positive comments in their profile. Trust has become an opportunity cost for leaving eBay—it's a brilliant feat of e-loyalty strategy. Other eBay trust tools include verification of eBay user, the Feedback Forum, Insurance and Authentication and Grading.

Maximize Data Collection Points. To maximize your data collection opportunities, collect data at every customer touch point—online and offline.

Online customer touch points include:

- Registration
- Sweepstakes and other promotions requiring customer data
- Transactions (purchase or request for data)
- Sign-ups (newsletters, email notifications, samples, coupons, partner offers, etc.)
- Customer profiles or user preferences
- Customer surveys (research related and entertaining content surveys)
- Customer service
- Entering and exiting URLs (URL linking to site, and link/entered URL to leave site)
- Web log files: pages viewed, categories searched, links clicked, etc.

Offline customer touch points include:

▦ Customer service by phone, entered in database
▦ In-store transactions and surveys
▦ Paper submissions (sweepstake or promotion entries)

The most important data collection point is the initial registration. Many times this registration process is more important than a first transaction, in that the act of registering indicates a customer wants to start a conversation or a relationship and that he or she is giving you "permission" to begin this process. If the right data is collected that can make the first and subsequent conversations exceed the visitor's expectations, it will go a long way toward building e-loyalty. And ensuring that you allow customers to update and modify their own profiles will not only keep the customer information up to date but will also engender more trust because customers know what information is kept online.

Perhaps you don't have a solid value proposition for registering or, because of the nature of your product, registration is unlikely. One of the second most effective ways to gather data is when you don't ask the customer for any information at all. Many successful websites use cookies and unique identifiers to make collecting customer-specific data seamless for the customer. Some of the Web tools for collecting customer navigation data include:

▦ Dumb cookies—cookie placed each time guest visits site to track one-time visits. Cookie counts can also indicate number of visits
▦ Intelligent cookies—unique cookie tied to a visitor ID on database allows websites to track and analyze visits to better target ads and promotions based on previous navigational preferences.
▦ Customer user names or passwords provided upon sign-in.
▦ Session IDs stored in URLs that are bookmarked and reused by the customers.

The fourth W: What *data should you collect?*

The three most important questions that drive "what" data you should collect are:

- ▨ What is the most important content to customize/personalize to drive e-loyalty?
- ▨ What types of data are needed to stimulate transactions and predict lifetime value?
- ▨ What data is needed to measure the profitability of your business model or fulfillment of your value proposition?

Customize/Personalize Valued Content. What you customize and personalize on your website should be driven by the e-loyalty drivers ranked highest by your high-value customers. For example, if loyalty to your website, product category or brand is most influenced by the offering, you would need to know certain demographics, psychographics and/or purchase preferences about a person to customize messages regarding your offering. By customizing/personalizing the offering messages, the messages will have relevance and a higher appeal to each customer or customer type. This is not to imply that you must always change your offering, but tailoring the language and emphasis of factors can make all the difference. For example, one of the e-loyalty drivers for Amazon is offering the largest selection of books. This e-loyalty driver was so important that they built their brand on the concept—that was smart! But this offering is only relevant if the website carries a large assortment of the books in a customer's specific area of interest. This is why Amazon collects data on book preferences for each customer and customizes recommendations, ads and referral lists that reflect specific book interests. This in turn demonstrates Amazon's large assortment of books in each customer's preferred book category. The e-loyalty fundamental of product offering, as demonstrated by the attribute of "large book selection," was established and then customized for emphasis, driving a deeper customer belief in this important e-loyalty driver.

The four categories of loyalty driver I discussed in part I were offering, quality, price, and image. After completing the e-loyalty driver research—which was described in the customer lifetime value modeling techniques covered earlier in this section—you should know which of these categories and relevant attributes are most important in driving e-loyalty to your website. I realize that by insisting on these predictive models I risk sounding like a research nerd, but look at it this way: without research, you could base your assumptions for e-loyalty drivers on trial and error. And if you guessed wrong, the warp speed of the Internet would give you digital whiplash, from which it might take months to recover. A smarter approach would be to spend a few weeks researching and analyzing customer loyalty factors, with the likelihood of engendering loyalty the first time increased by multiples of 100 percent.

Stimulate Transactions and Predict CLV. Even if you are a nonprofit website, you want to stimulate transactions of information on your website. So whether the transactions are informational, economic or even ecumenical in nature, you will want more of them. Collecting data that will enable you to stimulate these transactions and this increased interaction with the site improves your ability to build e-loyalty. The same is true for customer lifetime value. Even if you run a nonprofit site, you may want to rank visitors by level or kind of need—much like a triage process—and offer different services based on need or severity of need. So while my examples of transactions and customer value may sound profit oriented, they are equally adaptable to non-profit sites as well.

Stimulating transactions is both an art and a science. The "art" refers to the personalized customer experience possible only through the collection of customer data. The "science" is less customer-data intensive and refers to the Web applications that make the interactive experience seamless. Although this section is about what data should be collected to stimulate transactions, it would be shortsighted not to address the importance of mastering the science of transaction technology before you can improve the art of stimulating transactions. What follows is a short list of the most critical technical factors that must be in place before you can begin finessing your site with artful stimulation techniques.

- A navigational hierarchy that is intuitive to understand and easy to use
- A better than "good" search engine that has the intelligence to correctly narrow down a search, ascertain misspelled words, assume dual meanings and understand subsets of topics
- Tools for referring customers to complimentary content/products
- Back-end technologies that make using the content or e-commerce functions reliable and trustworthy
- Fast page loads that make transactions quick

With critical website technologies mastered, you can start increasing transactions by customizing/personalizing content to stimulate transactions. Once again, determining the predictors of customer lifetime value is frequently the most effective method for determining the factors that stimulate transactions. For example, if the number of employees in a business is directly related to customer lifetime value for your website, then determining how many employees a customer has and tailoring messages, discounts, and product selection based on the size of a company's employee base makes good sense. If the employee size was critical to stimulating transactions, you might need to customize the entire site navigation based on the size of a company's employee base. This customized navigation would also make it easier to customize product selection, pricing, shipping terms, added benefits and discounts without alienating smaller customers. It would allow you to treat your "best" customers best.

While the customer data points that drive transactions on each website will differ somewhat, here is a short list of common data points which drive transactions and predict customer lifetime value.

- Initial product purchased
- Size or amount of initial order
- Intended usage

- Home demographics (age, income, education, etc)
- Where consumer is in buying cycle
- Number of buying triggers present

You should collect data that predicts product preferences and whether a customer will have high lifetime value, including:

- Product preferences
- Predictive demographic data
- Predictive psychographic data

You should also collect data that predicts changes in value, including:

- Buying trigger points
- Changes in demographic data

Data to Measure Profitability of Your Business Model or Fulfillment of Your Value Proposition. You will need to collect data to measure the success against your company's overall goals and objectives or against the business model. So if your goals are to increase registrations by a particular target customer group, you will want to identify these customers when they visit your website. If your goal is to reduce customer support expenses by driving more customers to your website for customer support, then collecting data on the number of support users, the types of problem solved and the number of support contacts that ultimately were referred to a live support representative will be important in assessing your savings.

But there is also the issue of business model. I like to use the example of razor blades because it is easy to follow. In the razor blade business, there are three economic models that require the identification of very different types of data to be successful:

- The premium razor model, where profits are in the razor (customer data need will be buyer demographics, such as income, to identify propensity to buy premium razor products)

▦ The replacement blade model, where profits are in blade sales (customer data most important to profitability will be the number of blades used or frequency of shaves)

▦ The shaving services model, where profits are in the services (customer data will need to include how a razor is used—home versus commercial—and shaving habits of customer or shaving skill level)

The business model or profit model drives what data will be most important in identifying target customers.

Final Thoughts on Customer Data Collection Techniques. The point in the relationship at which you collect customer data can also influence what data and how much data can be successfully collected. Obviously, you won't be terribly successful if you ask a brand-new customer to complete a twenty-five-question profile without a pretty remarkable value proposition. Usually, the initial data exchange should include only the most critical data points that you need to track the customer and to provide customized/personalized content. Again, referring back to what data points are most critical in determining customer lifetime value will often point to the critical data collected. Keeping the initial data request short minimizes the risk of losing a customer because customers typically don't feel comfortable providing personal data to an online vendor with which they have little experience. Later, when the relationship is more established and some level of trust has been earned, additional data can be more easily collected.

As a general rule, customer data should be collected in several transactions rather than hitting the customer all at once with too many questions. An exception to this rule is when you already have a strong offline relationship, one in which customers already trust you and want to provide their profile information to make their online experience as rewarding as their offline experience. A good example of this situation is frequent fliers who are willing to complete an extensive profile on their favorite frequent-flier program's website. An interesting observation I have made is that in general, women are more willing to provide personal data than men are. In discussing response rates to long questionnaires with marketers working on women's sites versus men's sites, it is amazing how significantly higher the response rates are on women's sites. I don't know if this is because women more inherently trust a site devoted to women, or if women, being newer to the Web, haven't had bad experiences from providing personal data to an unscrupulous website.

The Need for Speed

One of the biggest changes in customer relationship marketing brought about by the Web is the way customers are able to drive change in companies. Customers are now calling the shots, telling companies what they want, and companies are being forced to respond to them. This has led to a whole new way of thinking about strategy, and the impact on planning is revolutionary. Net speed forces all kinds of corporate change like flatter hierarchies, shorter and more flexible budget cycles and, most of all, decision making being pushed out to the front lines—the Web managers. This power is due to the increase in direct sales as well as the instant feedback loop provided by the Web. Geoff Yang, a partner in the venture capital firm IVP/Redpoint Ventures, sums it up well: "It used to be that the big ate the small. Now the fast eat the slow."

The Web will continue to increase companies' need for speed, and the key to attaining this speed will be plans that optimize data collection from the Web as well as better data analysis and reporting tools that make synthesizing data faster. Data speed will ultimately become an important factor not only in building intelligent relationships with customers but in winning the online revolution.

So when planning the "art" of your customer data collection—where, who, when and what—you will also need to focus on the "science" of data collection—the analysis and reporting. When selecting Web applications for collecting customer data, tune into the back-end solutions provided by each application. Does it measure, analyze and report, or merely spit the data into Web files which may or may not be analyzed on a timely basis. The same rigor should be applied to all Web applications used on your site. And for businesses that have built their websites one application at a time, in a piecemeal fashion, consider procuring the consulting talents and integration tools from companies that specialize in integration of data and back-end transaction reporting. See this book's website at e-loyalty.com for a list of companies who specialize in integration applications.

Web data reports will soon be more of a driving factor in corporations than the weekly revenue reviews of yesterday. Analysis of pages viewed, columns read, products purchased, and so on, will not just drive the marketers of the company, but the strategy makers as well. Be sure your data collection plan meets the test of Web warp speed.

STEP 3: DEVELOP YOUR WEBSITE AROUND AN INTELLIGENT DIALOGUE

What Is an Intelligent Dialogue?

Many Web marketing pundits proclaim that you can't have a relationship without a two-way dialogue, and I would have to agree with that general statement. But for sites that want profitable long-term relationships, you will need to ratchet this requirement up to the level of an "intelligent" conversation. The problem is: what constitutes an "intelligent" dialogue when different types of customer are looking for different levels of conversation or relationship? This perplexing question sounds more appropriate for a psych textbook than a Web marketing book, but that's because Web interactions must sound, feel and act intelligent, or *human*, to create a relationship. It all relates back to the most critical factor in creating e-loyalty: humanizing digital loyalty.

Here is my human example of an intelligent dialogue. Let's say you and I meet at a seminar. The first day we exchange names, employer information and job responsibilities. The second day, you see me and greet me by name and ask how work is going in the e-loyalty business. When I remember your name and recall your business activities, we have reached the first level of an intelligent dialogue—we renewed our conversation based on intelligence gathered in our last conversation. Let's say we chat some more and you learn that my most loyal employee is my cocker spaniel Tara and that next week my ski trip to Colorado is forcing me to put her in a kennel. The following week, you want to get my favorable answer to your request to have me speak at the next meeting of Dog Owners with Loyal Cocker Spaniels. So you send me an invitation to speak and enclose a big rawhide bone for Tara to chew on while I am away skiing. You remember I will be out of town that week, so you tell me I can let you know my answer when I come back from skiing. You just took our conversation to a higher level of intelligence because you used the information that you learned about me to influence my decision regarding your proposal. I'll agree that cocker spaniel loyalty isn't the most intelligent part of my new friend's conversation, but he sure knows how to take the conversation up a notch. Was it bribery? Maybe, but the bribe meets my criteria of being directly related to what I value and to what his proposition is about—loyal cocker spaniels.

You get the idea; now let's take a look at how this intelligence applies to intelligent dialogues on the Web. There is a great print advertisement for a Web software company called MicroStrategy that makes the claim, "The difference is intelligence." The advertisement gives two great examples of taking intelligent dialogue on the Web to the next level.

> First generation e-business lets travelers book flights online. That sure beats the old way. Intelligent e-business lets airlines call ticketholders with real time information on flight changes, suggests alternatives and lets them use their keypad to book choices . . . all in the same automated call. No lines, no waits. Customers are happier.
>
> First generation e-business gives e-stock traders nice graphs. Very colorful. Intelligent e-business lets firms run continuous multiple analysis of client portfolios, alerts them by pager with time-sensitive opportunities and lets them buy or sell instantly with the press of a button. No missed profits, no regrets. Customers are richer.

What makes these digital dialogues intelligent is that they not only personalize information, but deliver it at the moment it's most useful and in a format that is timely, convenient and preferred by the customer. Taking customer data and using it to improve the Web experience is what makes an intelligent dialogue, which is an important factor in making customers loyal. I haven't used MicroStrategy's software, but I can tell this company understands intelligent dialogues. With 900 customers worldwide, it's clear that a number of companies agree with me.

Receiving permission to send email to a customer should not be mistaken for a relationship. Humans differ in what they perceive to be an intelligent conversation and in the amount of conversation required to feel confident that a relationship has begun. For some customers, the two examples above might translate into too much intelligence because it scares them or makes them uncomfortable that you may know too much about them. Other customers like me would marvel at a website that acted this intelligent. The degree of intelligent dialogue needed is influenced by factors such as the type of product offered, the sex, education and age of the customer, the pervasive culture of your target audience and basic human preferences. So identifying what constitutes an intelligent conversation on your website will require you to determine the following for your target customers and ultimately for each customer.

▨ What is the optimum frequency and vehicle for information exchange?
▨ What is the type of content needed?
▨ What is the depth of subject level desired?

The only way you can learn the answers to these questions is by talking to your customers and listening to their feedback. To begin the customer learning process, start by using qualitative focus groups to talk with your best customers, then use online quantitative surveys to confirm statistically what you learned from talking to a few small groups of your customers. This initial research will give you the information needed to know which areas of content are most important to customize/personalize, and to what degree. However, on an ongoing basis you'll want to constantly fine-tune your content strategy by having customers profile their needs/preferences so that customers can set the level of dialogue required. You can monitor the success of your customization/personalization strategy through response rates, content frequency on Web logs, email unsubscribe rates, customer churn rates (number of customers who never return), customer defection research (asking customers why they stopped frequenting your site) and comments from website feedback buttons. Using customer research and analysis of usage on your website to create the initial customization and/or personalization strategy and refine the amount of customization and/or personalization that is desired is paramount to achieving the right level of intelligence in your online conversations. One of the biggest components of this strategy is getting specific about what data and website functionality to customize and/or personalize.

Deciding What Content to Customize/Personalize
Deciding how to have an intelligent dialogue with your online customers is a more strategic way of approaching a common question I hear from seminar attendees: "What content should I customize and/or personalize?" The first half of this answer depends on whether you have the money to buy a good personalization application and whether you have a product, brand or experience which customers will find value in while spending time profiling their preferences. The amount of data collected also drives the customize versus personalize decision. For those of you who get the two techniques confused, here is a quick review.
Customization is segment-driven by:

- Letting customers choose Web content
- Serving Web pages based on customer customization choices
- Examples: Web portals MyWomen, BabyCenter,

Personalization is individual-driven by:

- Choosing content for customers
- Serving Web pages based on customer profile plus tracked Web use, interests and ad response rates

▨ Examples: Outpost, Excite, IBM Owner Privileges, Amazon, Jenny Craig Personal Counselor

Some sites like Yahoo! let the customer decide the level of customization and personalization desired. Yahoo! customers can customize their MyYahoo! by selecting what categories of content they want featured on their personal portal page. They can also take that one step further by selecting the types of articles they want in their news category or which stocks they want to watch in their stock quote category. The customer is in control.

Ideally, most websites will want to personalize as much on their website as they can afford and justify it through incremental value. But maintenance issues and expenses, given your specific content management requirements, should also be considered. Because personalization and content maintenance can be prohibitively expensive, customized content driven by customer navigational choice is more appropriate and, if done well, is almost as effective. It also has the benefit of not requiring customer profiling or registration—a process that can turn some customers away.

After surveying customers to determine their preferences and evaluating how much personalization you can afford, the second half of your customization/personalization decision will be driven by your e-loyalty strategy. The demographic, psychographic and behavioral characteristics that drive e-loyalty and customer lifetime value should be at the top of your list in determining what content should be customized/personalized. I describe how to determine CLV drivers in Step 2: "Identify the Customers You Want to Be Loyal."

Customization/personalization based on e-loyalty drivers

To maximize e-loyalty, you will want to concentrate your customization/personalization on the e-loyalty drivers and attributes that your most valuable customers value, namely, product offering, product quality, service or image. Making the attributes that drive loyalty to your website or product more personal and more relevant to your customer is one of the most effective ways to increase customer loyalty. If your loyalty driver research was completed with a large enough sample to ensure statistical reliability, then customizing/personalizing these drivers will have a direct correlation to increased loyalty.

As an example, consider the online sale of servers to businesses. Let's assume that the most valuable server customers value service more than any other e-loyalty driver. In this case, customizing service by product, at a minimum, will be imperative to your success—this means by model as well as operating system. However, personalizing service will be even more important to succeed in this competitive industry, so a personalization strategy that addresses personalized service on an as-needed basis will be more effective and more competitive. It may even decrease service calls due to the customer's ability to locate service information more quickly and using the correct information for his or her model. But a server manufacturer that really wants to increase the intelligence of this dialogue will add to this service personalized advisories that address the customer's model, his or her chosen operating system, specific software, industry specific requirements and usage demands. And to take this value-added concept up one more level, the company would personalize how often the advisories are sent and how the advisories are communicated; that is, the communication vehicle used to reach the customer (email, mail, phone or pager). Through this type of personalization the server manufacturer will start entering that second level of intelligent conversation which significantly turns up the volume on e-loyalty.

Customization/personalization based on customer lifetime value

Initially, some marketers can't understand why I don't recommend customizing and personalizing strategies that focus purely on transactions or product margins. I have found that websites focusing generically on customizing transaction-related content end up with a strategy based on products and not on most valuable customers. At best, this technique generates a site focused on average transactions, which results in more of the same: merely average revenues. Focusing on lifetime value drivers forces Web marketers to base customization/personalization on prof-itability—incremental profits from, and retention of, your most valuable customers. Using this approach, you will ultimately increase transactions, but the profits will be greater because your costs are lower since you are increasing transactions from a smaller transactional base of customers. This is frequently called "increasing share-of-wallet" rather than "share-of-market."

Referring back to the server sales website example above, assume this server sales website found that the two most important drivers of customer lifetime value were the size of company and type of business. At a mini-mum, this site would want to customize content via a navigation that focuses on small versus medium versus large companies. Within each company size category, the content should be customized based on type of company or application. This server manufacturer could use a product recommendation application on its website that collects customer-specific data and serves up recommendations with the product offerings, benefits, buy recommendations and service plans all customized to support the applicable business size and type. But let's take this CLV-based strategy up to an even more intelligent level of conversation. The site could gather CLV data in the same product recommendation application that would enable it to offer prices and benefits based on CLV, thus stimulat-ing e-loyalty among its most valuable customers or those customers with the potential to be high value. This in turn would increase profitability and reduce expenses by offering only premium pricing and services to the manufacturer's most valuable customers.

Deciding what content should be customized/personalized should be based upon making loyalty attributes more attractive, ensuring that potential high-value customers are treated "best" and keeping your most valuable customers loyal—all of which will ultimately increase incre-mental transactions. These principles are the science behind an intelli-gent dialogue, because they are based on customer research and modeling. But how you creatively implement these strategies is the art of the intelligent dialogue. I describe this "art" below in terms of sounding, acting and working intelligently.

Sounding, Acting and Working Intelligently

There are three other components to an intelligent dialogue which at first glance appear to focus on tactics, operations and the execution of your business. But as you'll see below, it's about how your company's "voice" sounds to the customer and whether your online tactics and business operations respect the customer. All have a direct relation to how intelligent your conversation with customers will ultimately be.

First you will need to "sound" intelligent, which directly relates to your customization and/or personalization strategy. But it is just as important that your e-business "act" and "work" intelligently. E-businesses must learn to use customer information intelligently throughout the company so they can react to customer needs more efficiently. This will in turn make the company appear to be an intelligent enterprise that customers respect. Through these three tactical areas, you will increase your company's overall IQ. Once you master your own strategy and tactics for creating intelligent dialogues, you can take my *Intelligent Dialogue IQ Test*™ at the end of this section.

Sounding intelligent

Sounding intelligent is all about the actual dialogue you have with your customers. Implementing basic intelligent dialogues can be achieved by following these steps.

Step 1: Show customers the value in a personalized dialogue or relationship.

▦ Tell them the added benefits they will enjoy
▦ Demo the customized/personalized application

Step 2: Ask permission to have a dialogue/relationship.

▦ Timing is everything; too soon is a turnoff
▦ For permission, use an opt in process (customer checks a box to receive communications), rather than requiring customers to opt out. (customer must "unselect" a checked box so as not to receive communication).

Step 3: Gather customer data and profile customers.

- ▨ Tell customers exactly what you will use the information for and what will be customized/personalized
- ▨ Promise not to share the information with others
- ▨ Reward customers for providing information

Step 4: Customize/personalize the dialogue based on customer data.

- ▨ Don't ask for information you aren't going to use because it will set personalization expectations that you won't deliver, ultimately disappointing the customer
- ▨ Customize/personalize data that enhances your brand's e-loyalty drivers and that are designed to enhance the experience for your most valuable customers
- ▨ Don't be afraid to indicate that recommended articles, products or other content are based on their current profile and product interests—it makes customers know you care

Step 5: Continue gathering data and increasing the intelligence of your dialogue.

- ▨ Use each customer touch point to gather additional data
- ▨ Increase the intelligence of the dialogue with each data point supplied

The type of data collected will drive your ability to personalize or merely customize your content and website offerings. Here is how the two techniques differ in the types of data required.

Customization is typically based on segment preference data such as:

- ▨ Product/service purchased
- ▨ Solution set desired

▩ Customer's lifestyle and general demographics like age group and gender

▩ Geography—localize information, ensure cultural sensitivity

▩ Business customer's industry

Personalization is typically based on individual preference data such as:

▩ Lifetime value of customer

▩ Customer's interests and more specific demographics

▩ Length of ownership and product life cycle

▩ Preferred distributor

▩ Customer interests such as Web pages viewed

▩ Product/purchase experience (databases, telephone logs, purchases)

▩ Subscription renewal or member anniversary date

To get more and more customer data, you'll need to identify customers on your website. There are several techniques to chose from, some explicit—whereby a customer knowingly provides data—and some implicit—whereby a customer does not necessarily know his or her surfing is being tracked—which can be used to customize/personalize Web content. Because the technologies and providers of these types of technology change so frequently, I have not gone into extensive detail on tracking technology in this book. However, for applications and companies that support these types of technology, see the resources section of this book's website at www.e-loyalty.com. Here are five common methodologies for using customer data to make content more relevant and thus sound more intelligent.

▩ Simple customer navigation to desired customized content— simple, but reliable

▩ URL link into website drives customized home page (e.g., for links from a women's website, customize a gender-specific home page that appeals to women)

- ▨ Explicit visitor-initiated personalization
  - ▨ member number
  - ▨ user ID/password
  - ▨ member email
- ▨ Implicit anonymous personalization
  - ▨ dumb cookies—not unique to visitor, so good only for single-visit tracking
  - ▨ smart cookies—unique to visitor for multivisit tracking
  - ▨ embedded URL saved in customer's "favorites"
- ▨ Intelligent agents—predictive responses based on the aggregated behaviors of a community of users

Once you have a sense of your customers' preferences and needs, there are innumerable ways to customize and personalize the content. It all depends on the products offered, the problems being solved and the interest level of the customer. As a starting point, here is a list of some of the general principles for using customer data to make your dialogue sound more intelligent.

- ▨ Speak to customers from their point of view.
- ▨ Tailor content to be more relevant to your customers' needs.
- ▨ Tailor creative style/tone to appeal to customer.
- ▨ Use pictures and stories to which your customers can relate.
- ▨ Develop product solutions targeted to customers' problems.
- ▨ Ensure links into your website start on pages with content targeted to the customers' preferences of the site from which they link (e.g., from a women's site to a page with content for women or pictures of women).
- ▨ Serve ads that are likely to target your customers' needs.

But customization and personalization shouldn't stop at basic web-site content. Think about these other opportunities to sound more intel-ligent.

- Let customers personalize navigation so they can get to their favorite areas of your website more quickly. One way to implement personalized navigation is to encourage customers to create links to content areas from their profile page (frequently called "My_____." as in "MyYahoo!" However, I prefer titles that include the visitor's name, like "Ellen's home page," because it really feels and sounds more personal and thus more intelligent.
- Shopping baskets that hold recently purchased items so the customer can check off a reorder quickly is another great personalization technique that clearly drives repeat purchases and e-loyalty. (PlanetRx is an excellent example of a personalized shopping basket.)
- Personalize sales promotions and premiums based upon customer preferences and customer value. You can use this technique to reward your best customers best, or to target best customers with promotions tailored to their buying habits on the Web pages they frequented most.
- Personalizing customer benefits, services or privileges based on customer lifetime value will not only make your resources stretch further but will also be more relevant to your targeted customers.
- Personalize rewards so they are more aspirational. Let customers build their own award chart from a list of award types that they are interested in, or hold an auction for exclusive awards to make the point requirements as customer-driven as possible. I wouldn't recommend a reverse auction for standard, ongoing reward charts because it doesn't provide the assurance customers need to be motivated by rewards. But for one-of-a-kind rewards, this process is fun and increases interaction with the program.
- Personalize cobranded offers with retailers and partners to bring the most relevant partners to your high-value customers. But be sure the promotion is clearly your offer, to avoid the perception that you are giving customer data to a partner. No matter how great a partner's award may be, it won't overcome a broken privacy promise.

Frequency of Dialogue. If you think the high response you received to your weekly email means you need to send communications twice a week, think again. This is the common misconception—that a 5 percent weekly response rate to direct email offers could become 10 percent a week by purely multiplying the frequency by two. More than likely, the number of customers who revoke their permission will far outweigh the increased response rate.

So how much email is enough, and how much is too much? You guessed it, there's no one answer. For news, it could be daily; for product information, it could be monthly. It depends upon the product and the interest level of the customer. For most product-related communications, the email should be driven by relevance rather than a schedule. For instance, let's assume you've promised your customers a weekly newsletter about your product, but some weeks there just isn't much news, so you are forced to fill the newsletter with information that is less relevant, timely or interesting. What happens should be no surprise: your readers value the newsletter less and less because it isn't consistently useful or valuable. Sending out communications when there is something timely, relevant and valuable could make two communications this week, but none next week, the right answer to your frequency dilemma.

At other times the right frequency is established in terms of the customers' attention span. Teen girls seem to like frequent, short email news on fashion. Teen boys can stay focused on four-page emails with endless detail on the latest software action games, but have no attention span for other topics. The key is to understand your customers' preferences for news complexity on your product or company and respect their attention spans. This could be best accomplished through special-interest newsletters from which customers select their favorite topic, thus controlling both the complexity of the subject and the frequency. Or it could be implemented via personalized messages saved on the news section of their personalized portal page from which they chose the topics which most interest them, thus letting the customer control the complexity and the timing of the messages.

Last, communication frequency should be driven by the purchase cycle. Your customer communications need to meet the interest level your customers have during various points in the purchase cycle and capitalize on these peaked interest levels to drive sales messages. Let's take the example of buying a car on a four-year payment plan. Upon first purchasing a new car, most customers have a high interest in learning more about the car, its accessories and about others who drive the car. But this interest level starts decreasing for most owners by the end of year one. The intensity and the frequency with which they want information decreases dramatically in years two and three. But in year four, when that last car payment is on the horizon, many car owners start focusing on their next purchase, and want to start receiving information to help in that decision-making process. If the customer was on a three-year payment plan, the cycle would obviously be shortened. For customers who lease, the process is even more predictable. This is one of the reasons why leasing has been so profitable for car manufacturers—they not only know the exact purchase cycle, they can also time the production of new cars and the resale of trade-ins. Here's the catch: some of the biggest exceptions to this rule are the most successful auto manufacturers. Take Jeep as an example. DaimlerChrysler has created a year-round, ongoing intelligent dialogue with Jeep owners through its Jeep Jamborees and other cross-country events. Owners want more information on the vehicles, the brand, the related events and other owners than most any other American brand automobile. Jeep has increased the interest in their product and thus the frequency of communications through a very intelligent dialogue. It makes me want to buy a Jeep just to get in on the fun.

Speaking in One Voice. When does a brand not sound like itself? Answer: when the brand has multiple product managers speaking for the brand in an uncoordinated manner. Sounding intelligent is about speaking in one voice, so you sound like one brand or one company in all your communications. If you have multiple agencies running your various communications, or you let product managers define their own voices, it can be very difficult to attain "one voice." Larger websites with diverse areas can run into this same problem. It's important that all product divisions know the extent of the relationship and all communications have the same brand and image.

Although this concept of "speaking in one voice" was the brainchild of Brierley & Partners' creative directors Howard Schneider and Robbin Gehrke, one of the most brilliant pieces of communication I ever saw was an internal booklet for employees produced by IBM, simply titled "One Voice." It was a guide for all employees, but the focus was on corporate communications, marketing and advertising. The purpose of the guide was to ensure that the company brand was presented consistently, to ensure that marketing personnel echoed the same key brand messages and, most important, to ensure that all employees understood the one-voice strategy so that all their actions reflected a singular brand positioning. It was brilliant in conception and execution and would have made the Brierley inventors proud. IBM's metamorphosis from a stodgy hardware company into a leading Internet services company is partly due to the branding strategy behind this one-voice concept.

But the question most websites struggle with is what voice to use? Most important, the voice should be human. The feel and voice of a real person can have a remarkable effect on building loyalty and trust—and converting browsers into buyers. Founders frequently lend their voices to their website, and for those few short months when the founder either writes or reviews every word, that website has the voice of an individual. That genuine voice is a powerful thing to customers looking for a personal connection in a digital world. Big businesses will continue to look for technological solutions to make the online sales experience as "human" as possible, but their answer can be as easy as hiring the right individual to talk to customer segments. For example, iVillage.com hired Harriet Rubin, the Princessa herself, to be their voice of working women. And Yahoo! bought MountainGreetings because they couldn't capture the greeting card market without the voice of the most successful online greeting card company.

Maintaining one voice has an even more important role in maintaining a consistent relationship with customers. If the personal checking department at my online bank tells me that I am one of their most valuable customers and allows me "special" privileges that I cannot extend to my online business accounts, I quickly realize we have no real relationship at all. To speak in one voice means extending or grandfathering a customer's preferred status across product lines or, better yet, building the customer relationship program around the multiple product lines to begin with.

The same principles of "speaking in one voice" hold true for websites that service households rather than individual customers. If my husband and I both buy groceries from our online grocer, but use different Web passwords, the grocer should "household" the data by our mutual address to recognize us as a single buying household, not two separate customers. If we both buy groceries online, but my husband gets preferred treatment that I don't get, I might jump to the conclusion that his preferential treatment is due to his gender, or worse yet, his "bedroom eyes." The same can be true when business-to-business websites give one department preferential treatment and not another department—the rational for why isn't clear to the customer. You get my point—know with whom you have a relationship, and speak in one voice to all those who share that relationship.

The principle of speaking in one voice is so simple in concept, but it becomes harder and harder to implement and maintain as a website or e-business expands. And unfortunately, as your website and customer relationships expand, the consequences of breaking this fundamental loyalty rule also expand. Your mistake is not limited to one area of your company but is amplified over the entire Web operation, resulting in customer alienation toward your entire website. To plan a strategy to help ensure you speak in one voice, see my recommendations later in this chapter for creating a customer contact strategy based on a customer focus, not a product focus.

Acting intelligent

Spamming. Spamming your customers or potential customers by sending unauthorized email is not intelligent! Need I say more? If you are sending email without permission from an "opt-in" or a clearly marked "opt-out" process, you are spamming. To avoid spamming, using an opt-in permission marketing process is your safest bet. Opt in requires customers to actually check a box that indicates they want to receive email or other communications from you. A less preferred method is opt-out, which involves requiring a customer to "uncheck" a box that gives you permission to send communications. Marketers using the opt-out technique hope that customers will overlook the prechecked permission box, particularly if they bury it at the end of the Web page. Marketers using the opt-out technique think permission is more about facts, and less about a customer's perception or belief. That's why the biggest problem with opt-out techniques is that if a customer doesn't believe he or she gave you permission, it still feels like spam to the customer. When customers think you spammed them, it really doesn't matter that you "think" you had permission—you just lost the customer. Opt-out marketers are betting that the incremental revenues generated; from communications will outweigh the ill will that is generated; sometimes this is used as a shortsighted acquisition strategy with the backdoor for retention left wide open.

More often than not, websites that use opt-out strategies are trying to please investors who judge a website by the amount of customers registered rather than customer loyalty measures. I recently heard a Garden.com marketer claim they had 800,000+ customers registered, which sounded very low to me, but after a few questions I found that Garden.com makes it a point not to push registration and doesn't require registration for most of its services. They are consciously limiting their database to a "qualified" list of high-value customers. Because they know their database has predominantly high-value customers, they can justify the mailing and customer service resources because their return on investment for the mailing is higher than if a true "mass" mailing to "average" customers were executed. So is Garden.com's database somewhat smaller than other successful e-commerce websites? Why yes! But is it of more value? Certainly! Web marketers like Garden.com are working the Web like a fine-tuned direct marketing machine.

But even with the best opt-in techniques, some customers will forget they gave you permission to communicate with them. This is why it's best to confirm the source of your permission in each communication, and periodically remind your customers what they signed up to receive. Here are two good examples of the reminder and unsubscribe process. The first is from Sega's online gaming site (Note: I am not a registered or paying member—i.e., I'm a low-value customer—thus there is no personalization).

> Hello HEAT.NET Perimeter members. You are receiving this email because you asked to receive it when you signed up with HEAT.NET. If you would prefer not to receive it, please see the end of this message.

The second is from the Full Sterne Ahead newsletter. Note the fun tone and, for those of us with short memories, the added touch of reminding me where I gave the permission.

> You're receiving this e-mail because, once upon a time, you subscribed at the Target Marketing of Santa Barbara Web site http://www.targeting.com for the Full Sterne Ahead newsletter. To unsubscribe, simply reply to this with the word "unsubscribe" in the subject or body and I'll never darken your e-mail box again.

Permission Marketing. Given Seth Godin's great book, *Permission Marketing,* and the many articles on the subject, I have included only the most important aspects of permission marketing below. However, my short treatment of the subject should by no means lessen its importance. Permission marketing is a critical aspect of starting a relationship and demonstrating trust. For that reason I mention the topic here and several other places in the book.

What permission marketing is:

▦ At a minimum, permission is given when a website includes an opt-in (or opt-out) basis on its customer registration which gives the customer's permission to send communications.

▦ However, the best uses of permission marketing include some terms around the permission, whereby a customer identifies him- or herself and gives you permission to communicate when and how you have specified.

▦ Most important, it is a trust not to violate the privilege of hosting the customer's data.

What permission marketing is not:

▦ It's not permission to email as often as you like.
▦ It's not permission to call when you only mentioned email.
▦ It's not permission to lend the names or to send partner email as your own.

The advantages of permission marketing:

▦ Your email/mail are more likely to be opened and read.
▦ You can personalize messages without turning customers off by sounding "too personal."
▦ It allows greater frequency of communications—within limits.
▦ It allows you to prove you are trustworthy, and then customers will provide additional data—ideally resulting in better targeted messages.
▦ Customers will be more open and appreciative of being offered rec-ommendations based on their preferences because they expected their data to be used in this way.
▦ If used correctly, it can provide a profitable partner-marketing rev-enue stream.

Privacy Policies. Start off your privacy strategy with a great rule of thumb: the more you know about a customer, the greater your obligation to respect his or her privacy. A privacy policy or statement is your promise to keep customer data confidential. Sometimes just as important is to reveal what data is tracked. One of the easiest ways to share tracked data with customers is to list this data on their profile page. Listing tracked data on a profile page has two benefits. First, it allows customers to update or correct their data at any time, which means better data hygiene. Second, it can motivate customers to register or set up a profile page, which generates a greater number of profiled customers. To act intelligently, websites should adhere to the following privacy policy standards.

- Make the privacy policy easy to access whenever asking for data and always link to it from the home page.
- Be sure it is clearly written in "customer speak" and not "lawyer speak."
- Disclose all data-gathering practices, including profiles, cookies, web log analysis, transaction tracking and surveys.
- Clearly identify what information is collected.
- Explain how information will be used.
- State that you won't sell, rent or trade information without permission.

Working intelligently

To sound and act intelligent to your customers, you will need to create a strategy for customer communications, frequently called a "customer contact plan" or "communications strategy." This customer contact plan is an extension of permission marketing in that it acts as a planning tool for customer communications. But in many respects it is also the backbone of customer relationship management in that it helps marketers track and understand customer preferences. And to the financial analysts in your company, it will be a tool for optimizing the return on investment for each customer by tracking response or buy rates. But ultimately, it will make you sound and act more intelligent with respect to your customers.

A customer contact plan should use the following principles to truly make your company work more intelligently.

- It should be multidimensional.
- It must be customer-oriented.

▩ It is managed by a segment manager, not a product manager.
▩ It should act as a planning tool.

Multidimensional. A contact plan needs to be multidimensional to track the entire customer conversation. This means that it needs to include all types of customer communication, from all customer contact points, and should include data on both directions of the conversation. Here are some examples of the types of communication that would be planned and tracked.

▩ Advertising—mass, targeted and customized/personalized
▩ Publicity—where articles should appear to reach target customers
▩ Data acquisition—all types of data request (registration, surveys, etc.) and data supplied
▩ Customization—customer preferences supplied, data that was customized and response to past customized content
▩ Product offers—customers' preferences, what was offered, what was purchased
▩ Promotions/sales—specific offer, when sent, customer response
▩ Sales transactions—purchases and returns
▩ Partner offers—specific offer, when sent, customer response
▩ Rewards and recognition—type of reward and data awarded
▩ Customer service—customer initiated, help provided
▩ Customer feedback—whether by email, phone or mail and how responded to

Customer-Oriented, Not Product-Oriented. Probably one of the biggest problems large corporations face in customer communications is control within their own company. More often than not, each product group creates customer communications with a disregard for other communications being sent from their own company. This problem can multiply when you have a retail sales channel and a direct sales channel that don't coordinate customer communications. Customers who are bombarded with email and mail from product managers and multiple sales channels soon start to understand why the company's prices are so high. If this isn't happening in your company—and I hope it isn't—I'm confident that you've been on the receiving end. Either you're angry to have your service fees spent on postage, or you're tired of the email cluttering up your in-box. The second most common communication mistake is when a customer buys a product, only to receive a sale notice on that same product one week later—that drives angry calls to a help desk and turns a satisfied customer into a disloyal customer.

To avoid talking to your customers in multiple "voices" requires that your customer contact plan be built around the customer and not your products. It needs to track all communications by customer and consolidate communications from multiple product managers. Only through a customer-oriented contact plan will the customer feel like there is one relationship and that the messages received are coherent. From a purely tactical standpoint, it will also ensure better tracking of response rates, since you will know the sum total of all communications that influenced a customer response. Last, from a relationship-building viewpoint, you will be able to more accurately tailor communications to customer preferences.

Managed by a Segment Manager. A customer-oriented communications contact plan typically requires that the plan be managed by customer segment managers and not product managers. I'm sure there must be some exceptions to this rule, but I don't know of any. Product managers inherently look out for their product over other products, and customer segment managers inherently do what's best for the customer and the group of products. They act as customer advocates, while at the same time tracking total value and optimizing profit per customer. For companies where the lowest-margin products have the squeakiest wheels, a customer segment manager will filter out the noise and ensure that high-margin products are heard loud and clear. This may sound elementary, but for those of us who have worked in large companies, we know this phenomenon to be true.

Once you have your customer contact plan managed by a customer segment manager and oriented around customers, you'll obviously want to personalize communications whenever possible to appeal to your customers' unique preferences, needs and problems they want solved. But just as important is maximizing the return on each customer by differentiating messages based upon customers' current revenues, lifetime value, share-of-wallet, or potential profitability. When you're ready to take your intelligent dialogue to the next level of personalization, this intense customer focus will make it easier for you to tailor individual messages for relevance, select communication mediums that meet your customers' preferred communications style and time the messages to be most useful.

Acts as a Planning Tool. While a customer contact plan will make you sound more intelligent to your customers, it will also make your business planning become more intelligent. Here are some of the ways a customer contact plan will help your business planning.

- ▦ It balances types of contact (email, postal mail, telephone, in person) to appeal to customers and to reduce communication costs.
- ▦ It controls sequence, type and frequency of contact.
  - ▦ specifies the timing and the type of message based on purchase life cycle, lifetime value and potential value
  - ▦ establishes optimum communication frequency based on customer preferences, response rates and unique product characteristics
  - ▦ disciplines a company to adhere to the time and patience required to build a relationship with a customer through a series of communications
- ▦ It includes rigorous testing.
  - ▦ allows testing with smaller groups before assuming more email is better
  - ▦ facilitates message optimization by customer segment/preferences to maximize response rates
- ▦ It ensures a "total" customer profile to maximize lifetime value.
  - ▦ makes cross-product marketing more likely

▨ consolidates communications to minimize the number of contacts, thus increasing the value of communications
▨ It allows planning by segment, but communicates by individual customer.
▨ allows better management of customer segments
▨ enables extensions into new customer segments
▨ It helps extend existing customer programs to your website.
▨ It migrates offline programs to an online medium for instant program access and lower customer service costs.
▨ It enlivens customer programs with localized content and more interaction.

Take the IQ Test

If you think you have mastered an intelligent dialogue by sounding, acting and working intelligently, then ask yourself the following questions. If you have mastered an intelligent dialogue, you will answer yes to these questions.

1. Have less than 10 percent of your customers revoked their permission for you to communicate with them?
2. Do you receive feedback from customers with phrases like "your website is just like me," or "this is exactly what I have been looking for," even though these customers have distinctly different interests?
3. Has customer feedback indicated that your information is relevant, interesting and useful?
4. Have your customers ever complained when a newsletter was late?
5. Is the length of time a customer spends on your site increasing?
6. Is your customer churn rate decreasing?
7. Do you use an opt-in strategy for gaining permission from customers?
8. Can a twelve-year-old understand your privacy policy?
9. Do you know the optimum frequency with which your customers want to hear from you?
10. Are customer segmentation plans incorporated into your communication plans?

11. Does a customer advocate or customer segment manager manage the contact plan for your customers, rather than a single product manager?
12. Do product managers need permission from the customer communications manager to send customer communications?
13. Does your communications plan currently track all customer points of contact, or do you have future plans to add these customer communications?
14. Have your customers ever asked to receive your communications more often?
15. Are the majority of your customers willing to give more information when asked?
16. Are the response rates on your emails increasing?
17. When surveyed, do 75 percent or more of your customers report that they usually or always read your emails?
18. Is your loyalty program incorporated into all your customer programs?
19. Is one of your success measures cross-sell and up-sell from customer communications?
20. Have recent measurements of repurchase, referral and up-sell/cross-sell increased?
21. When your best business partner asks to embed customer identifiers into your Web page links to their site, do you always say "no"?

STEP 4: DESIGN YOUR WEBSITE FOR YOUR MOST VALUABLE CUSTOMERS, NOT YOUR AVERAGE CUSTOMERS

Let the Needs of Your Most Valuable Customers Drive Web Design
One of the biggest pitfalls with many websites is that Web design and features are developed for what the average customer wants. Designing for average customers will do just that—satisfy *average* customers, ultimately yielding *average* profits. What's the point of expending all that sweat

equity if you build relationships with average customers, only to lose your best customers? Designing for best customers means thinking through each process in your website—the content, advertisers, product sold, tone etc.—with your best customers' preferences and needs in mind. I'm not advocating alienating average customers for best customers, although in some cases where you want to focus solely on the top-tier customers in an industry, this strategy might be appropriate. But normally you want to develop special features and benefits for your best customers, ones that perhaps you can't afford to offer to all customers. This will require setting up alternative navigation channels or customized/personalized pages that limit certain benefits for your best customers. Whether your Web offering is exclusive to your most valuable customers (MVCs) or merely more appreciated by your best customers, the key is to design your Web offering so that your best customers get the experience they desire.

For companies where the old rules of product-focused marketing seem to permeate business decisions, a Web design process based on customer needs—not to mention their most valuable customers' needs—is a difficult stretch. Without a customer focus, these companies start by organizing their website around products or corporate groupings of products because they've always approached product advertising through isolated acquisition efforts, and initially they think of the Web only as an extension of advertising. Typically it is the Web design firm that suggests improvements to their website usability by focusing on how customers shop, not how products are organized internally. This ignites the kindling. And without knowing it, the Web design agency fans the flames by recommending a navigation based on problem solving or solution selling that combines multiple products. The good intentions of the Web design agency are the igniter of an embroiled debate amongst warring product groups. Web efforts force companies to think like a customer, and the ensuing corporate struggles to let customer-focused marketers lead the organization are healthy battlegrounds. But I have ceased to be surprised that these revolutionary corporate changes can start by asking for agreement on website objectives and navigational strategy.

But don't think dot com start-ups that are more prone to begin with a best-customer–based design are innocent of letting business operations affect customer focus. Approximately four to six months into a dot com start-up, I've frequently seen the train jump track. The dot com founders find themselves wined and dined by hopeful partners, pulling their attention toward the latest sexy Web application or a partner marketing revenue deal that seems too good to be true. Before they know it, they are planning to add several new unintended features, channels, services or other diversions, and can't seem to make the new business model hold together. There is intense difficulty in the concept of "just say no" when an offering doesn't serve your MVCs. Many start-up executives are guilty of these powerful diversions, and I have personally been in the advisory role of telling several dot com founders that a proposed partner deal is good, but not for the target customers—the MVCs. So even at a dot com start-up business, marketing and design decisions need to be continually refocused by asking whether the proposed site feature is important to the target audience.

The most obvious Web elements that are enhanced with a most valuable customer approach are advertising, content, communications, community and retention programs. But your MVCs should affect much more, starting with your website objectives all the way through e-commerce and finishing with customer support. Below, I lay out the eight most critical design features that should be based on the preferences and needs of your most valuable customers.

Website Objectives
In Step 1: "Clearly Establish Your Goals and Objectives," I illustrated how a business's overall goals and objectives must be made more specific to define the goals and objectives of an e-loyalty program. To take this one step further, you should delineate e-loyalty goals by tailoring them to ensure your MVCs are retained. For example, a goal of simply retaining customers would be made to specify the goal of retaining MVCs, and then using objectives to define who those customers are and what your quantitative objective is. In markets that are large enough, you might

even want to retain high-value customers at the expense of average customers. The travel industry is a good example. For new travel agencies
trying to break into the highly competitive market of travel planning,
offering travel services for the very frequent traveler by limiting benefits
and services only to gold and platinum members of airline programs
could be a successful high-value niche strategy. The entire travel enterprise would be focused on the needs of best customers: very frequent travelers.

Just about every type of Web strategy can benefit from a most valuable
customer focus. Website goals that are extensions of a bricks-and-mortar
business strategy can benefit by using the Web to service best customers
or to capture a group of high-value customers previously missed due to
their preference to purchase via catalogs. The goal of increasing customer satisfaction through improved customer service is a natural application, since the Web allows you to offer various levels of service
depending on a customer's value. For that matter, the Web can be used
to differentiate discounts or free shipping depending on customer value,
which will in turn allow e-businesses to increase profitability. Whatever
the goal of your website, delineating that goal and the respective objectives by focusing on your MVCs will lead to higher retention of the right
customers and ultimately increased profits.

Advertising/Acquisition Plans

Advertising and acquisition plans are marketing elements that really benefit from a more targeted message to a website's MVCs, but many advertising agencies are still fighting to buy mass media for the masses—the
average customer. To truly take advantage of a "best customer" approach
in your acquisition strategy requires smaller media buys with more targeted messages—a technique that large ad agencies have avoided in the
past to maintain their buying thresholds of network airtime. The most
successful advertising is that which targets the most valuable target audience with messages about the specific loyalty drivers that appeal to this
target audience. This is because loyalty drivers are the reason customers

buy a product as much as they are the reason why a customer becomes loyal to a product. For example, if service is the most influential loyalty driver for your MVCs, a website needs to do two things: focus on the proof points of great customer service in their acquisition campaign and then focus the majority of their resources on ensuring that customer service is the one of the best features of their website.

Here is where most advertisers will jump up and point out that "advertising is about building a brand, it's about awareness!" But the keys to building a brand online have to do with mastering the best customer interaction (navigation, usability and service), not just building the image. Online branding is more about ensuring that each customer's experience is the best than about reaching as many eyeballs as possible. Online branding is more about proving the image than espousing it, because the Web allows customers to test a brand positioning faster and more thoroughly than bricks-and-mortar retailers will ever experience. So websites that claim they are "the best" at anything had better be prepared for grueling side-by-side comparison tests that will happen at the speed of a click. On the Web, customers are less concerned with image, and more concerned with brand. The exceptions are those brands that have already proven themselves offline, like Barnes & Noble or Lands End. These websites did enjoy an instant web audience with very little advertising, but don't think for one moment that they didn't have to prove their navigation, service and product selection. The only difference is that these established brands have the luxury of being given a second chance by loyal customers, but they know a second or third foul-up will mean that loyal customers will defect to Amazon and Style.com.

Sure, awareness is important, but awareness of brand alone doesn't drive customers with the success rate that awareness of loyalty-driving attributes do. It goes back to one of the main sources of customer churn: why keep attracting customers that don't value your most important online features? Your acquisition strategy and your branding should be an extension of targeted sales points to each of your most valuable customer segments. Luckily the Web is more about targeted eyeballs, than massive eyeballs, anyway. There are relatively few venues on the Web capable of reaching millions, and even if they do, customers are trained to focus on areas of most interest, navigating down special interest paths, ignoring your untargeted ads. The ability to target customers' interests and needs makes the Web the perfect medium to execute finely targeted messages, tailored to each of your MVC groups. Through this targeting technique customers see that a brand is focused squarely on their needs or preferences, which in turn stimulates customers to begin a personal relationship with a brand.

Customer Profile Strategy

A customer profile strategy is your plan for registering customers and collecting data from them that can be used to make their Web experience more personalized. Building a customer profile strategy based on MVCs is kind of a "no-brainer." In Step 2, I covered how registration and profiling tools should collect data that can be used to identify your MVCs. So designing a profiling strategy around your MVCs should make perfect sense.

You will need to ask for data in a sequence, frequency and format that match the expectations of your best customers. If your MVCs tend to be more leery of supplying personal data than other customers, then your profiling strategy should be to ask for data only after you have proven that you can be trusted, and then only through a series of short data requests. Once customers see the value of providing the data, they will be more likely to provide it. On the other hand, if you are women.com and find that your best customers think of your business as a woman-to-woman conversation where they can "share" personal data to enhance the exchange of dialogue, you will find it easy to collect not only greater quantities of data but very personal data as well. There are few sites that collect as much data and as much personal data as women.com. They are the pros because they know their customers well and have earned their trust.

While working on several children's websites, I have learned that having children under thirteen years of age as your most valuable customers poses a set of unique issues to consider in a profile strategy. In April 2000, the Federal Trade Commission began enforcing the guidelines contained in its publication *Children's Online Privacy Protection* Act (COPPA), which requires verification of adult approval either using a digital signature or having the parent call an 800 telephone number. The double email permission process previously used to gain parental permission is no longer adequate. The double email process required a website to send an email to a parent, who then replied with the permission, and the website would reverify the permission with confirmation email to the parent. The problem lies in the homes where children and parents share the same email address. Websites targeting children will have to weigh the expense and privacy risks of profiling children with the benefits of being able to profile children for personalized content.

More important, your profiling strategy will need to collect the data necessary to identify your most valuable customers through the shortest series of questions possible. At the same time, this initial profiling request will need to collect the minimal amount of data required to provide a customized or personalized experience that will make the interactive experience compelling enough that customers want to come back for more. Not an easy strategy to master the first time, so I'd advise starting with very few profile questions and slowly adding more, or test customer reaction to adding more before increasing the quantity of data collected.

Content
If your website is correctly targeted to your MVCs, these customers should see themselves in your website. Upon visiting your website, they should immediately feel like they belong there. To achieve this requires designing your graphics and content to match the style and tone of your MVCs. This requires a full understanding of the MVCs' preferred style and tone. Are they most comfortable with conservative or edgy prose? Are they looking for a quick, solution-based visit or do they prefer a leisurely, entertaining experience?

Your customer's Web experience level should also drive design decisions. Inexperienced Web surfers may not understand embedded links or navigational shortcuts, and links will need to be overt. If you visit a few children's gaming sites, you will quickly learn that this experienced audience picks up on implicit links embedded in photos and graphics better than most other Web users—in fact, they prefer the navigation to be somewhat of a surprise. On the opposite end of that continuum are busy women using the Web to save time. These women want a clear, no-frills navigation that leads to fast problem solving or information gathering.

I've worked on several sites where the MVC is a woman, but we didn't want a clearly feminine design that might discourage their male customers. This is where websites reach a critical juncture: either design a site for women and be the best site for women or build navigational channels into your site based on gender differences. Using solid strategic marketing skills, either strategy can be effective. With a strong brand that can be carried over multiple channels and still prevail, the channel strategy can work. However, an unknown brand using a multichannel approach has to be careful not to make the mistake of trying to be something for everyone, only to end up being "not exactly" what anyone wants. In arguing for a purely female-oriented site, there is a large enough female population on the Web to justify websites built solely for women. Since customers expect more personalized experiences on the Web, a website that specializes in women makes a better long-term approach. Hifi.com and HerHifi.com are good examples of separate gender channels.

Men, women, teens or seniors all have preferred navigational styles that can be loosely applied across the segment. Granted, not all customers in a demographic segment act alike, but if your website or areas within your website are targeting a specific segment of Web user understanding the Web navigation, page scanning and scrolling habits of the majority of the customers in a segment can prove invaluable. To get more specific data on a target group of customers, research software is available that measures eye movement patterns to identify left-to-right or top-to-bottom reading habits of your targeted customers. At a minimum, research on Web logs can help identify navigational preferences like singular linked pages versus hierarchical searches. And the expectation of customized or personalized home/portal pages to speed navigation through a website also differs dramatically among customer groups.

Most websites are designed based on industry-wide reports on Web usage patterns and preferences. Although these types of report can be helpful in weeding out the terribly unsuccessful Web design techniques, when strictly adhered to, the preferences of average users may not meet the expectations of your MVCs at all. A bit of research on your own target audiences could save a lot of money on subsequent redesigns and will mean a better chance of achieving e-loyalty the first time around. After all, you may not get a second chance.

Customer Communications

Your communications with your MVC should sound very different from your communications with your average customers. It's much like the experience of going to a restaurant that knows you as a frequent customer. As a valued diner you would be greeted by name; some restaurants even keep a list of spouse names to ensure they greet everyone by name when possible. You would probably hear comments like "it was great to see you" and you'd be asked if you wanted your usual table. And the pinnacle of best customer romancing would come when the waiter asks if you'll "be having the usual." When the dinner is over, there might be a complimentary dessert, but there's always a profuse round of thanks, with the wish that they will see you soon. The experience is great because it's personal and you are treated like a highly valued customer. The communications, the choice of words and the sincerity are all driven by the fact that you have a relationship and you are a most valuable customer. The same is true for the Web and all other customer communications. Explicitly thanking customers for being great customers is fundamental in building a lasting relationship. However, it also creates an expectation that your entire business knows a customer is valued, and you need to be prepared to carry that through all customer touch points by everyone "speaking in one voice" to the customer.

There's another important point regarding the restaurant example above. I bet restaurant patrons who experience the most valued customer treatment described above *never* complain that the restaurant has invaded their privacy by remembering too much of their customer data—that is, their names and dining preferences. And I have yet to see a restaurant post a privacy statement on their front door, relieving them of any legal ramifications from waiters tracking and using patrons' preferences to ensure personalized experience. One reason we don't see privacy statements on restaurant doors is because customer data is used only to enhance the dining experience and to make the customer feel valued. Even though many chain restaurants have been tracking customer data for years, mailing discount postcards and birthday offers, we haven't heard from enraged customers, because they use the information to improve the restaurant experience and don't invade the customers' privacy.

A seemingly personalized experience can take place at any size eating establishment or website. Case in point: My mother recently walked into a Jack-in-the-Box and was asked if she "wanted her usual?" Amused and intrigued, she answered, "Yes." Turns out she got exactly what she always orders, even though she had never been to this location before. It could be that "Jack" knows senior citizens like my mother always order the 99 cent burger with water. But regardless of the reason, it really made her day even though she knew there was no way they really knew her. As a matter of fact, she was eager to go back. Many websites also use aggregated data to customize content. One leading PC manufacturer's website tracks registered users' surfing patterns. If a customer surfs pages on educational products on one visit, the next time that customer logs onto the home page the featured content is about educational products. It frequently happens on health sites; you surf women's health issues and on your next sign-in the home page features women's health issues. The website feels like you "belong." The point is that when a Web customer knows her or his data is being tracked and aggregated in a way that makes the content and Web experience richer, the customer is less bothered by the idea that personal data is tracked or remembered.

Another critical component in personalizing content for MVCs is to show you understand them by speaking their language. Speaking the customer's language means learning to drop the "corporate speak" and communicate in human terms or, more important, the terminology used by your targeted customer segment. College kids don't talk like adults, any more than teens talk like their grandparents. Even in a seemingly similar category such as women's finance, you'll find websites like Cassandras-revenge.com that have a much more feminist and intellectual tone than iVillage.com's content, which is more conservative and targeted to less knowledgeable investors.

The first step in learning to talk in your customers' tone and style requires dropping a corporate tone, which I call "corporate speak." One of the best books that advocates throwing out corporate phrases and talking to customers like human beings is *The Cluetrain Manifesto*, which is also available at www.cluetrain.com. These pundits of humanity started out by listing their ninety-five rules for humanizing corporate communications on their website, and it ultimately resulted in a best-selling book. Here's how the authors of *The Cluetrain Manifesto* explain the need for human conversation.

A powerful global conversation has begun. Through the Internet, people are discovering and inventing new ways to share relevant knowledge with blinding speed. As a direct result, markets are getting smarter—and getting smarter faster than most companies.

These markets are conversations. Their members communicate in language that is natural, open, honest, direct, funny and often shocking. Whether explaining or complaining, joking or serious, the human voice is unmistakably genuine. It can't be faked.

Most corporations, on the other hand, only know how to talk in the soothing, humorless monotone of the mission statement, marketing brochure, and your-call-is-important-to-us busy signal. Same old tone, same old lies. No wonder networked markets have no respect for companies unable or unwilling to speak as they do.

But learning to speak in a human voice is not some trick, nor will corporations convince us they are human with lip service about "listening to customers." They will only sound human when they empower real human beings to speak on their behalf.

While many such people already work for companies today, most companies ignore their ability to deliver genuine knowledge, opting instead to crank out sterile happytalk that insults the intelligence of markets literally too smart to buy it.

If you visit cluetrain.com or read this book and do not laugh at the appalling examples of corporate speak, then you are probably guilty of corporate speak yourself. The problem is that some corporate marketers and their supporting agencies have been speaking this sterile language for so long that they don't know to speak any other language. So finding a creative agency that understands how to write for human beings and how to adapt the tone and style that matches your best customers can prove much harder than you realize.

The third step to master in talking with your most valuable customers is never to forget who they are—frequent customers you value. When you are talking exclusively to your best customers, whether on personalized Web pages or through personalized emails, you will want to adopt a writing style that assumes they know your product but still like to have their smart buying decision reaffirmed. I can't count the number of times I have rejected copy for a frequent customer program brochure because it insulted best customers by talking to them as if they didn't know the products, or worse, as if we didn't know these were our most frequent customers. The copy devoted 50 percent or more to hard selling the customers and never thanked them for their continued loyalty. Keep loyal customers loyal by reinforcing their decision to be loyal. You can do this by serving up hard facts through product surveys and other measurement vehicles, or you can reinforce their decision by featuring successful individuals who also made the same smart buying decisions. But the most important way to keep loyal customers loyal is by thanking and rewarding them for their loyalty.

Community

By visiting a few chat rooms, you can see how the importance of matching the style and tone of your MVCs also applies to community-building tools. Just look at the difference between chat rooms on a women's portal like women.com or a men's portal like ESPN. Women prefer to use chat rooms to poll other women for suggestions and guidance. Men use chat rooms for bragging rights or to announce their decisions or opinions in order to see if others support or reject their beliefs. The desire to have decisions affirmed may be universal, but the means of attaining that affirmation are frequently very different. So managing a chat room to appeal to the preferred chat style of your MVC can be another important content component in your strategy to retain targeted customers.

But, buyer beware! There is too much hype over the potential of online communities. One community software vendor advertisement that concerns me claims, "They stick with us. They'll stick with you. Build your community in 30 days or less." In addition to the fact that you can't build instant customer interest in a community, the whole use of the word "community" is another growing genre problem that contorts Web marketing. These software vendors obviously view community as merely a software tool. It's not the definition I use. The online community is a place where customers with similar interests meet to interact, much like a geographically based community. The Web applications that enable this customer interaction include bulletin boards, chat rooms, messaging, customer recommendation postings, postings from "ask an expert" and, in some cases, polls and auctions. When used correctly, the main objective of hosting these communities is not selling—although that can be a by-product—but to let customers share experiences in order to enrich their lives and businesses or to validate their own beliefs, purchases or even loyalty to a brand. It seems too many websites can't keep the hard sell out of their chat rooms.

In examining communities on the Web, I find most of them to be woefully lacking. Either customer submissions are too quickly addressed by the moderator so that the entire "conversation" is merely a reflection of the company talking, or the place is a ghost town. Companies that try to overmanage chat rooms and bulletin boards by responding to every posting themselves have truly missed the point. Their customers come to share ideas, but get a candy-coated hard sell instead—the community may appear to live on, but the participants are really corporate stand-ins. Chat rooms opened with the best intention of letting customers express their concerns still die off, due to the fact that many products or services don't warrant chat rooms. Are you really surprised that housewives didn't want to talk about ketchup after all? The money would have been better spent on making content more interactive with the product by using Web tools that provide recipes for using what's in your refrigerator and a bottle of ketchup.

I've had both good and bad experiences with community tools. In some cases it can be very beneficial to let customers interact, but in many situations your money will be better spent by selling dynamically, providing richer product content, implementing online service desks, recommending additional uses for your products or offering advice from experts. Kate Delhagen, a senior analyst at Forrester Research, Inc. (www.forrester.com) and coauthor of a recent report titled "Community Pipe Dreams," echoes my advice in her report. Delhagen thinks that most brand marketers and retail sites seem to be hoping to use community-building features as a misguided attempt to build brand awareness. She points out that while Harley-Davidson riders may enjoy participating in chat sessions about their lives and motorcycles, such "brand-lifestyle identifications" are rare. "Unless you're really advanced and have the selling thing down cold, you should forget about trying to build a community around your products or brands," Delhagen says.

Putting up a chat room simply so consumers can talk among themselves is a risky proposition. Even monitored chat rooms/bulletin boards can ultimately backfire on the companies. The typical course of conversation I see in chat rooms begins with comments about how great the product is. This then leads to customers asking "how to" questions among themselves. But soon the participants start to see trends in product failures, and the chat room then turns on the company for not doing something about product deficiencies. Or even worse, two customers report that their problems were treated very differently by customer service (e.g., one got a replacement, the other was told that it wasn't covered under the warranty) and then the chat room members join together against the company. Companies must be active in the chat rooms/bulletin boards to quickly right the wrongs, even if they are merely "perceived" wrongs, before the conversation reaches an explosive point. Otherwise, every customer who enters the chat room/bulletin board will get an earful (or eyeful in this case) on why they shouldn't buy the company's products. Try taking the angry messages off the bulletin board and you will just fan the flames. It can get worse. I've even seen class-action suits start on bulletin boards and employees act as innocent customers in their competitors' chat rooms in an effort to stimulate customers to bad-mouth their competitors. So community builders beware.

I will grant you that customers' feedback from chat rooms/bulletin boards can be very helpful to companies in improving products, but the companies must be prepared to monitor the chat rooms 24/7 and right all the wrongs (perceived or real) as they surface. There is a loyalty principle that a customer with a problem that was solved quickly will be more loyal than a customer who never contacted the company. On a one-on-one basis, using excellent customer service support, I emphatically agree with this principle. But the odds of loyalty being increased start to decline very quickly when customer problems are announced to the entire customer base. Offering customers private chats with online customer service reps and using self-help diagnostic tools might be much safer, more efficient ways to collect customer feedback and solve customer problems.

Bottom line: I would advise against implementing chat rooms and bulletin boards unless you have a clear relationship marketing strategy that includes directing topic discussion through the use of experts. This requires scheduling talk times on given subjects and attracting customers with noted experts. And you will need to plan weekly, if not daily, updates as well as full-time monitors to keep the topics on track and screen postings for foul language and clearly inappropriate comments. Having these types of directed presentation with customer Q&A sessions can be extremely effective in building loyalty to your products and brand, but it does require a serious commitment by your website management to fund the efforts correctly. Here are two great examples of directed online communities.

1. REI.com combines product and safety advice from outdoor adventure experts with bulletin boards for customers to exchange

tips on best locations. The combination keeps disgruntled customers in a one-on-one chat with REI customer service, but
allows customers to exchange ideas and provide their own advice
on localized topics that REI couldn't cover completely.

2. WebMD.com holds live events with health experts and then has
short Q&A sessions following the events. This ensures that the
advisory portion of the website is medically oriented (not customer supplied), but provides interaction with experts for visitors.
Visitors can also share experiences on bulletin boards, but postings are moderated to ensure visitors don't provide others with
questionable advice. The right mix of directed interaction and
medical content ensures the safety of its visitors and the reputation of the website.

Before I leave the subject of community, I want to address other interactive tools that can make the Web experience richer, but which don't
meet my definition of community. There are many interactive, relationship-
building applications improperly lumped into the "community" category
that are more accurately described as content used to build relationships.
Relationship-building applications, like email newsletters or advisory services, self-help "rooms" with a library of aggregated content, self-help
diagnostic tools, virtual reality tours, Web-to-TV/radio interaction, advisory services, calendaring and even reward programs have been herded
into the expanded nomenclature of "community." Don't get me wrong;
these are all good tools, but let's keep them safely corralled into the rela-
tionship- and sales-building barns so there aren't false expectations that
these applications can't maximize sales. Regardless of the categorization,
these Web tools also need to be tailored to the needs of your best customers and accomplishing this requires much the same tactics as true
communities: survey your best customers for appeal on each selected
application, include content relevant to these best customers; deliver the
content in a style and tone that matches these customers; and remember
that these vehicles provide the perfect opportunity for thanking these customers.

Retention Programs

Here is the second "no-brainer" in this list of website features that should be developed based on the needs of your most valuable customers reten- tion programs. But you would be surprised how many retention pro- grams are directed at the masses—average customers. For retention programs to focus on MVCs they have to start with MVCs. This requires using them for program research, not a random sample from your cus- tomer base. You'll probably have to fight your research manager on this point, but it's important. To passify research managers, I've frequently conducted tandem groups of most valuable customers and average cus- tomers. From this research you need to use the most important loyalty drivers for your most valuable customers, to determine what type of retention program will be most likely to retain them. In other words, you need to determine what type of program will best deliver the features, services and benefits that your most valuable customers want in return for loyalty. Then you can build out the selected loyalty program with personalization features, benefits and rewards that will appeal to these most valuable customers.

The goal of these MVC retention programs should be to treat the best customers best. This is especially important with reward programs. Reward programs that are targeted toward best customers will have design features that optimize resources by limiting rewards to best customers, and will make the program aspirational. I will cover loyalty program designs more fully in Step 5, but here are a few examples to illustrate reward strategies that focus on MVCs.

- A point program with award levels attainable only by high-spending customers
- Membership programs that require minimum frequency or spend- ing to be eligible
- Unadvertised programs that quietly upgrade shipping methods, offer exclusive benefits/invitations or send thank-you gifts to MVCs
- Special access channels on a website that offer exclusive informa- tion, but are limited to "established clients" or members

▦ Pricing schedules that ensure high-volume customers receive significant discounts

▦ Interstitials (pop-up windows within a window) that offer special benefits/discounts, but which don't pop up until the tenth visit

▦ Interstitials that pop up only when the order totals a certain amount.

It's important to remember that when a retention program is successful at making customers more loyal, it can typically be a successful acquisition tool as well. In these cases where the retention program is used to acquire customers, it is even more important that the program be targeted to the needs of MVCs. Otherwise the program will acquire average customers and not best customers.

E-Commerce and Customer Service

For years, successful bricks-and-mortar retailers have been developing merchandising schemes to attract the best customers. So it puzzles me that this strategy isn't adopted more often by online stores. Your best customers have shopping preferences, and identifying these preferences as well as adopting an e-commerce design that matches these preferences is one of the secrets of creating e-loyalty for your online store. To develop the depth of customer understanding required to define the shopping preferences of your best customers begins with customer research. Here are some basic shopping preferences you will need to define through customer research and transaction tracking of your most valuable customers.

How do my MVCs make buying decisions? (Drives the basic store layout, merchandising and the information emphasized)

▦ Quality versus price?
▦ Features versus intended use?
▦ Benefits versus style?
▦ Brand versus functionality?

What are the purchase patterns for my MVCs? (Drives how you sell the products, merchandising, payment processes and distribution)

▨ Single component purchases or bundles?
▨ Auto refill, product sampling or upgrades?
▨ Cash or finance?
▨ Buy ahead and stock the product or always buy "just in time"?

When do my MVCs shop? (Drives inventory decisions as well as customer service support strategies)

▨ Morning, noon or night?
▨ Weekly, monthly or quarterly?
▨ Are there seasons or events that drive buying?

What products do my MVCs want/need/buy most often? (Drives inventory)

▨ Inventory products based on MVC purchases
▨ Decide which products to customize/personalize based on MVC transactions
▨ Develop product bundles based on MVCs most commonly combined products
▨ What accessories do MVCs buy or need based on other purchases?

How do my MVCs want to navigate the online store? (Determines basic navigation as well as the need for customized and personalized navigation)

▨ Product type versus product use?
▨ Consultative selling versus price-oriented selling?
▨ Advisory versus self-knowledge?

What information does my MVC need to make a buying decision? (Drives product information quantity, quality and presentation style)

- How much and what information do they need?
- What information is needed to create a solution or to solve a problem?
- How much and what type of content is needed to develop a solution/solve a problem?
- Which product data do they need most often? (This determines the content listed on product page versus subsequent pages)
- Do they need product demos? Do demos address MVC needs?
- Is talking with a customer service rep needed to close the sale?

What service needs do my MVCs have?

- How important is delivery method?
- What delivery assurances are necessary?
- How immediate are MVCs service problems?
- Do MVCs want to talk to a service agent or do they merely want their problem solved via email?
- What level of service can my MVCs receive at competing websites?

I could go on for pages with the possible types of data companies might need from MVCs to drive e-commerce strategy and design decisions. But this list should give you enough ideas for developing your own more specific and comprehensive list.

Your MVCs' shopping patterns should also drive pricing and service policies in your online store. In fact, this is one area where personalization can really be used to maximize revenue and minimize expenses to increase profitability. Here are some examples of how pricing and service strategies can be optimized around your MVC.

- ▦ Offer higher service levels for purchasers of your higher margin products.
- ▦ Where resources are limited, reserve live customer service for MVCs.
- ▦ Provide exclusive service hot lines for MVCs.
- ▦ Send thank-you cards with discount coupons to MVCs.
- ▦ Offer discounts based on customer lifetime value, volume ordered or purchase frequency.
- ▦ Adjust shipping prices to include expedited shipping for MVCs.
- ▦ Develop special sale areas for MVCs.
- ▦ Offer extended sale prices to MVCs.
- ▦ Offer advance purchase opportunities from new product lines.

The pinnacle of customer loyalty occurs when your customers are so loyal that you can charge a price premium without significantly affecting sales. While this may not be an MVC pricing technique, your ability to implement premium pricing will be driven by the extent of their loyalty.

STEP 5: FORMALIZE AN E-LOYALTY PROGRAM FOR YOUR MOST VALUABLE CUSTOMERS

You're cool! You have a million customers registered on your website. The initial public offering was a great success and your stockholders love you. But where is the relationship if customers don't return? You'll read in other books that loyalty can't be bought. I agree that a reward program cannot be a successful loyalty tool without a quality product and good customer service; the basic business offering must be at least on a par with competitors. But it's obvious that these authors have little experience with the strategy or the metrics behind successful reward programs, or they would understand the loyalty they drive. In industries where the product offering is difficult to differentiate, or where price has historically been the only incentive tool, reward programs can be most effective. And never before has it been so difficult to maintain a differentiated experience or product offering than on the Web. The Web can neutralize operational differences and market reach between the "big guys" and the "little guys." Revolutionary enhancements on your website are detected immediately by your competitors and often matched within days or weeks. This new, ultracompetitive landscape, combined with the ability to build customer relationships more economically than ever, make the Web the type of environment where loyalty programs can really unlevel the playing field.

Much of the disdain for reward programs lies in the assumption that rewards must revolve around points, miles, prizes or other monetary incentives. Some of the best loyalty programs use soft benefits as their most effective loyalty tool. Finding the right rewards to motivate loyalty is an art and a science that combines the psychology of your customers with leveraged award values to provide awards that have a greater perceived value than actual costs. The facts do prove that *many* reward programs have failed—but understanding why some succeed and others fail is critical. I've evaluated and disassembled enough poorly designed or poorly executed programs to tell you that more often than not, it was the program designers who failed, not the reward program concept. Too often companies believe that designing reward programs is simple. They charge out on their own, creating programs that are "too rich"—generating unacceptable liabilities and unaffordable program costs—or that are improperly communicated—leading to poor participation rates or customer dissatisfaction. Because of design flaws like these, many programs have to be scrapped; and as you can imagine, terminating these programs causes some ill will among loyal customers.

There are many great examples of offline reward programs that enabled companies to acquire and retain customers despite extreme competition and high customer churn rates in their industry. Because the Web is so new, there are only a few Web programs that have used rewards successfully. Here are just a few examples.

- ▨ After sixteen years, airline miles still drive airline or hotel choice and influence hundreds of purchases in other categories where companies use miles as their reward currency of choice.

- ▦ Sportsline.com used a point program featuring access to unique online sports events to create an overnight success that caused executives of the established ESPN.com website to lose more than one or two nights' sleep over a dropping market share.
- ▦ American Express and the Citibank AAdvantage credit cards manage to charge $50 and $75 annual fees in an industry where "free" is the norm. Without a substantially different product offering—other than earning miles—you have to attribute this success to rewards.
- ▦ In 2000, iWin.com and many other similarly reward-based websites climbed the website ranking charts faster than any other e-business category. That they rose so quickly is impressive, but the fact is that customers continue to frequent the sites due to reward-generated loyalty.
- ▦ The fact that MyPoints' and NetCentives' clients continue to pay high fees for point program services certainly attests to the success these major e-retailers have had using point programs to stimulate sales and retain customers.
- ▦ Neiman Marcus customers, who can shop anywhere, continue their loyalty to the InCircle program in return for invitations to exclusive parties and trendsetting fashion shows. The reward of "exclusive access" seems to be priceless.

But here is where reward program naysayers really must have coat-checked their brains. Do you think that the Jupiter and Cyber Dialogue research reports all misunderstood customers who said they would be 56 percent and 33 percent more likely to frequent a website if it offered points or miles? I think not! Okay, enough soapboxing on my part—you get the message. Reward programs really do work, but only when developed around sound relationship marketing principles, and only after basic service features are reliable.

The branding of a loyalty program can be just as critical as formalizing the rewards. Building loyalty without some sort of moniker to refer to this loyalty phenomenon is like trying to differentiate a product that you sell only by its generic name. The e-loyalty brand (AAdvantage, MyPoints, Gold Club, Best Customer Club, etc.) is what I belong to and where my relationship resides. I don't head to the front of the airline ticket counter line and say, "I'm an American Airlines customer"; I say, "I'm AAdvantage Platinum." Naming the program is particularly important when a company has multiple products or sub-brands they want to cross-sell under one loyalty program. When an envelope arrives with "American Airlines" in the left-hand corner, I toss it. But when an envelope arrives with the golden letters of AAdvantage prominently placed, I open it to get my goodies. I know that the red, white and blue branding means I'm receiving an anonymous sales message, but the gold branding means I'm valued and I will be rewarded for my loyalty. Car rental companies and hotels have understood the power of these golden-branded envelopes for years, and pay dearly to ride on the name of the AAdvantage program. The same is true as online programs establish themselves. Devoted MyPoints fans religiously read their emails from MyPoints to see which retailers are offering the next big point earnings opportunity. But if a retailer issuing MyPoints sends his own email, that email might never get read. It's the MyPoints brand and the relationship expectations that get the email opened and read. So the formalization can be as simple as a name, or as complicated as membership in a point program.

The types of formalized e-loyalty program range from service, to content, to access or prestige and sometimes include monetary rewards driven by point schemes. Formalizing an e-loyalty program makes it clear to customers where the relationship starts and stops. It provides a springboard from which to communicate, and it provides a vehicle for attracting partners to share in your e-loyalty expenses. Step 5, "Formalize an e-Loyalty Program for Your Most Valuable Customers," will not only convince you of the value of a formalized program but will also explain the techniques for selecting the right loyalty program scheme.

The Benefits of a Formal e-Loyalty Program

I've already discussed some of the benefits of formalizing an e-loyalty program, but here are a few more generic benefits.

▦ Creates a sense of relationship that can be referred to by name

▦ Makes it clear where the relationship starts and stops

▦ Provides customers with an incentive to have their transactions tracked, thus providing you with a greater degree of permission marketing from your customers

▦ Provides the ability to regularly recognize a customer's loyalty

▦ Acknowledges a customer's MVC status in every interaction

▦ Includes communication vehicles that keep the dialogue going

▦ Provides a vehicle to attract higher partner revenue streams

By the way, if some of the points above appear on your new proposal for starting or expanding a loyalty program, it won't be the first time I've seen my list of benefits pushed under senior executives' noses. However, you'll need to develop some more specific benefits of implementing a formal e-loyalty program, such as those that follow.

▦ Provides a mechanism for limiting more expensive customer service benefits to MVCs

▦ Provides a clear rule for discount pricing policies

▦ Stimulates customer registration or profiling on your website

▦ Rewards customers for providing additional/extensive customer data

▦ Gives sales reps a tool to incent big companies for consolidating their spending on your website

▦ Allows you to identify your MVCs so that you can use their suggestions to improve your e-business, manufacture the most desired products, ensure inventory of products critical to retaining best customers, etc.

Types of Reward Program

There are a number of different types of formalized e-loyalty program design that can be used to reward loyalty and/or incremental spending. But let me first make it very clear that rewards don't necessarily mean points or awards with clear monetary value. Rewards can be any type of hard benefit (monetary value) or soft benefit (personal value). Hard rewards/benefits are what you are probably most familiar with: points or miles for every dollar spent, goods given at specified spending thresholds, buy twelve and get the thirteenth free, and so on. Soft rewards/benefits come in many forms and are frequently the most aspirational and the most difficult for your competitors to copy. Soft benefits/rewards include access to an exclusive online event, use of privileged information, a moniker on your gaming profile page denoting to other gamers your prestigious skill level, the right to host a special chat room or game room and many others. In fact, the most successful rewards are frequently soft rewards because they are more personally meaningful and directly enhance the product experience. Whether soft or hard rewards are used, the key is to ensure the reward is highly desired by your MVCs and difficult for your competitors to match. If your competitors can easily match your program, you haven't created anything but an additional cost of doing business.

Before I discuss how to select the right program model, let me give a quick review of the basic types of e-loyalty program and some examples.

Service Programs. These programs either provide special services as their point of differentiation, or they give their MVCs special VIP services that enhance the website or product experience. The service could include a special VIP customer service email address, phone number or access to service reps using live online voice applications. For content-rich websites, a service program might include personalized guides assigned to MVCs to help them find topics of interest. Here are some current service program examples.

- *Hertz #1 Gold Club.* This is the mother of all fee-waived service programs. MVCs get fee-waived memberships in the #1 Gold Club.
- *Ebay.com.* Under eBay's SafeHarbor™ program, customers have their own service rated. Traders who value the service record they have built on eBay are reluctant to defect to other auction sites because the opportunity cost would mean starting with no service record, and thus lower bids. The SafeHarbor program is not exclu-

sive to MVCs, but the service is what makes eBay customers loyal; and because the value builds with customers' transactions, it's difficult for competitors to match. That combination makes a very intelligent e-loyalty design.

▨ *Outpost.com.* Outpost.com uses free overnight shipping as its service differentiator, but it can't really be defined as a formalized loyalty program. As Outpost.com becomes more established, and like other online retailers is forced to become profitable, the company would be smart to discontinue the blanket policy of free overnight shipping, and place all of its MVCs into a best customer program that has free overnight shipping as a primary benefit.

▨ *Fidelity.com.* Fidelity.com built a formalized service program for account holders by combining their basic services into their Gold Star Services. The program provides competitive features like stock quotes, personalized pages with portfolios, a stock evaluator and other useful applications. But they've created a best customer program for accounts with $100,000 or more invested called Preferred Services and a Premium Services for customers with $500,000 or more invested. The level of personalized service increases with the service program qualifying tiers. So far, customer loyalty to Fidelity's service has allowed Fidelity to avoid participating in the discount trading wars that its competitors—e*Trade, Ameritrade, Datek and others—have started. The same can't be said of some of the other established brokerages that are hearing the sucking sounds of customers' assets being withdrawn and transferred to discount brokerages.

Information and Advice Programs. These programs use information or advice to enhance a product service or customer experience. Information as a benefit can be based on quality or exclusivity of information, such as is the case with research reports and financial evaluations. The authority of the writer can also make the information more valuable, as is the case with several video game reviewers and medical author celebrities. Even content quantity can be a value factor if information, such as news articles, is aggregated into newsletters or special interest rooms to make the news more relevant and the medium time-efficient. Here are some examples of information and advice programs.

▓ *IBM Owner Privileges.* When I began designing IBM's consumer loyalty program, I found that several service features were unique and that the quality and timeliness of product information were above average for the industry. Marketing each of these advantages separately had not been effective, so I bundled them into a formalized membership program and added advisory services. The membership program, IBM Owner Privileges, not only increased recognition of the service and information benefits increase but increased the perceived value as well. Offering the membership program as a buyer's privilege also increased registration, allowing IBM to gather information on their customers. That program is now used to sell IBM products directly to consumers.

▓ *TheStreet.com.* Selling Web content is a difficult business model, especially in the crowded field of financial websites. But the founders of TheStreet.com understood what investors wanted in a financial news source: "financial reporting and analysis that is current, insightful, honest, uncompromising and objective. News so current it puts you virtually on the trading floor." The community features and information are the product, just as they are with many financial sites, but the quality and timeliness make them TheStreet.com's source of loyalty as well.

▓ *Garden.com.* This site does many things right, but the membership requirement behind their premium advisory services is worth noting. There is plenty of advisory content throughout Garden.com, including a Garden Doctor advisory section with static advice. But to get interactive advice from a horticultural specialist, you have to be a registered member of the site. Garden.com knows their MVCs are serious gardeners, and serious gardeners want to access experts. By offering the expert service, they not only attract potential MVCs but are also able to identify them, track them and treat them as MVCs.

▩ *Sales.com*. Developed by Siebel Systems as a sales rep community to support their sales products, Sales.com became so successful that it was spun off into a stand-alone business that offers advisory services to sales reps. Most of the advice and services are for members only, and the site features both free and paid premium memberships. The membership requirement not only incents registration but sets expectations that the site is about belonging to this sales rep "club" of insider information. But even more brilliant is the fact that the sales advisory tools and services offered to members are loyalty builders in that the more customer or daily task information a sales rep enters, the higher the quality of advice and service. Defecting would mean having to reenter this information into a new website—something most sales reps don't have time for.

Discount Programs. This type of program is fairly straightforward. Members receive coupons or instant savings on selected products or from program partners. The concept can be used as a general membership program, or can be an exclusive benefit for best customers. Here are some examples that illustrate these two program applications.

▩ *FreeShop.com*. While FreeShop.com is a discount provider, it has created a program called Club FreeShop that sends members emails with opportunities for free or discounted items in the categories for which they sign up. The separate membership to Club FreeShop creates a greater perceived value over a simple sign-up registration form that most other discount sites use. Before being merged into Yahoo!, YoYodyne was the master of membership programs for discounts.

▩ *AA.com*. AAdvantage members receive access to special fare sale information.

▩ *Schwab.com*. Schwab offers its best traders participation in its Active Trader Commission Discounts program, which has a tiered discount program based on quantity of trades.

▣ *Bluefly.com.* This e-business uses discounts as its general sales model. While the discounts drive loyalty to the website, this program can feel more like a pricing strategy than a customer program. As discount sites become more popular and are required to be more profitable, we will likely see membership fee requirements to buy from these discount websites. The annual member fees will present both a higher perceived value and an opportunity cost of defecting, which will in turn drive loyalty.

Community Programs. These programs revolve around letting customers interact with one another. Recall that my definition of community involves customer interaction, not just one-on-one communications between the customer and the website. Chat rooms, bulletin boards and customer opinion postings are all techniques for creating this interaction. But what drives loyalty from community is a feeling of belonging or identifying with the group. When successful, communities can even be extended to the point where customers believe the community cares about them. Here are some of the better known Web community programs engendering loyalty to the brands that host them.

▣ *HarleyDavidson.* This motorcycle manufacturer's community is so successful that the community is more about a spirit of independence and adventure, shared by all, than it is a motorcycle club.
▣ *Amazon.com's Oprah's Book Club.* This community not only increased book sales, it is credited with raising literacy rates.
▣ *Apple.* Apple is the king of community in the hardware industry. Their long-time users are fiercely loyal. The only problem with this community is that it revolves around graphics, advertising and publishing, which unfortunately has not been a large enough user group to grow Apple's market share.
▣ *SmartGirl.com.* I call this the intelligent teen girl site. Its community of teen girls has an incredible sense of belonging because they create most of the site content themselves.

Access Programs. Successful access programs generate an emotionally driven loyalty by providing customers with an avenue to exclusive events, people, openings or information to which they otherwise couldn't gain access. This type of program can be a particularly strong loyalty driver because it is typically based on an emotional response, such as status, exclusivity, power or even lifetime wishes. Access programs are typically combined with either a membership fee, a point program or a spending/frequency threshold program that tracks customers to determine qualification for access. Below are some uniquely different programs— uniqueness being common to successful access programs because it appeals at a deep emotional level and is therefore harder for competitors to match.

▦ *Neiman Marcus.* The InCircle Program at Neiman Marcus is one of the oldest and most successful access programs. The program offers customers points that can be redeemed for classy trinkets, but that's not what these customers value. They value invitations to exclusive in-store parties, high-visibility receptions at the symphony and opportunities to meet top fashion designers.

▦ *Sportsline.com.* SportslineRewards Plus uses access to unique events to make customers loyal to its website as well as its point program. Access to events such as live chats with Tiger Woods, an interview with Magic Johnson or, best yet, the chance to win Michael Jordan's used Chevy Blazer (who'd a thought?) all give members experiences they couldn't get access to on their own.

▦ *AOL.* AOL is in many ways using an access loyalty model to retain customers. AOL has partnered with or acquired many good sites, so that much of the related content is available only from AOL. AOL also offers customers free access to content that other websites normally charge for, such as with AOL's partnership with *Business Week* that allows AOL customers to view gratis what Business-Week.com visitors must pay for.

Entertainment Programs. These programs generate loyalty purely on their ability to entertain their customers. The entertainment could be in the form of humor, games, jokes, trivia, video clips or other forms of online entertainment. Here are a few examples.

▨ *Fool.com.* I would be remiss not to mention these two kings of entertainment. The Motley Fools have built loyalty to an entire financial media enterprise based on their entertaining approach to financial planning.

▨ *Uproar.com.* This is a targeted marketing website that keeps customers loyal by letting them play games for free. To play the games, visitors must profile, or in some cases give their names to Uproar partners.

▨ *Moviefone.com.* You could go to any localized portal and get movie listings, but at Moviefone.com you get a wide selection of movie trailers to view and advance notice of movies. For movie buffs, the entertainment of live video makes them more loyal to Moviefone.com than a localized portal such DigitalCity.com or CitySearch.com.

▨ *Reebok.com/Nike.com.* Both of these sports apparel companies have successfully used entertainment to keep customers returning to their websites. Reebok.com has used extensive games with new versions and sequences appearing each week. Nike.com hooks a viewer by using an unfinished humor scenario on television, which refers viewers to the website to see the "exciting conclusion." Once the customers are on their site, Nike keeps them coming back as the story continually unfolds like a well-planned soap opera.

Point programs. These programs need no explanation. The velocity with which point programs are sweeping through the Web is blinding. Old currencies like airline miles are still popular, but proprietary currencies and new Web-wide point currencies are also gaining popularity. Here are examples of currency that are winning customers.

▦ *ClickRewards* uses points, transferable into the airline mileage program of your choice

▦ *MyPoints* gives points redeemable for awards (company manages an open-Web program as well as proprietary versions of the program)

▦ *CyberCash* gives points redeemable for cash

▦ *Alladvantage* reward currency is monetary currency of the customer's home country

▦ *Sportsline.com* is a proprietary program offering points for participation.

Unanticipated Rewards. This is a tricky program category because by definition its unscheduled rewards don't sound like a formalized program; however, when strategically administered, customers learn to expect the "unexpected." Unanticipated rewards are used to thank customers for a specific behavior and can also be used to stimulate incremental transactions. Giving a discount coupon for every fifth transaction or for every $500 spent or for trying a new product or service are all strategies for giving unanticipated rewards. These rewards can also be tied to product cycles or buying cycles so that the unanticipated reward reminds the customer of a given product when they are most likely to be in the decision-making or buying cycle. One of the most compelling reasons to use unanticipated rewards is that they are perceived by customers to be a more sincere "thank-you" than awards earned from point or frequency programs. Identifying examples of unanticipated reward programs is tough since they are never advertised and are normally not discussed, because to do so would reveal the very planned strategy of this seemingly impromptu thank-you. But here are a few examples.

▦ *American Express.* For years cardholders would receive impromptu thank-you cards from American Express which would enclose a dollars-off coupon for dinner at a local restaurant. Of course the coupon was stimulative for both AMEX and the restaurant.

▦ *BN.com*. I'm a frequent customer of Barnes & Noble and have noticed that some of my shipments include a generous dollars-off coupon. My shipment at Christmastime included four coupons for $10 off a $10 purchase that I could give to my friends as gift certificates (nicely executed as an unanticipated reward and a viral marketing tool all rolled into one communication). I haven't determined if the coupons are event-driven or seasonal, but they certainly generate incremental recommendations and spending on my part.

▦ *PlanetRx.com*. When you buy your first order from PlanetRx, the shipment arrives via overnight delivery at no extra charge. The company doesn't promise this service, but it believes in the theory that first impressions are lasting ones, so it gives the unanticipated benefit of expediting shipment on the first order. PlanetRx also uses generously sized product samples in fancy packaging for unanticipated rewards. As marketers we know this is a simple trial promotion, but PlanetRx is smart enough to position the samples as unanticipated "gifts." And these gifts all serve to stimulate sales of new products.

How to Select the Best Reward Program Strategy for Your MVCs

I wish I could give you an easy answer on how to pick the right reward program for your customer base, but quite honestly, program design really does require experience with the strengths and weaknesses of each program type. Now I don't say that because I consult on this topic every week, but because I have seen many companies attempt this process and implement the wrong programs due to a lack of experience. The other essential ingredient for success is to have a complete and thorough knowledge of your customer base, and typically my clients don't know enough about their customers even to begin the design process. This is why most of the program design projects I complete begin with a more in-depth analysis of the customer data than had previously been undertaken, or it requires executing primary research to learn more about the targeted customers. Even with program design experience and customer knowledge, the reward program design process is still difficult in that it requires analyzing and optimizing multiple selection criteria simultaneously. Here are some of the steps you will need to take to select a program design.

- Determine which program models will optimize your business/ website goals and objectives.
- Develop a customer segmentation that identifies who the reward model needs to retain (i.e., MVCs).
- Determine which reward models enhance the critical drivers of loyalty (i.e., product offering, quality, service or image).
- Evaluate each selected program model to ensure it does not adversely effect critical margin drivers or business processes that drive profitability and operational efficiencies.
- Determine which program model best matches the purchase frequency and best rewards the desired behavior.
- Determine which program models appeal to your MVCs.
- Analyze your competition's loyalty efforts to evaluate successful reward models.
- Forecast program costs and incremental profits for preferred models to determine if the program model is affordable given your product's margin or specified program budget.

The first three selection criteria bulleted above were explained in Steps 1 and 2 earlier in this section of the book, so I won't cover them again. But the remaining selection criteria need more explanation, which follows.

Critical margin drivers and business processes

While I always advocate that companies should give customers the rewards they want, not the rewards companies want to give them, this principle if taken to the extreme will compromise your basic profitability model. The reward program design needs to complement your business model. For example, if you are in the shaving business, you need to consider whether you are in the razor, blade or shaving services business.

▦ If you're in the razor business, then rewarding customers with
blades makes more financial sense and it keeps customers using
your product.

▦ If you're in the blades business, rewarding customers with blades
would have a negative impact on your profitability model; whereas
if you reward customers with a new proprietary razor, it not only
protects your blade sales margins but also keeps customers loyal to
your proprietary blades.

▦ If you're in the shaving services business, what your customers
might want most is a free shave after every ten shaves; however, you
need to weigh the opportunity cost of forgoing the profit margin on
each eleventh shave against the cost of buying a shaving-related
reward. Ideally, you would want to recruit a reward program partner that reduces your cost of providing customers with shaving-
related rewards (e.g., expert advice on men's skin care, aftershave,
cologne, skin care products, etc.).

The shaving example helps to illustrate the need to consider business
processes. Here are a few current Web models and the business processes
that must be considered before selecting a reward program.

▦ *Advertising Web model.* On a content website sponsorships and
advertising comprise a significant portion of revenues. Therefore,
any reward program that stimulates click throughs on advertisers' or
sponsors' messages will enhance the business model.

▦ *Fee/membership Web model.* For sites that operate on a membership fee, the program needs to stimulate customers to renew their
subscription each month/year.

▦ *High-margin e-commerce model.* Almost all reward programs will be
financially feasible for this model, but will the customers feel all
reward models are appropriate? High-end retail customers won't
learn difficult program rules or self-manage a tracking process, but
will respond well to point programs that are fully automated and
offer rewards that are compatible with their status and taste (partic-

ularly soft rewards that offer them access to something they wouldn't ordinarily be able to buy).

▦ *Low-margin e-commerce model.* On e-commerce websites that have trouble moving customers from browsing to buying, the product margins can't support a program based upon expenditures. The program design needs to reward trial or conversion on the first few orders, while implementing a different type of loyalty tool to retain customers who are comfortable with buying online.

Purchase frequency and desired behaviors

Purchase frequency should drive program concept design. This is because infrequently purchased products require a completely different approach than replenishment goods (e.g., a frequency-based program). The same is true if your best customers purchase substantially more frequently than average customers (e.g., the ubiquitous frequent flier gold program model). Because frequent purchases involve much more frequent interaction with a program it is easier to use the program as a loyalty tool that reminds customers of the reason they remain loyal (e.g., credit card mileage programs). A website that enjoys a high frequency of visits is able to reward nonpurchase behavior such as trying new features, reviewing new products, voting on new product enhancements, visiting more frequently, viewing more pages or any other desired behavior. While the reward for these types of nonpurchase activity might only be pennies or fractions of pennies, many customers find mere fun in earning these points or the monthly total point earnings is enough to keep their loyalty.

The difficulty lies with infrequent purchases—automobiles, household appliances, durable goods, etc.—where customer interaction is typically limited to service issues when a loyalty program isn't in place to stimulate more positive customer interactions. Automobile manufacturers tried to use credit cards to incent loyalty, under the guise that the card would create more frequent interactions and that it would instill an opportunity cost. While these cards may have been effective on some customers, like my mother, who would have purchased a Ford-Mercury product despite the credit card, they aren't effective for customers who want to consider other brands. Thus, the only customers who these cards made loyal were already loyal. The credit card rebate became nothing more than a discount that reduced the margin on purchase by their best customers.

For infrequent purchase categories, the lease is one of the most successful loyalty program models because it maintains a monthly dialogue with customers and allows manufacturers to know when a customer is considering a new purchase. Frequently, leases also involve financial "hook" that make repurchase more advantageous. These types of financial hooks follow the loyalty design principle of creating "opportunity cost" that I describe later in this book.

Appeal of the selected program models

Not all program models appeal to all customers. In particular, the reward of information can be tricky. Information rewards work only within a carefully crafted program, in select situations, where either the product itself turns information into power (programs for gamers that give tips and advice) or the information is critical to the customer's needs (health updates on a disease or stock market changes for investors).

The appeal of earning points that can be redeemed for awards appears to many to be somewhat universal, but doesn't always appeal to a given customer set because of the operational requirements, the belief that it doesn't fit with the product or purely cultural appropriateness. The best example is Air Miles, which launched a grocery program whereby customers earned miles for purchases. The program bombed in the United States but was a huge hit in Canada, where it still operates successfully today. Americans didn't think points belonged in the grocery store and weren't willing to deal with the program's operational requirements for mere pennies on the dollar. Points for dollars spent in casual dining chain restaurants also didn't make the record books. The difficulties in executing the restaurant program consistently nationwide were too great and diners didn't perceive the rewards as substantial enough based on the total check price they were paying.

A second area of consideration is reward programs for children. If you think online registration rules for children are too restrictive, then you aren't going to like the fact that some states require customers to be eighteen years old to participate and that all states require parental permission. Children's purchase patterns are typically driven by so many factors other than loyalty to a website or brand that other loyalty programs which affect their emotional buying behaviors can be more successful. Anyone who has taken a teenager shopping knows the difficulties of teen buying behaviors. There are two exceptions to my advice. The first is when points are used to influence *where* a purchase is made, not *what* is purchased. The teen market represents a significant percentage of discretionary income, so I am sure awarding teens points for shopping with a website's partners or affiliates will become commonplace. The second exception where point programs for children really work is when points are rewarded for game play. The thrill of winning becomes much greater when points are awarded, and the thrill isn't consummated until the winnings are spent in the online store.

Evaluate competitors' programs

There aren't too many industries that don't have some type of loyalty program in place. For some industries, like travel, the loyalty currency of airline miles is so entrenched that no other program has been successful in competing with miles. By the same token, miles for travel are so commonplace that to differentiate, companies have created gold and platinum tiers on their programs to provide their best customers with other benefits. The mileage currency is slowly permeating the Web as well with programs like ClickRewards, MyPoints and e-Centives signing up more and more companies for this common currency.

Implementing a reward program in an industry where there are already loyalty programs requires an in-depth study of current program reward values and an understanding of what is working and what isn't. Determining reward value can be difficult. For hard rewards the evaluation requires you to understand what customers perceive the award to be worth, regardless of the manufacturer's suggested retail price (MSRP).

For soft benefits that have no MSRP, assigning a value can be almost impossible, which is also what makes them such an effective aspirational component as well as an effective way to make your program difficult for competitors to match. To see an analysis of a point program valuation, go to the website (www.e-loyalty.com) that supports this book, where there are several reports on reward program evaluations. Determining which programs are working and which programs are not requires some creative research. Here are some of the techniques I have found useful in getting the inside scoop on a program, some of which would have made Sun-tzu proud.

■ Enroll in all your competitors' programs and all programs similar to your own that are offered in other noncompetitive industries. Assign a staff member(s) to participate in these programs and report his (their) findings.

■ Formalize a program that rewards your employees for supplying information on competitors. When your employees obtain the help of friends and family in your search, your reach will become larger than you expect.

■ Subscribe to a news service that tracks news (press releases as well as published articles) on your competitors' programs. Advertisement and direct mail clipping services are also important in picking up information that didn't make your news search.

■ If the company has a bricks-and-mortar establishment, quiz employees on the success of the customer program, then compliment the manager on what a great program it is. You'll frequently find he'll gush forward with program success stories that he is proud of. (This is one of my personal favorites and has been so successful for me that I have had clients pay me to use this technique for gathering information at several competitors' establishments. It proves that Southern charm goes a long way in gathering marketing intelligence.)

■ Use the reward program customer service desk (most effective if it's a live call) and talk to the service rep about your problems, requests, reward choices, and so on, then ask if your requests are different than other customers participating in the program.

▦ Always attend seminars where your competitors' marketing managers are speaking. Frequently, you'll gain information from the presentation itself, but you can also use the Q&A session to ferret out additional information. It's amazing what companies let their marketing staff say at seminars, and you should take advantage of it.

▦ Recruit research participants from a website frequented by your competitors' customers and ask them about their satisfaction with your competitors' programs. I have even uncovered customers participating in a competitor's test program using this technique; it gave my client an important advance view on his competitor's next move.

▦ Become a client of the major Internet analyst companies such as Forrester Research, IDC (International Data Corporation), Jupiter Communications or Cyber Dialogue and you will uncover information in their white papers and research papers. More important, you'll gain access to analysts who have contacts in every industry and can help you with competitive information.

▦ Hire a marketing analyst away from your competitor. While I don't advocate this last technique, I see it done all the time. Just be aware that if this individual is willing to spill his or her guts to you, he or she won't have trouble doing it a second time with your company's information.

Affordability of program

Before you get too far down the road with your new reward model, be sure to have an experienced reward program analyst price out the program. This includes both the operational expenses as well as the forecasted reward costs. While the operational expenses can be developed by a less-experienced marketing manager, the forecast of awards redeemed is both a science and an art. It's a science in that many of the forecasting techniques are basic business modeling techniques, but the art comes into play when you need to develop assumptions that drive the model.

This is when experience with various programs and the behaviors of different customer types come into play.

Point program operations can be very expensive due to the software costs. This is why several point program managers, such as MyPoints and ClickRewards, have made successful businesses out of being outsourcing vendors. As I tell every client who wants to implement a point program, there are many other reward programs that are just as effective as points but have much lower reward and operational costs. Programs that feature special services can quickly become exorbitantly expensive if the most costly of these services is not limited to best customers.

One last note on affordability. Many companies test the affordability of a program design based on whether it can be launched within an initial fixed budget. Successful reward programs that can be proven to retain customers and generate incremental revenues should be budgeted based on a percentage of incremental revenue (i.e., value of retained customer and incremental purchases stimulated by the program). This budgeting logic frequently leads to expensing a reward program based on fixed and incremental expense components, with the fixed component not charged against the program budget. The fixed component might include things like the marketing staff and advertising and database expenses since these expenses would be incurred regardless of what type of marketing program is implemented. The incremental expenses generated by the program would include items that the company would not buy if it weren't for the reward program (e.g., additional web development, award costs, program specific emails, etc.). These incremental costs should be limited to a predetermined percentage of product revenues established to fund the program. Typically the percentage of revenues devoted to a reward program is between 2 and 5 percent. I have seen two programs with costs as high as 7 percent and 10 percent of revenues, but neither of these programs still exist today. I'm certain that the programs were "too rich," resulting in a negative ROI when measured against incremental revenues. For a full budgetary model for forecasting reward programs, see the program budget and forecast modeling tools at www.e-loyalty.com.

But don't overlook savings as a source of revenue. Partner, sponsorship and advertising revenues generated by the program should also be credited against program expenses. To estimate savings, simply calculate the difference between the cost of the marketing project with and without the partner participation. Post the difference as a credit against expenses. Whenever possible, these types of revenue opportunity should be used to make the program self-funding. I'll cover this more fully in part III of this book.

When Not to Select a Reward Program Strategy

I've been known all my life as a rule breaker. So I have no problem breaking my own rules for formalizing a reward program. There are a few businesses where an ongoing, formalized reward program doesn't make much sense. My favorite example is ketchup. I don't think ketchup brands need formalized reward programs unless all children eat like my niece, putting ketchup on everything. But even with all that ketchup consumption going on in my brother's house, the kid is brand indiscriminate, so there's little hope of appealing to kids who fall in and out of dozens of eating hang-ups. There just isn't enough long-term intense interest in the product, or the possibility of a serious relationship, to warrant a program. Ketchup brands would be smarter to participate in established customer reward programs as partners and sponsors rather than try to build momentum in their own program. Or maybe they should just pay more sitcoms to feature ketchup-thirsty munchkins—that seems to be where kids pick up most of their peculiarities today.

There is so much "noise" in the marketplace created by companies competing for the relationships of customers that it's not realistic to think that every brand can have a successful reward program. Brands need to first ask if customers *want* to have a relationship with their product or company, and then determine whether the company has the money to raise their program high enough over the noise level to be noticed. Much like ketchup, there are many package goods or replenishment brands that customers value and trust, but they don't think a reward program is appropriately matched to the product. A number of grocery programs have been launched, but just as many have failed due to the low margins of the industry. It will be interesting to see if the e-grocers can generate a higher margin that will support a reward program. Packaged goods manufacturers have created every variety of box-top collection program you can think of, but these programs have never really changed the loyalty landscape. One of the few packaged goods reward programs that has the breadth and depth of brands and industry penetration necessary genuinely to stimulate loyalty is the Betty Crocker Red Spoons program. But I'm afraid my lifelong dream of turning that program around will never materialize as long as Betty Crocker continues to ignore the program's potential. Most package goods manufacturers will find it more effective to participate in online reward programs that aggregate brands into a single program.

Healthcare and prescription brands are another area where loyalty marketers have to tread lightly. Customers are rightfully suspicious of drug companies that want customers to be more loyal by taking more of a prescribed product. Any type of point program launched by a brand rather than a retailer would appear more as an addiction program than a loyalty program. The exceptions are drug programs that offer the reward of information to improve your health and move you off the drug. I've seen successful programs for a smoking-cessation product and a sleep aid that actually coached customers through a drug dosage program with the goal of moving customers to a "medication-free" state. The ability of health websites to generate loyalty for healthcare brands is why many health-related websites with strong pharmaceutical partnerships are poised to meet with financial success.

Businesses that are required by law to treat all customers equally may also have difficulty implementing a successful program that rewards best customers best. Too often the programs can't adequately incent the most loyal customers and therefore have limited financial success. Utility companies fall into this category, which is why companies in this industry have launched and discontinued more reward programs than any other industry I can think of. The legal restrictions governing these companies make program strategy difficult. In several cases, even when loyalty program specialists were brought in to design the programs, failure was inevitable when the utility company turned the programs over to general ad agencies who didn't understand program strategy, economics or communication requirements. MCI's partnership with AAdvantage has been the only program with real staying power, and much of this success can be attributed to the MCI product and the experienced partner management staff at American Airlines who coached MCI through all member communications and program changes. For utilities of any type that don't first build consumer trust through product quality, customer service, fair pricing and honest communications, no reward program is going to be successful.

One industry in which you probably wouldn't think of creating a reward program is charity fund-raising. But with a careful and tasteful strategy the industry is ripe for reward programs. For years, local charities have used the reward of "exclusive access" as a means to drive charitable giving. As a case in point, an invitation to the exclusive fundraising event like the Cattle Baron's Ball is more certain after a generous donation to that social group's charitable cause. The standard ploy of status-conscious individuals desiring access into exclusive social circles like this has frequently been to donate substantial sums. It wouldn't take much creativity to turn these concepts into a formalized program to stimulate charitable giving. Instead, most national charity programs have used the tactic of guilt and shame as their fundamental tool for stimulating giving— yuck!

Key Design Principles for Optimizing Your Selected Reward Program Model

Once you have selected the best reward program model, it's time to optimize that model for your best customers. There are hundreds of design elements that will need to be optimized as you develop your program. Some design principles are obvious, like designing program features to appeal to your MVCs. But some design principles are less obvious to those unfamiliar with designing loyalty programs. Here are eleven program design principles for a successful e-loyalty strategy.

1. Give customers what they want, not what you want to give them

If you think this design principle is one of the obvious ones, it's because you haven't been in my shoes. Far too often, companies want to give customers that which costs the least, such as low cost or discontinued products, personalized Web features that they should give all customers by virtue of the Web medium, or even worse—whatever they have too much of in the warehouse. And surprise, surprise, customers don't find these products desirable.

Giving customers want they want in a service-related program is even more critical for e-business. So if your service program concept doesn't meet a customers' expectations—whatever they may be—change it, enhance it or deliver it differently. Given the speed and interactivity of the Web, the explosion of customer choice, the emergence of new competitive pressures and the expansion of customers' expectations for service, just giving customers what they want might not be enough. You must be able to anticipate needs, solve problems before they start and offer responses to mistakes that more than make up for the original error. In short, you will have to provide a service program that goes beyond customers' expectations and really wows them.

Whether it's rewards, service access or any other type of reward or benefit, to keep customers loyal and ultimately generate incremental sales or transactions you have to give customers what they want, not necessarily what you want to give them. The only way to know what customers want is to ask them, and the only way to anticipate what they want is to know them well.

2. Make it aspirational

If you are to generate incremental transactions of any kind, the reward not only has to be something the customer wants, it needs to be aspirational. In other words, the reward must go beyond "okay" and be highly desirable. One of the most successful ways to build aspirational qualities into your reward program is to implement membership or reward tiers so that customers can "aspire" to earn a certain level of membership that is accompanied by benefits, status or access they desire. Again, some of the most effective aspirational components in a reward program are soft benefits. Some reward programs don't even enroll customers until they have met a purchase threshold or have met some other quantitative standard.

3. Create an opportunity cost

A strategy that creates an opportunity cost is one of the most important, and yet one of the most overlooked, components of a successful reward program. There must be a perceived opportunity cost to the customer for not concentrating all their transactions on a website or for defecting from the website. Here are some common opportunity cost strategies used in e-loyalty programs and websites that have implemented the strategy well.

- ▦ A superior level of service earned by being a best customer. These customers would have to forgo this superior service if they defected (AA.com)
- ▦ A superior level of personalization built through multiple customer interactions would be lost and a customer would have to start as an unknown at a new website (Amazon.com)
- ▦ Upgraded shipping or free shipping for best customers (VictoriasSecret.com)
- ▦ Point balances that cannot be transferred to other point programs (Sportsline.com)
- ▦ Access to interviews with celebrities (CDNow.com)
- ▦ Preferred service accounts for account holders with $200,000 or more invested (Fidelity.com)
- ▦ Lower stock trade prices after thirty or more trades (Schwabb.com)
- ▦ Membership that gives customers exclusive information that provides customers an advantage (TheStreet.com)

4. Use personalization as a program differentiator

You can learn a lot about customers by having them tell you which rewards they are most interested in. For example, family-oriented rewards suggest the customer has a family. Many times the rewards will suggest favorite hobbies, sports, retailers, and the like. For years this type of information has been used to select awards which incent the greatest number of customers. But the Web allows you to actually customize, or even personalize, an award program.

You can customize rewards by:

▓ Creating award charts that are customized to certain customer segments

▓ Creating reward program areas that feature program news or awards that appeal to a segment of customers and then encourage customers with similar interests to interact

▓ Giving best customers access to an exclusive reward area that has unique awards

▓ Sending emails that feature awards most likely to appeal because they are based on their award preferences to date

▓ Tailoring award charts based on customer data

You can personalize rewards by:

▓ Letting customers personalize their own award chart by selecting the awards of most interest and building them into a personal award chart on their home page

▓ Letting customers personalize their awards by bidding on awards at an auction

▓ Fulfilling individual needs by personalizing award charts using one-to-one principles; i.e., the customer submits his/her award ideas and those which are accepted are put into the customer's personal award chart

▓ Sending emails that feature awards in which a customer identified an interest

▓ Customizing communications to feature other customers who redeemed the same award in which the customer is interested

▓ Offering reward program promotions that earn a reward specified by the customer

By personalizing your reward program, it will become more difficult for competitors to match your program. A posted award chart is fairly simple to match, but a personalized reward chart viewable only by the customer becomes far more difficult to match—both monetarily and emotionally.

5. Create opportunities for personal involvement and interaction with your company

Use the program to create a sense of personal involvement. The most direct involvement a customer can have is to participate in new product design and new program improvements. Loyal customers want to be involved in making your product better, because it, in turn, improves their experience. Simply letting customers interact with your company's management might also give customers the sense of participation they want.

At other times, interaction with the program itself is what customers desire; this frequently includes customer-to-customer interaction. Loyal customers want to meet others who are happy with your website and/or products so they can validate their decision or enhance their own product experience through tips and advice from more experienced individuals. As I discussed in Step 4, this "community" experience can be very effective in building a relationship between a customer and an e-loyalty program, but it needs to be carefully directed to be successful.

Here is one of the most important ways to create involvement: "localize" your program. Yes, I do mean geographically, in both the physical and virtual senses. For many customers, an online program is more like a virtual program—not really real. When I launched the IBM Owner Privileges program, customers didn't really feel the program was real until they received a mailing—a tangible. Many customers have the same feeling. One of the first online game networks, Sega HEAT, regularly hosts game tournaments in cities around the nation for players to meet each other and actually see and touch Sega HEAT. These players meet online every week, but the opportunity to meet other players physically makes the relationship more real and the bond stronger. To compete with bricks-and-mortar stores, many successful websites are now building "token" bricks-and-mortar locations to reach out to their customers and make the relationship more real. Gateway Computers was the first to initiate this strategy, and it's rumored that many others are to follow. The localization component becomes particularly important for websites with high-ticket items. Websites that feature designer jewelry and furniture are likely to be the next Web successes that localize their relationships.

One industry that is certain to build bricks-and-mortar locations is interior design retailers who sell wallpaper, paint, blinds, fabrics and other related products. These direct order retailers are running the local retailers out of business by selling at 50 to 80 percent off retail prices. But the Web direct stores need their competitor's bricks-and-mortar stores because customers have traditionally gone to them to browse wallpaper and other product books, then ordered online or by phone. Using bricks-and-mortar stores enabled the direct sales companies to avoid any type of showroom or the purchase of expensive wallpaper books. The problem is that interior design products, such as wallpaper, paint and fabric, are extremely hard to buy without seeing first. The intermediate step will likely be that websites offering interior design supplies will let customers order samples to be mailed to their home; however, this will increase the expense of their low-cost operations, and customers are likely to see the prices on interior design products creep back up. Smart Web retailers will partner with the local stores to create a "local" presence and create a new business model that combines the two.

If you can't localize your program geographically, there are several techniques for creating local versions of your program.

- Create awards that are local (local theater, concert, sporting event tickets).
- Use testimonials from customers who live near the customer receiving the testimonial messages.
- Create chat rooms for customers within the same geographical locations to meet or create bulletin boards that discuss product/service features that are specific to a geographical condition (cold/snow in the North and hot/sand in the South).

▥ Use local celebrities within your program (feature as customers or use to promote program features).

6. Treat best customers best

Customers aren't equal and shouldn't be rewarded equally. They know they aren't equal, even though low-value customers will initially tell you that it isn't fair for best customers to get better benefits. Once you explain the magnitude of difference in their spending, these low-value customers may still grumble a bit, but you aren't going to lose their business over the fact that they are jealous. So you shouldn't be afraid to treat best customers best. State clearly the advantages and benefits of being one of your best customers, and the qualification for being a best customer. Treating best customers best not only shows real gratitude to your best customers, it also creates an aspirational component that will stimulate potential high-value customers. As I've pointed out previously, treating best customers best also ensures that your marketing expenditures are spent on those customers who will provide the greatest return on your investment.

The Web allows reward programs to take this concept to the extreme by varying pricing, awards, product selection and more, based on a customer lifetime value. Many websites are blatant in their best customer pricing, showing two prices for every item (the regular price and the members-only price). Posting award charts with much more exciting awards for members is another way to reward as well as inspire customers. But all of these practices also work when communicated only with best customers; in fact, creating some mystique around the members-only benefits can make the best customer tier more aspirational.

7. Convey genuine gratitude

Successful programs convey genuine gratitude for customers' loyalty, unencumbered by a sales message. You simply need to thank them regularly. It's one of the most important motivators for repeat purchases. This could be a simple email, but it sometimes has more impact as a mailing with a small gift. As for your most valuable customers, you need to routinely recognize them as "best" and thank these customers profusely.

But just as important, you need to demonstrate that you value their continued loyalty. This means waiving service fees, crediting accounts for service problems or misunderstandings and upgrading the product whenever possible. There are many ways to demonstrate you value loyalty online. Here are just a few.

- Don't just "welcome" customers back to your home page; thank them for coming back.
- Develop thank-you interstitials that pop up based on frequency (interstitials are browser windows that pop up within the Web page being viewed).
- Develop personalized thank-you messages on your order confirmation page.
- Send emails with thank-you gift certificates.

8. Know the return on investment of your program before launching

As a loyalty program designer, I live by these two rules: if you can't measure it, don't design it; and if it doesn't have a positive return on investment (ROI), don't launch it. The only time it's appropriate to launch a program with a negative ROI is if that program supports a separate business objective that is critical to the business. I've discussed the benefits of forecasting the incremental costs and revenues of a program on previous pages and I will discuss the process for determining ROI in more detail in the latter half of this book. But it is important to note again that you need to know the ROI of your program *prior* to launching, not after.

9. Always have an exit strategy

Even the best-laid schemes of mice and men can go afoul—the same is true for reward programs. Even the smartest reward strategy can be made obsolete by a competitor's actions, especially when those actions disregard basic profitability measures. I have always abided by the rule that "your reward program is only as competitive as your dumbest competitor." This means that if your competitor establishes reward values at a rate substantially higher than your own—even to its own financial detriment—your program is no longer competitive and you will either have to match the competitor's program or create a new one. This is also why making programs and rewards so unique that they are difficult to match is so important.

Given the stupidity of your worst competitor, the changing dynamics of the Web or even your own possible business transformation, you will need to have an exit strategy that can be invoked if the need arises. An exit strategy should include several strategic decisions.

1. How will we "turn off" the rewards?

   ▩ Use a future date identified and published or "at will"?
   ▩ What are our legal rights and assorted issues?
   ▩ Will we use a phased or instant approach?
   ▩ Are there strategies for limiting the program to MVCs rather than completely discontinuing the program?

2. How will we notify customers of our rights and our intentions, now and then?

   ▩ In our current program, how do we communicate our legal right to change or discontinue the program so that our customers clearly understand and our legal counsel is satisfied?
   ▩ If we stop the program in the future, what communication vehicles will we need to use and how can we ensure all customers are properly notified?

3. What steps can we take so as not to lose loyal customers?

   ▩ How will we communicate the message and how much notice will we give?
   ▩ How will we compensate customers with reward currency unredeemed?

4. If we need to make the program of higher value in order to compete, what will we do?

  ▦ What are our most effective reward tools?
  ▦ What are our least costly reward tools?

You always hope you don't need your exit strategy, but it's important to have one and to ensure that your current program strategy keeps the exit strategy viable.

10. Give Your Offline Program New Life on the Web

If you're a bricks-and-mortar business launching a new Web presence, there are many ways you can use the Web to enhance retention by extending your existing customer programs to the Web. For those stores that have split their business into offline and online components, don't make the mistake of trying to run two separate loyalty programs as well. It's just too confusing for your customers and only serves to illustrate your disjointed business strategy. Besides, for those customers who have positive offline relationships with your company, you can use the customer loyalty program to migrate them to the Web using the existing and trusted relationship.

Use the Internet to give customers access to your program and their accounts. American Airlines has demonstrated the value of this strategy by enhancing a number of AAdvantage program features. It may be as simple as taking a previously mailed newsletter and making it come alive on the Internet with customized and localized features. The Web makes multiple customer newsletters affordable. And don't stop at customizing just the content; customize and personalize coupons and sale items in the newsletter as well. Neiman Marcus has done a good job of this by taking their basic customer mailings as well as their InCircle program newsletter online and making the content more local by store and more interactive for customer personalization.

Several companies with extremely successful service programs have extended these programs to company websites. Jeep is an outstanding example of how a company can take a very successful customer program, "Jeep Jamboree," and bring it into the homes of all Jeep owners. The original Jeep Jamboree concept is a leading example of customer interaction and localization, enhanced through a virtual jamboree event. Fidelity.com is a good example of taking a recognized customer service program to the Web, and the strategy seems to be holding against the bargain brokers. But my favorite transition from offline to online is Whirlpool. I own a number of Whirlpool appliances, so when I had trouble with my Whirlpool washing machine, I knew the drill. Here's my true Whirlpool loyalty story.

My washing machine broke down days before I had weeklong guests arriving. I needed to get my machine repaired quickly if I was to win the Martha Stewart award for hosting guests. Previously I had called Whirlpool's 800 telephone number and they recommended a repair service near my house. But I thought I'd check the Web first. I was right; the Whirlpool site quickly referred me to a list of local repair services. Unfortunately, none of them could come before my guests arrived. But I remembered seeing a navigational path on the website that asked if I wanted to "repair it yourself" or "find a serviceman." Though I wasn't a big appliance repair person, I was desperate. The Whirlpool site featured an excellent diagnostic tool that identified the problem and the part that needed replacing. It then gave me the websites of several parts suppliers who could get me the recommended part. I scanned for the one nearest me with overnight delivery. Bingo! I thought I was in the clear until I thought about installing the darn thing. But again, remember that the website offered me two navigational paths: "install it yourself" or "find an installer near you." I dreaded my decision, but I took the path less traveled—I clicked "install it yourself." To my surprise, Whirlpool had created installation instructions, complete with step-by-step photos that even I could follow. To make a long story short: the part arrived the next day, I promptly gave the instructions to my husband (who actually read them) and my guests had clean sheets. I don't know which part would have made Martha most proud: the fact that I had my guestrooms perfectly attired or that I repaired the washing machine myself (not like she would do it herself, but she sure would enjoy recommending it).

The point is that Whirlpool took its reputation for great customer service offline and improved the experience online. The only thing Whirlpool could do to make me more loyal is to offer me a "best" customer service status reward in which my part was shipped overnight for free because I own more than four Whirlpool appliances.

11. Recruit Partners to Make Your Program a Success

The success of an e-loyalty program strategy should be defined through several different measurements: loyal behavior (repurchases/return visits, incremental purchases/visits and referrals), customer satisfaction, and/or the degree to which a program is self-funding. After years in the loyalty business, it has become easier for me to achieve the first two successes, but the third, designing a self-funding program, always takes a little more creative thinking and lots of networking. A self-funding program is one in which incremental revenues that are directly attributable to the program cover the majority of the program expenses. There are several ways of creating self-funding revenues.

- Use program tactics to generate incremental revenues from customer transactions (content or purchase related)
- Develop marketing partnerships (e.g., the partner might buy points, pay for access to communications or provide rewards at less than cost in exchange for brand awareness)
- Sell exclusive Web page sponsorships (this could be a simple branding effort or the sponsor could provide added value in content or discounts)
- Sell advertising opportunities throughout the program's Web pages and within member communications
- Develop affiliate marketing, which involves linking to affiliate websites in return for a percentage of revenue spent by your customers. But you shouldn't limit affiliate marketing to your reward program;

it should be a part of your overall business model. The reward program should simply provide additional opportunities for promoting affiliate marketing opportunities.

■ Reduce marketing expenses by sharing costs with partners or using barter deals, which should be viewed as a revenue stream (e.g., shared research projects, joint mailings, bartered website advertising, free samples used as gifts, co-sponsored promotions, etc.)

But within the full range of revenue opportunities, I encourage clients to focus on true win-win partnerships. Using the fullest meaning of the term, you should work with partners as if they were business partners, not merely marketing partners. By sharing information on customers, success measures on promotions and general business issues, the partnership becomes more rewarding than the revenue generated suggests. True partner marketing usually generates the greatest share of revenues, significant cost savings, unique opportunities that are truly priceless and the ability to create significant enhancements in your reward program. This is why I call this self-funding process "partner marketing" and treat it as one of the most important aspects of the program strategy.

Women.com is becoming one of the most respected partners you can have on the Web. Gina Garrubbo, Anna Zornosa and many of their peers at women.com truly define the epitome of Internet win-win partnerships. Companies that partner with women.com get access to the many different women.com research vehicles that analyze women's behavior on the Web. This information is not available to purchase elsewhere, and even with unlimited research dollars an outsider to the online women's market couldn't tap into the millions of women that women.com gets feedback from every day. Women.com not only coaches its partners in best strategies for optimizing the partnership, but in an effort to enhance its partners' proprietary websites it also shares its knowledge of website design and promotions for women. And the benefits don't stop there, Women.com also brings its partners together so that they can create additional contacts and joint marketing opportunities that increase the effectiveness of their marketing and reduce the expenses by sharing costs. And what does all this hard work get women.com? First, it is known as one of the best partners on the Web, so attracting high-caliber partners is no problem. It is also able to share much of its research expenses with partners and ultimately the improved strategy, partner relations and increased marketing funds lead to better enhancements of the women.com network. Marketers who think sharing partners is the industry standard need to take some lessons from the women (and men) at women.com.

Test Your e-Loyalty Program Design

So you think you've mastered reward program design, eh? I applaud those of you who have put this book to work and designed a strategy of your own. But before you get too confident, here is a short list of test questions to ensure your confidence is well founded. For those of you who cheated and skipped the lessons behind these test points, I can only encourage you to read them. As I've explained before, there's an art and a science to reward programs and few companies or marketing agencies have truly mastered it all.

In case there is any doubt, ideally, you want to be able to answer affirmatively to the following questions.

- Is the navigation personalized and does it sell?
- Does it build a competitive advantage that is difficult to match?
- Does it target MVCs and treat best customers best?
- Does it offer what MVCs value most?
- Does the program model selected match the targeted customers' expectations?
- Does it create an opportunity cost for defecting?
- Does it capitalize on the purchase frequency and the purchase cycle?
- Does it speak in the customers' language?
- Have you established communication processes and standards that ensure the entire company "speaks in one voice"?

▓ Is it self-funded through incremental sales and partner revenues?
▓ Does it facilitate a one-on-one relationship with the company?
▓ Does it seize every opportunity to optimize relationships with customers?
▓ Is it integrated throughout the site as well as the business?
▓ Is it simple to understand and participate in?
▓ Does it have a positive return on investment?

There are many ways to test your strategy prior to launch, but the most important test is with your MVCs. Always allow the time and money required to test your strategy thoroughly—the cost of not testing can be significantly greater.

STEP 6: PERSUADE YOUR CUSTOMERS TO WANT A RELATIONSHIP

At this point, I hope you've mastered Steps 1–5; you have your e-loyalty strategy on paper and heads are nodding—affirmatively. Too often this is the point where marketers start feeling very confident and hand the program communications over to an internal or external advertising agency not trained in loyalty marketing communications. This kind of confidence can prevent marketers from understanding that their entire success is now in the hands of an unskilled creative team. It's not a "build it and they will come" Web world out there, and even the most ingeniously designed loyalty program won't convince customers to return to your website without the proper amount of persuasive copy. But if you are using a creative team unskilled in loyalty creativity, you might want to share Step 6, "Persuade Your Customers to Want a Relationship," with your creative staff. And if you could slip a copy of this section under the door of that pesky senior manager who keeps rewriting your loyalty program copy, that might be of benefit as well.

Persuading customers to want a relationship doesn't entail merely acquisition-related marketing. Persuading customers to have a relationship has three stages.

- Convincing customers to start a relationship
- Maintaining and deepening the relationship
- Optimizing the relationship

Each stage plays a critical role in building loyalty to your website.

Starting the Relationship

To start the dialogue and ultimately the relationship, you first need to convince customers to try your website. It's important to distinguish between starting a dialogue and starting a relationship. Just because someone registered on your website doesn't mean you have a relationship—this is merely permission to start the dialogue. To have a relationship, you first have to have trust, so the length of time it takes you to engender trust is about how long it takes to start a relationship. Sometimes merely the act of a customer "raising his hand" to join your customer program is a sign that you are starting a relationship. But I'm jumping ahead of myself. First you need to attract them to your website. If you know your customers, contact them directly and give them an incentive to visit your website. Adjust the incentive across customer groups based on customer lifetime value. If you don't know your customers by name, use advertising techniques such as the ones that follow to drive customers to your website.

- Run banner ads on websites your targeted customers frequent to link customers to your website.
- Use TV/cable/radio/print advertising targeted to your best customers to achieve brand awareness of your URL.
- Use Web promotions and sweepstakes to encourage trials.
- Partner with companies that can give you access to their customers through their permission marketing programs.
- Create buzz around a unique website feature that will be picked up by the press from your publicity initiatives.
- Use reward programs like MyPoints that have millions of customers who can be incented to try your website.

Once you've persuaded the customer to visit the site, don't forget that first impressions are everything. So if you don't have a home page that readily helps newcomers quickly see all the benefits of your website, you might want to offer a website tour through the use of an interstitial (a pop-up browser window that uses a window-within-a-window technique). Persuading the customer to complete a short registration or profile is the first step in initiating the dialogue. But this action should not be construed as a relationship unless the customer gives you the rights to much more—as in the case of signing up for a formalized reward program where customers are tracked and communicated with regularly. A simple website registration is merely an opportunity to gather more intelligent customer data so that you can engender trust and the customer will ultimately initiate a real relationship. I want to remind you again that whenever possible, the initial registration should collect data that can be used to determine a customer's potential lifetime value, so that you will know the amount of marketing resources that should be expended to persuade a customer to try various website features.

You'll need to help customers see the value in a relationship with your website as quickly as possible. But customers are savvy, so you won't fool them with overhyped discounts and commonly attained sale prices. Rather than bribe customers, put the emphasis on demonstrating program value. Use trial memberships, virtual tours and testimonials from other customers or notable individuals to demonstrate specific value points. And whenever possible, personalize the all-important answer to every customer's question, "What's in it for me?" When the customer does agree to start the relationship by signing up for your loyalty program or supplying personal information so that you can personalize content, you need to reciprocate by giving the customer a reward. And you need to do so as quickly as possible. For example, if I sign up for your newsletter, don't just send me an email thanking me; include the most recent issue of the newsletter in the email as well. Provide immediate gratification whenever possible.

Maintaining and Deepening the Relationship

Just as trust is the foundation of starting a relationship, it remains critical to maintaining and deepening a relationship. With the goal of earning and maintaining trust at the forefront of all communications, you're ready to maintain the relationship through orchestrated communications and thank-yous. The communications will need to be a series of intelligent dialogues that become smarter and smarter with each interaction. The thank-you gestures will need to be sincere gratitude accompanied by rewards that customers want. The balance of intelligent dialogue and rewards targeted to individual customer needs is what maintains and ultimately deepens an online relationship. If your business can't reward customers with what they want, then find a partner who can.

This process is no different from any human relationship. When we start a relationship that we don't get much out of intellectually or personally, and the relationship is not rewarding in that it doesn't enhance our lives, we either discontinue the relationship or merely decide not to deepen the relationship.

When a customer relationship matures, you need to ensure that you are acting as though you are providing service to the customer, not selling to him or her. This distinct difference will become very apparent to your customers. Ensure that you continue to convey genuine gratitude, unencumbered by a sales message. Simply thanking customers is one of the most important motivators for repeat purchases. And when it comes to your MVCs, you need to profusely thank them, recognize them as your best customers, talk to them as experienced customers and demonstrate that you value their continued loyalty.

When you are communicating and rewarding loyal customer relationships, consider where the customer is in the product life cycle and how this changes the nature of the relationship. If he just started the product life cycle, then reinforcing his smart buying decision is important. If in the middle of the life cycle, he may appreciate learning new ways to use the website or enhance performance. And if he is near the end of the life

cycle, then focus on how you might reward this loyal customer for recommending other customers. If a subscription period marks the end of a
life cycle, then address subscription renewal benefits.

The customer life cycle is also important when designing rewards and
benefits that match customers' changing needs. You should develop customer thank-yous to complement these life cycle stages. Another way to
enhance the effectiveness of a thank-you or a reward is to localize the
reward whenever possible. Using localized events (online features sorted
by geographical relevance) or simply gathering customers from the same
area into a chat room can remarkably increase the value of your actions.

With your eye on the customer's life cycle, strive for a long-term relationship, not a short-term relationship. All marketers think that long-term
relationships are their focus, but often their program strategy doesn't
reflect this objective. For example, as you create an opportunity cost in
your e-loyalty program, make the opportunity cost grow over time or
enhance it with additional spending or interactivity. This can be as simple as a personalization engine that becomes more and more intelligent
with each interaction, thus creating a more enhanced experience with
each visit. Or it can be as complicated as a reward program that has multiple earning tiers that customers earn over time and which provide
higher and higher reward or service levels.

As in any relationship, there are going to be some bumps and bruises
along the way. Even with all the technology in the word and a darn-near-
perfect database manager, you will make mistakes and your customers
won't like it. But the key to maintaining a solid relationship through these
mistakes is to acknowledge your mistakes or inadequacies and use the
opportunity to build stronger loyalty. There have been many customer satisfaction studies done over the past ten years that analyzed customers who
contacted a company about a problem and those customers who had no
problems at all. Customers who contacted a company about their problem
and had it successfully resolved were more satisfied than customers who
never encountered a problem. Smart companies use their customer's service problems as an opportunity to prove that they care and that they can

be trusted to do what is right for the customer. Since trust is the foundation of all successful relationships, it shouldn't be surprising that great customer service improves relationships and thus e-loyalty.

Optimizing the Relationship

Optimizing the relationship entails using customer relationships to generate incremental revenues, to acquire additional loyal customers or to improve your product, business or services. While I don't mean to *use* customers in the manipulative sense, optimizing your relationship will require you to *persuade* customers to spend more or become evangelists for your program. And to show your appreciation you must reward these customers. Optimizing the relationship must be a win-win situation to be effective and requires a great deal of trust on the part of the customer. So in all your relationship-building and -optimizing endeavors, your actions and intentions must continue to earn and keep the highest level of trust possible.

Many relationship marketing tools can be used to generate incremental revenue, acquire referrals and stimulate feedback. Here are some examples of tools that can be employed to optimize the relationship.

Tools for generating incremental revenues include:

▦ Discount promotions that generate incremental revenue without cannibalizing current spending and profits
▦ Promotions that double the reward value of specific online behaviors (ads clicked, pages viewed, products reviewed, purchases made, new features tried, etc.)
▦ Tiered membership levels that increase rewards and benefits as a customer's value increases
▦ Product or content recommendations based on a customer's previous purchases or content viewed
▦ Special members-only retail areas that can improve margins on liquidated merchandise
▦ Variable benefit programs that meet customers' changing needs

Tools for enhancing your product, service or business include:

▨ Volunteer feedback programs (online buttons, chat rooms, bulletin boards)
▨ Formal feedback programs in which customers participate in exchange for rewards (surveys, customer advisory panels, etc.)
▨ One-to-one product development/manufacturing programs in which customers can develop their own product specifications in return for advance ordering or larger orders

Tools for developing customer evangelists and lowering the cost of customer acquisition include:

▨ Member-get-member programs or promotions (should include the ability to reward a customer for recommending another customer using either promotion codes, a relational database or other tracking mechanisms)
▨ Web tools that allow visitors to reach out to nonvisitors (instant messenger tools, tools for sending articles to friends, coupons that can be given to friends)
▨ Promotions that allow members to extend a temporary visitor membership to friends

The degree to which you can optimize the relationship will ultimately depend on the customer data you collect, the effectiveness of the communication channel you open and the intelligence level of the dialogue you're having. This holds true for all three of your optimization objectives.

To generate incremental spending you'll need to:

▨ Be able to differentiate between high-value and low-value customers
▨ Know which customers have a greater share-of-wallet than you are receiving

- Personalize your promotions
- Time your messages to match buying cycles, product cycles or life cycles
- Understand how customer cycles affect size and type of purchase
- Predict repurchase rates and best purchase times
- Use the strength of the relationship as a buffer against competitor discounts
- Have an open communication channel that can be used to drive temporary demand for discounted, discontinued or overstocked product/services

To persuade customers to help you acquire new customers you'll need to:

- Know which types of customer are best at recruiting high-value customers
- Determine which rewards stimulate your customers to become advocates
- Have a communications vehicle that is read by the majority of your customers

To employ the help of your customers in improving your business you'll need to:

- Know how to rank customer feedback based on customer value so that your enhancements don't satisfy the wrong target customer group
- Participate regularly in your online community so that customers learn to trust your presence and will be more forthcoming with suggestions and feedback
- Develop and actively promote feedback vehicles
- Track transactions to improve inventory or bandwidth efficiencies
- Track customer life cycles and capitalize on these changes to improve profitability through both program spending and pricing

Without a plan to optimize the relationships you build with customers, you will forgo the most beneficial part of your e-loyalty strategy. The financial benefit of reducing customer churn to increase profits can be magnified if you extend this process to optimizing existing customer relationships. Optimizing relationships grows your share-of-wallet for each customer rather than constantly relying on an expensive marketing objective of increasing your share of customers. Developing customer relationships also generates higher revenues through lower marketing expenditures, and that means better profitability.

STEP 7: CONSTANTLY IMPROVE E-LOYALTY BY LISTENING AND MEASURING

The interactivity of the Web is stimulating more and more customers to take an active role in directing a website's offering by how it talks to customers, how it delivers its services and other critical business features. Using feedback from customers to provide a more personally rewarding experience for them is what will differentiate the successful sites from the not-so-successful sites. Marketers unwilling to move from product-driven marketing to customer-driven marketing will have a tough time with this new business model. But the inevitability of this model is forcing all of us to develop better feedback tools and to become better listeners.

Your customers are constantly telling you what they think of your website, your products and your brand or company image. All you need to do is learn to measure this feedback, to analyze it and, most important, to listen. Compared to man's best friend, humans haven't exactly excelled at listening. I'd even go out on a limb and venture that one gender generally listens better than the other. But the Web can make up for any flaws we may have in our genetic dispositions by tracking not only what visitors deliberately tell us but what their actions or behaviors tell us as well. I've provided a variety of Web "listening" techniques below with suggestions on how to use this data to improve your ability to create e-loyalty. Some will be familiar to you; still, I hope that seeing the entire list of options for listening and measuring will not only make you aware of new areas where you could improve but also serve to remind you that your customers see these mechanisms as megaphones aimed at management. So whether they vote with the click of a mouse or through cutthroat criticism in emails, your customers are talking to you. The question is, are you listening?

Stimulate Customer Feedback

While telemarketing research calls during the dinner hour are probably not the best way to obtain customer feedback, there are many less-invasive techniques that you can use to get your customers to give you feedback. Naturally, as you build a relationship and have more frequent dialogues with your customers, they will be more likely to *want* to tell you what they think about your products and your website. You'll find some customers are so in love with your website that they want to talk all the time — sometimes annoying, but frequently very helpful. The key is to make feedback mechanisms easy to use and positioned near interactions that are likely to generate feedback. This way, when the mood hits your customers to speak their minds, you'll be ready to listen.

Ask for feedback

When you have a real need to know, ask! The science of deploying a Web application to ask for feedback can be that simple. Many Web applications exist that will effectively solicit feedback. Pop-up boxes (interstitials) and emails with surveys attached are most effective because they create a fairly random sample. But if you can get customers to use feedback buttons, bulletin boards and chat sessions, these can be more effective since they can be interactive, allowing you to delve deeper into the reasons behind the opinions or suggestions. But *persuading* customers to respond is the art of customer feedback and requires a real knowledge of your customers' needs and preferences.

Make feedback convenient

Make providing regular or spontaneous feedback as easy as possible. If you have a fairly loyal customer base or visitors who are passionate about the subject, then a simple embedded link or button titled "Tell us what you think" and linked to a survey or email tool will attract adequate responses. But as a bare minimum, give customers the tools to send you feedback on every page. A simple link titled "Contact us" on the bottom of every page is fairly standard.

Anticipate the need for feedback

There are many situations where either the interactive tools, the content or the targeted customers will stimulate more feedback on a website, and you will need to anticipate these needs if you are to satisfy your visitors by building the infrastructure to respond and learn from this feedback.

Web Applications. There are some transactions on a website—content or money oriented—that are more likely to drive customers' need for feedback. For example, downloads, e-commerce, and more complicated Web applications are more likely to result in usage problems, which inherently drive feedback or the need for customer service. Anticipate the need for feedback on troublesome applications by placing links to service reps or programming a pop-up window (interstitial) to appear when a customer tries to abandon a shopping cart, download or other Web function before reaching completion. Use a simple phrase such as "Not satisfied with this shopping experience? Tell us why." Or the feedback could be linked straight to a Web master's service desk using the phrase, "Having a problem with this mortgage estimator? Tell us about the problem you encountered."

Content. The content itself will increase the need for feedback. For example, content containing hotly debated issues or controversial subject matter drives feedback. Your customers may feel that you are giving too much time or space to one side of an issue. Instances where customers interact with other visitors, such as game sites and sites allowing visitors to critique one another's Web submissions, also drive feedback. Typically visitors on these types of sites want you to chaperone a troublesome visitor, which might be handled more effectively with online game referees or moderators than with feedback buttons. The key here is to know when immediate feedback is needed versus delayed feedback.

Targeted Customers. The target audience can affect the degree to which visitors want to provide feedback. For example, parents frequently want to provide input on websites for children, and it is extremely important for sites to be sensitive to parents' needs if they are to receive parental permission for their children to interact with the site. So feedback buttons specifically for parents versus children would be very smart in these situations. Seniors have proven themselves to be some of the most frequent providers of extremely helpful feedback. Managing larger amounts of detailed content will be an extra challenge that websites attracting large numbers of seniors will want to be prepared for. But websites that support a niche of specialized products or content closely watched by a group of avid followers will receive the most feedback. Here are a few examples: websites supporting avid hobbyists, sites supporting professions such as photography where standards are frequently debated, or sites that feature support groups. These types of "vertical" websites that target very specific subjects within a broader category will become more and more prevalent as critical mass is reached in more and more of these areas. After all, that's the beauty of the Web technology—it let's you reach the largest mass audience possible on the most obscure of topics. Because visitors to these sites will be more passionate about the subjects, the need for feedback will increase as will the need to fine-tune your offering to meet exactly the needs of these groups. In these situations, customers truly will drive the website offering. So make sure your feedback mechanisms are in place.

Once you've selected your feedback mechanisms and have a plan for acting on that feedback, follow these basic rules in persuading customers to provide feedback.

- Tell customers you value their opinion.
- Tell customers why you want to know the information.
- Tell them what you are going to do with the information.
- Promise to keep their identities anonymous.
- When using a standardized survey tool, and the topic is appropriate, tell customers how their preferences compared with other customers.
- If the information request is lengthy, provide a reward, but don't try to ask for everything at once. Divide up the survey questions into manageable bites.
- Don't ask for anything that can be answered or inferred by other means.
- If responses are provided on a bulletin board or chat session, be sure to monitor the postings and actively participate so that the feedback remains constructive and that any customer issues that are exceptions are resolved and don't become reflective of your overall business or customer service.
- Don't ask the same customer too often unless he or she volunteers to provide regular feedback.
- Thank them, thank them, thank them.

Though I've laid out a number of effective means for generating feedback from your customers, I want to add this important note of caution: don't ask for feedback if you aren't going to act on it. Few things can increase the bond in a customer relationship than for you to act on information he or she provides, whether it be personal information or constructive criticism to improve your website and/or products. But the reverse is true: few things are more damaging to your customer relationships than not acting on feedback, with the exception of providing a podium for customers to tell other customers you didn't respond to the feedback. This is why collecting feedback in an open forum like a chat room can be a very risky proposition if you don't intend to respond. With the collection of data comes the responsibility of action.

Measure Participation in Your Customer Programs
While the sheer number of registered visitors won't give you a handle on the degree of customer loyalty you have engendered, it will provide feedback on your persuasive tactics and the appeal of your offering. So start out by counting the number of visitors registered, but don't take that number to the bank, even if your investors are duped by sheer registration numbers. The gross total of registrations will serve as the basis from which you measure active participation, but the real measure of loyalty to a program is in subsequent behaviors and their frequency. Below is a short generic list of measures that home in on e-loyalty. You will obviously want to tailor these to meet your specific web model or customer program.

■ Out of your customer base, what percentage actively participates in your program offerings? "Active" will be relative to the average and above average frequency for your site and the number/types of activities in which customers can actively participate.
■ What percentage of customers responded to surveys? Having a large percentage of customers who want to provide feedback is a good indicator of "ownership," or a shared interest in making the website better.
■ What percentage of registered visitors return to visit the site again? Return daily? Weekly? The frequency will depend on your content topics and update schedules.
■ What is the response rate to direct marketing offers for incremental purchases or transactions? This can be a tricky number to decipher. A very loyal customer may be receiving 100 percent of share-of-wallet, so lower numbers may mean saturation. On the negative side, low response rates to incremental purchase offers could represent a disloyal customer base that buys only when it has to. The answers will depend on the type of product, the price point and possibly supplementing this data with live customer feedback.
■ Are customers actively participating in referral programs? This is the highest form of loyalty—to have customer advocates for a web-

site. High numbers in this area are a very good indication of e-loyalty. If you have low participation, do some research to determine if the incentive was adequate and the referral process was user friendly.

▧ What percentage read your emails, and does it value the information? I gave some tips above for identifying readership levels and determining the types of content that customers value. Obviously, high readership is a positive indicator of interest, value and usually loyalty.

▧ To what degree are your customers satisfied with your program? More important, to what degree do they believe that the program adds value to their lives? Don't forget, satisfied customers defect everyday. So identifying a deeper point of value will be important in judging the importance of your program in their loyalty consideration factors. Ultimately, the repurchase is the strongest indicator of e-loyalty.

Analyze Email Unsubscribe Logs

I frequently hear email advocates say that you should keep sending email until you receive too many "unsubscribe" requests. Well, how many is too many? And if too many customers are unsubscribing now, could that represent the tip of the iceberg for a larger group of unsatisfied recipients who haven't bothered to unsubscribe? It could be too late if you used this tactic as an indicator. I propose you attack this email frequency question with better listening skills and a lot more strategy.

First, you must keep in mind that each customer's email frequency need is different. You generally won't be able to categorize email preferences by demographics, needs and other customer differences and expect to optimize email results. So why not start out by asking how often each customer wants to receive communications from you on various subjects? Customers may want to receive all your emails on product recall news regardless of frequency, but they may want to read about new product development ideas only once a month. Every product, website, topic and individual will be different. This doesn't necessarily mean you need to write hundreds of different newsletters; perhaps you can automate the grouping of information/articles based on a rules-driven email system that selects the right email based on the indicators you place on a customer's profile. In an effort to build a personal experience you'll want to capitalize on their differing needs, and this will require a tailored email strategy.

Next, you'll want to track customers' readership of your emails. Granted, you won't be able to track readership exactly, but there are several techniques that can give you benchmarks on readership. For instance, you can make some news available through embedded links within your email; by using a unique URL, the number of linked customers can be tracked. It's always more convenient for readers to have the entire newsletter contained within the email, but using teaser links to a few articles, or links to attractive offers, will give you an opportunity to actually track readership and interest levels. Occasionally you'll want to include a positive reply option to let readers vote with their mouses; be sure the email server can handle this type of volume. Or if you have readers who are more active participants, ask them to reply to the email with a subject line selected from a list of options, which allows them to vote on preferences or simply to send a vote of confidence on the value of the emails. Better yet, provide a link to a short survey on email preferences.

Once you have these readership measures in place, focus on analyzing the nonreaders through analysis of your "unsubscribed" logs. Do you see a correlation between certain email news topics and unsubscribed counts? Or are certain customer segments "unsubscribing" more often than others? Perhaps you need to tailor your content to better meet the needs of this segment. Do you receive unsubscribe requests most after a certain number of emails have been received, or after a given frequency? Either your customers require a few copies to realize they don't like the content, or too much frequency ruins the value. But even as valuable as these logs can be, asking customers about the value of your emails prior to defection is still the more strategic approach. So give that readership survey a little more thought and action.

Anonymous Customer Tracking
  Track customers' online behaviors using server log data
  Server logs are great listeners. They record just about everything you could want to know about your customers' preferences, critical search paths, opinions of your offering, decision-making processes, first link to your site and much, much more. Using various log-analysis software programs, you can hear visitors' feedback loud and clear. Here are a few ways to use server logs to measure the effectiveness of your e-loyalty efforts, but ideally, your log analysis will need to be tailored to measure your specific loyalty techniques and your unique website design. Hopefully these ideas will stimulate you to design the perfect listening techniques for your website.

1. Where did your customers come from?

    ▨ What URL or link brought them to your site? This will give you insight into what sites are best at driving visitors to your website, but just as important, it will give you insight into your customers interests or demographics. If an interest in gardening is correlated with links to your site, you might consider a sponsorship with Garden.com. If a customer comes from women.com, you can safely assume that she is a woman. If he comes from a sports website, you can safely assume he is interested in sports (I bet you thought I was going to do some stereotyping here? Not me!).
    ▨ If first-time customers are consistently typing in your URL, then it is safe to assume that your marketing and publicity efforts are successfully persuading customers to try your site.
    ▨ The keyword used most often to find you on search engines also gives you some important marketing information. First, you should be sure you list your business website under those keywords on as many search engines as possible. Second, you should consider adding more content related to that keyword. If I found your political site based on the word "vote" rather than "Republican," it might not mean much since both are likely to

be prevalent throughout the site. But if the name of a lesser-known Republican were a frequent keyword used to find you on search engines, you should get an interview and additional content on this political candidate while he or she is still in the limelight.

▦ Banner tracking is also helpful, not just in the rating of banner effectiveness, but what happens after a customer links to your site from a banner. Test the stickiness of linking from a banner to your home page versus from a banner directly to a content/ products related to the banner. It's usually a given that direct links work better, but not when a website brand is a complete unknown. Customers may want to be familiar with the website itself before becoming too engrossed in a shopping process.

2. What types of navigational path do your customers use?

▦ Do customers prefer to find products by type of product category or user needs? If most of your customers find your laptop products by clicking on mobile computers, unlike government customers, you know that type of product is more important to most customers than what the product is used for. However, I wouldn't recommend killing the user-type navigational path since choice is still most important. It might make you want to spend more time on simplifying the identification of products via the quickest possible route.

▦ In selecting a shampoo, the navigational path "hair care→ women's shampoos→color-treated hair" tells you more than a straight link to shampoo: that the buyer is a female, and might likely be cross-sold on hair coloring products.

3. What were customers' answers to diagnostic tools? With a diagnostic tool you can help your customers find the perfect solution, but you can also learn a lot about customer needs and preferences. Keep in mind that a stringent privacy policy would not allow you to

track this information by individual customer, but aggregated data is typically well within privacy policy promises.

- When using a financial tool, what was the income distribution level?
- When using a product customization application, what were the preferences, needs and specifications selected most often?
- On your parenting site, which polls are answered most often: those about babies, children, teens, young adults or grandparenting? The answer could give you directional data on the ages of your visitors' children or grandchildren.
- Which self-help bulletin board or chat room topics are most frequented?
- When recommending vitamin supplements, which ailments are customers trying to remedy most?

4. Where did your visitors leave you?

- What page did they leave on?
- Did they leave on an advertising link from the page? What link?
- Did they type in a URL? What does that URL tell you about customers who leave before transacting? That they have different interests or needs? That they have mistaken the identity of your site?
- After the completion of a transaction? This is what you hope to see the most of, but don't count on it.

5. At what point/page do customers bail?

- Is there a repeated navigation path for defectors?
- Are customers more likely to jump to another site from a specific page or type of content?

■ If customers typically get through the entire product selection process but abandon their cart after reading your warranty page, this is great feedback on your warranty offering.

Analysis of aggregated customer data

Analyzing the data on all of your customers and comparing it to each individual customer is termed "collaborative filtering." This technique harnesses the information from the masses to predict the actions of an individual by matching the characteristics, needs or behaviors of an individual to a group similar to him. Net Perceptions, a developer of collaborative filtering software, calls this using "community knowledge." I call it "predictive modeling"—a technique relationship marketers have been applying to direct mail for years. It works very much like the customer lifetime value analysis I described in Step 2 of this book. In identifying most valuable customers, I determine which customer characteristics/demographics are most predictive of high value and set those characteristics as the predictive filter for high value. All customers who have the same characteristics as my MVC group are assumed to be MVCs until they prove otherwise. In collaborative filtering, you look at the characteristics/demographics of each visitor and match them to all customers on your database with the same characteristics/demographics, high value or not. You then *average* the data for this group of customers to develop a predictive model for what this new customer will want. This requires making the leap of faith that because this new customer "looks like" these other customers, he or she will have the same preferences, need the same things and respond to offers in the same manner as his or her cyber-twin. Obviously there is some danger in relying on the law of averages, which is why in Step 4 I advise you not to design your site around your average customer. I am the exception to most marketing averages. Expecting me to act like others with my demographics could result in a bigger disadvantage than the advantage of better targeting other customers. Nevertheless, I strongly recommend the use of collaborative filtering tools, but advise you to limit your assumptions to those with the highest degree of correlation, and therefore the highest likelihood of predicting preferences. Here are the types of data that can feed collaborative filtering software.

Actions. Includes data from Web log entries that track which areas a customer visits and for how long. Analyzing this behavioral data can sometimes provide more insightful data than if the customer had talked to you personally.

Transactions. Includes tracked purchases as well as information requests from diagnostic tools that recommend content, search engines, downloads and so on. For this information to represent the totality of a customer's transactions (e.g., a complete picture of your share of the customer's wallet), it should include offline transactions as well.

Implicit Information. Includes data that a customer actively provides through profiling, surveys, entertainment polls, product selection tools and other tools that capture preferences. Not all customers have the time or are willing to fill out surveys, so tracking 20 percent of your customers (assuming that number is statistically significant) and then assuming the other 80 percent of your customer base will act similarly may generate useful targeting based on averages.

The value in all this expensive modeling software is that it provides data that will enable you to predict the individual needs of customers, which provides customers a more personalized experience and a more profitable interaction for your web business. Predictive modeling is also of great benefit when a customer doesn't provide detailed personal information or when collecting that information is unlawful, as is the case for children who don't provide parental permission. Using this modeling technique to personalize content so customers feel the site has content/products that match their needs will make customers more loyal and thus more profitable.

■ If customers see content, advertisements or product recommendations, that match all their needs, they are more likely to identify with and be loyal to the site.

■ If customers receive offers and promotions that best meet their needs, they are more willing to transact and buy on your site.

A secondary value in this type of predictive modeling is that it helps you decide where to expend your limited resources.

■ If most high-value customers frequent a particular area of your site, or they buy a particular product, you might try to determine if trial of this content/product stimulates transactions. And the opposite is true: if one area of your site tends to attract only unprofitable customers, then develop tactics for transforming this content into more profitable customers or remove it from your website.

■ If a customer doesn't track as a high-value customer, but has the characteristics that match other high-value customers, you may want to incent this customer more generously because he or she has the potential to be high value.

Specific customer tracking

With a customer's permission, tracking her behavior on your site can provide the type of specific feedback needed not only to personalize her experience but to measure her e-loyalty as well. The benefits of tracking individual customer data and providing a more personalized experience are much the same as those I listed above for collaborative filtering models, with the critical difference of not relying on averages. With customer specific data, you know what the customer wants and you don't have to risk assuming she acts like her cyber-twin. Using personal identification technology (personal cookies, passwords, embedded URLs saved in a "favorites" folder, etc.) you can track and log the customer's selections and transactions on your website and post this data by customer ID on your database. You can use this data to determine your customer's preferences (e.g., visiting five women's product's pages indicates an interest in women's products), then put an identifier on that customer's profile that indicates an interest in women's products and serve content/product offers accordingly. The number of identifiers on a customer's profile is limited only by the amount of computing engine you are running on your website. However, simply being accurate on a broad preference point like women's products versus men's products can produce a huge leap in tailoring content, while precision-tuning preferences into too fine a granularity may not generate the incremental profitability needed to justify the expense. So don't be discouraged if you can't afford the powerful tracking engines because sometimes common sense and a good knowledge of your customer applied to a less-sophisticated modeling tool can produce admirable results.

Analyze Customer Service Logs and Reports

Customer service logs from telephone centers have always been a great resource for collecting customer feedback, but they are only as good as the service rep who logged the call. Given the turnover in customer service centers and the lower grade of employee that service centers sometimes attract, the data that gets logged usually isn't as reliable as you would like it to be. Probably the most abused entry by customer service reps is the most valuable one: "type of problem" or "reason for call" entry. Online customer service can provide a much greater source of customer feedback if parts or all of the interaction is automated and logged. Even if your website employs live, online service reps, using a problem identification questionnaire to start the interaction can better direct the inquiry, save valuable online time and be an invaluable source of customer data. Here are a few areas to analyze that offer you a starting point in identifying valuable feedback in your own customer service logs. Just remember that analyzing these logs is as much an art as a science, so you'll need to don your Sherlock Holmes hat and become creative in using this data.

■ What are the most frequently viewed Q&A topics? This can help point out weak language in instructions or even product defect points.

■ Do certain areas/features/products drive more service contacts? Check your server log for most common links to service. This could be a result of poor instructions for a Web application or a faulty product or service that doesn't meet user expectations, but all areas would need to be addressed. However, it could be merely a consequence of the type of user who buys/uses the product/content. Less-savvy users may be drawn to certain areas or features on your site, or buy certain products/services more than other types of visitor. Try building tutorials for these customers or make the areas of your website that these customers frequent more user friendly for novices. On the other hand, some products might just attract chronic complainers, which should stimulate you to reevaluate your choice of target audience and the level of customer support your business model can handle.

■ Do service contacts per one hundred visitors substantially increase during peak usage periods? If so, your server may not be handling transactions adequately.

■ Do the self-help navigational logs indicate customers leave before getting to solution pages? If so, there could be a problem with usability.

■ Is the self-help function tried before contacting live service reps? If not, the self-help link may not be easy to find and/or use.

■ How many customers come back to customer service/help areas more than once in a day? A high incidence of multiple access per customer indicates that customer problems are not being solved on the first attempt. This would suggest that the help/service tools are not meeting the needs of the customers.

Routinely Conduct e-Loyalty Research

You need to implement a plan that regularly solicits feedback from your customers in an unbiased and statistically significant manner so that these measures can be tracked and your progress monitored. To do this effectively involves conducting primary research at least quarterly. Shortly after a website launch, you may want to conduct this research every two months. But beware of the standardized, product-oriented research spit out by the majority of "old school" research groups. Too often, working with these researchers is like listening to a conch shell — if they want you to hear the ocean, you will. But to really hear the ocean, you have to go to the ocean. There you'll find that the ocean has many different sounds, but you'll hear only those that you listen for. Too poetic perhaps, but too often I find that Web research projects are ramrodded by the overbearing rules of research Ph.D.'s who forget that we are trying to measure unpredictable and sometime irrational human behavior, not scientific behavior. Here are some research objectives and measurement standards that I find helpful in determining the *true* effectiveness of an e-loyalty strategy.

Measure changes in loyalty to the site and specific features

- Loyalty to website measured in terms of behavior (visits, return visits and referrals)
- Loyalty to website features measured in terms of usage (trial, continued usage, referral)
- Loyalty to website measured in terms of trial and usage of competing websites or products (i.e., the share-of-wallet customer gives you)
  - Heard of competitors?
  - Tried competitors?
  - Used competitors? How much?
- Loyalty to website measured in terms of a perceived opportunity cost of defecting
  - Which features would customers not give up to defect?
  - What is the perceived cost of switching from your site to the competition?

Monitor loyalty drivers

You do this for two reasons: (1) to see if there is an increase/decrease in importance of each driver and associated attributes; and (2) to measure your success in delivering on the loyalty driver attributes customers value most. Remember that the importance of each loyalty driver—price, service, product quality and image—is not the same for all websites.

1. Which loyalty drivers are most important in producing the desired loyalty behavior(s), and what attributes of your website influence each the most?
   - Price—identify associated attributes
   - Service—identify associated attributes
   - Quality—identify associated attributes
   - Image—identify associated attributes

2. How is your website performing against the attributes of your most influential loyalty drivers?
   - Price or value
     - belief that prices are fair or that prices match values
     - belief that prices are lowest or "a good deal"
   - Service satisfaction
     - the importance of service features such as packaging and on-time delivery
     - the importance of service rep response rate
   - Quality of product, whether it be content/goods/services
     - perception of quality
     - concrete experience or proof of quality
   - Image of website and management
     - belief that your website/product/service is the best or a leader in the field
     - belief that your website cares about customers
     - belief that content/goods/services will improve their lives
   - Overall customer trust, which incorporates five loyalty drivers:
     - belief that the website wouldn't break promises (e.g., selling customer data)
     - belief that the website offers only the best content/goods/service
     - belief that content/goods/services will be delivered as offered

- ▓ belief that the website will do what's right for the customer
- ▓ belief that if a customer needed help, the website would be there

Identify any new customer lifetime value predictors
- ▓ Track your high-value customers' demographics and psychographics against your lifetime value model's predictors.
- ▓ When your site expands to include new customer segments, validate your lifetime value predictors.

Identify new user segments
- ▓ You may have intentionally expanded your user base to new segments, in which case you'll want to measure the effectiveness of this expansion.
- ▓ You may have unintentionally expanded your user base, in which case you'll need to identify the new segment(s) and ensure that you are creating a relevant message for these customers.

Identify additional customer needs
As more and more customers understand the potential of Web interactivity, their expectations and needs change, too. What customers said they wanted when you launched your site versus months later are probably substantially different, and will continue to evolve as customers learn enough to imagine what is possible.

- ▓ Track changing customer needs.
- ▓ Track customers' Web experience levels.
- ▓ Track changing customer expectations.

PART

Making e-Loyalty a Reality for Your Website

THE SUCCESS OF AN E-LOYALTY PROGRAM DOESN'T END WITH A
GREAT PROGRAM STRATEGY. IT'S ULTIMATELY DEPENDENT ON THE VIABILITY
OF THE IMPLEMENTATION PLAN AND A MARKETER'S ABILITY TO DRIVE THAT
PLAN TO COMPLETION . . . WITH THE ORIGINAL STRATEGY INTACT—
A FEAT MORE EASILY SAID THAN DONE.

Developing an Implementation Plan for e-Loyalty

GETTING STARTED

At this point, I am assuming that you have completed the seven-step
process of creating your e-loyalty strategy, and you are ready for implementation. So I won't cover strategy development in this part of the book.
In Part III, "Making e-Loyalty a Reality for Your Website," I lay out my
proven process for implementation, which includes the following nine
steps:

Step 1: Develop and Test e-Loyalty Concepts to Finalize Your
e-Loyalty Strategy
Step 2: Develop an Initial Business Case to Test the Details of Your
Program Concept
Step 3: Create a Customer Contact Plan
Step 4: Develop a Partner Strategy
Step 5: Determine Resources Required, Best Sources and Associated
Costs
Step 6: Finalize the Program Forecasts and Budget

Step 7: Adopt an Extended ROI to Justify and Defend Your Budget
Step 8: Develop a Plan for Measuring Success
Step 9: Develop a Viable Timeline with Implementation Leaders

These nine steps can be applied to the two most common implementation scenarios: creating a new website around e-loyalty and integrating an e-loyalty program into an existing website.

Creating a New Website Based on e-Loyalty

After I give a seminar, I almost always get the question: "We're developing a new website now. When should we start developing our e-loyalty strategy?" Thinking of your website strategy and your e-loyalty strategy as separate entities is a fundamental problem of many Web business owners. Your e-loyalty strategy should be integrated into all aspects of your website. In many cases your e-loyalty strategy is your business strategy. So my response to this commonly asked question is this: "You should be developing your e-loyalty strategy as part of your business strategy and your Web design strategy, even if you don't plan to implement the e-loyalty tactics until after the website is launched. Your e-loyalty plan should drive many other business decisions. So if you haven't started your e-loyalty strategy now, you need to start as soon as possible."

Not too long ago a client asked me to submit a proposal for e-loyalty research. The proposal covered customer segmentation and identification of e-loyalty drivers as well as testing e-loyalty customer programs we had been discussing. I received a call after my client had reviewed the proposal and she told me she had decided to do some research on website features and usability before starting any loyalty research. This Web marketer didn't understand that separating e-loyalty from her business development was a critical mistake. First, she was expending thousands of dollars developing a beta site without knowing what her customers' loyalty drivers were; that is, what features were important in building loyalty with this type of service. Second, she planned to test a beta website against a random customer sample since she didn't know what her target segment looked like. This mistake would have caused her to develop a site for her average customer, not her target customers. And third, she wasn't going to get an accurate reading on the appeal of this site without including the customer loyalty features. In this way, money and time are wasted on website development every day because companies fail to understand the importance of building e-loyalty into the business development and website planning processes.

It's unrealistic to think you can launch a new e-business with all the features you ultimately plan to implement in place on launch date. E-loyalty features often aren't implemented until after the website has been up for months, and that's okay. But it's not okay to wait until your website is up to *start* planning your e-loyalty strategy. In some cases it's smart to delay implementation of an e-loyalty program or a set of features until after the site has some measurable traffic and transactions. One client I advised to use this delay strategy found he didn't need the expensive e-loyalty program he had previously thought was necessary. Another benefit of delaying the launch of an e-loyalty feature includes the ability of taking "before" and "after" snapshots to measure the direct effect it has on success measures.

Integrating e-Loyalty into an Existing Website

If you didn't plan your e-loyalty strategy before you launched your e-business, fret not. It's not too late to incorporate e-loyalty features and programs. However, don't think that by adding a choice application or two you will instantly generate greater e-loyalty. E-loyalty is a way of doing business, not a type of Web application, so you'll need to add e-loyalty principles to your e-business philosophy and strategy. Consequently, making your site engender more e-loyalty might take more overhauling than you imagined. The major downside to developing your e-loyalty strategy after the fact is that your business model or your current partnerships may prevent you from implementing the best e-loyalty program strategy. Another downside is adding effective features that might conflict with preexisting Web features.

In using the implementation steps outlined on the next pages you will need to evaluate how each process is affected by your current website strategies and features. However, I would add a word of caution: do not let your existing situation prevent you from implementing an e-loyalty program that will clearly differentiate your offering and make you more competitive. The Web is about change. I don't know too many websites that didn't have a major overhaul after the first six to twelve months, and many Web businesses enhance their websites with significant changes every other quarter. So if implementing the perfect e-loyalty strategy requires a website overhaul, weigh the benefits against the expense of time and money. Or at a minimum, schedule your e-loyalty program to coincide with the next big website overhaul—it's sure to be just around the corner.

STEP 1: DEVELOP AND TEST E-LOYALTY CONCEPTS TO FINALIZE YOUR E-LOYALTY STRATEGY

Once you've developed several e-loyalty concepts that meet your objectives, you'll need to evaluate the concepts at a broad level through internal analysis. However, no e-loyalty concept should graduate from your initial list to this evaluation phase if the concept doesn't support your goals and objectives and seem viable for your targeted customer segments.

To start this initial evaluation, evaluate e-loyalty concepts based on any major implementation issues and strategic support required. Next, develop a list of major requirements for each program concept to ensure that each concept is operationally viable, given the available resources and your access to the required technology. And naturally, you'll want staff members that are most familiar with your customers to evaluate the concepts based on general appeal and compatibility. This last subjective phase isn't intended to substitute for real customer reactions, but simply to weed out any glaring mismatches.

In order to take these concept finalists to research, you'll need to develop the programs more precisely to include the level of detail needed for a customer to evaluate the program. For example, if you are researching a point program, your research will be useless unless you develop the point valuation information. Customers won't embrace a reward that they don't know the value of—or worse, they'll tell you they love the idea because they assume the points will be worth much more than you are able to provide. To communicate these program details you'll need to develop a positioning statement and sample program description copy to test the concept. Many researchers think that this step is unnecessary, but I've moderated or sat through enough of these research projects to know that customers can't make the leap from business plan descriptions to their own lives. They need to see the program in much the same way it would be presented to them on the Web; otherwise, they won't provide realistic feedback. When business descriptions of your program are used, you'll hear comments from research participants such as "they only want to implement this program so they can get us to buy more." For these same reasons, it is extremely important to develop positioning statements that introduce the concepts—much like the content you would use to persuade customers to consider joining the program. How you position a program will have an enormous bearing on the appeal and a customer's impression of your intentions.

Now you're ready for research. There are many effective research techniques, and the one you select should really be driven by the type of program you are testing and the availability of your target customers. Some programs test better offline, but most can be effectively tested using online research methodologies that provide interactive capabilities. If your website isn't up, you probably don't have customers yet, so testing concepts can be trickier. First, you'll need to conduct the initial round of research to prioritize your target audiences and identify your most valuable customer segments. For more information on selecting a research methodology and to see a list of vendors that offer online interactive research, check our website at www.e-loyalty.com.

Based on your research results, you'll probably be ready to fully develop a final Customer Relationship Marketing (CRM) program concept. But I would advise planning a second round of research much later in the implementation process that tests final creative ideas and Web usability.

STEP 2: DEVELOP AN INITIAL BUSINESS CASE TO TEST THE DETAILS OF YOUR PROGRAM CONCEPT

After fleshing out the details of your e-loyalty plan, you'll want to test your assumptions by developing a broad business plan with estimated revenues and expenses. This process should be one step higher than a "back of the envelope" analysis, but not as exacting as your final forecasts and budgets will be in Step 7 of this implementation plan. Your objective in evaluating your concept is to ensure that the program model is capable of generating a positive ROI. So if your concept is a customer service program, you'll need to determine what level of service can be provided to given percentages of your customer base that you've identified for these benefits. Or if you are developing a point program, you'll need to determine what percentage of revenue you can afford to earmark for rewards and how you can subsidize rewards to make them both affordable and of high enough value that they have measurable appeal.

Here is a list of the types of analysis and considerations you would want to complete at this phase of your implementation.

- ▩ Outline your e-loyalty business plan.
- ▩ Develop a list of strategic issues to be addressed.
- ▩ Determine if a pilot program or test case will be needed.
- ▩ Recommend a broad strategy for acquisition, customer communications and rewards.
- ▩ Develop broad brush budget estimates.
- ▩ Develop revenue and membership forecasts to include partner revenue streams.
- ▩ Complete a cursory ROI analysis.
- ▩ Develop a preliminary timeline and project schedule (to be updated in Step 9 based on final program requirements).
- ▩ Develop a program exit strategy.

STEP 3: CREATE A CUSTOMER CONTACT PLAN

In Step 3 of my "Seven Steps to Designing an e-Loyalty Strategy," I demonstrated the importance of using a customer contact plan in order to create an intelligent dialogue. It's also an important part of the implementation plan because it identifies the various communication requirements needed to support the e-loyalty strategy. These communication requirements will give direction to creative agencies, Web developers and budget planners. The broad components of this contact plan will need to include strategies for implementing the following:

- Acquisition plan (advertising, publicity, promotions, etc.)
- Online content
- Online transactions
- Membership/customer communications
- Customer service plan

Each of these five contact plan components must be developed in order to identify requirements for each. Here are the types of details you'll want to include for each communications plan.

Include all forms of communication vehicles employed. For example:

- Onsite content
- Push content
- Email
- Postal mail
- Telephone
- communications through third parties
- Live interaction online or via phone
- In-store merchandising and takeaway collateral

Include all types of customer contacts required. For example:

- Advertising

- Publicity
- Data requests
- Product offers/sales
- Promotions
- Sales transaction process
- Partner offers
- Rewards and recognition
- Customer service
- Customer feedback

Include the type and frequency of contacts.
Include techniques for localizing content.
Include the required variations for each communication. For example:

- By customer segment
- By individual customer preferences
- By preferred communications medium
- At preferred frequencies

Include the testing and measurement requirements to ensure a closed-loop process that measures the effectiveness or response rate for each communication.

Another important element in your contact plan is to identify techniques for ensuring that you "speak with one voice" so your customer dialogue will *sound* intelligent. The three most important areas to focus on in order to achieve this "one voice" standard are:

- A creative strategy that covers branding, graphical standards and tone of voice
- A process for funneling all communication tactics (online and offline) into a single contact plan to achieve one voice
- A database strategy that outlines the requirements for tracking all customer contacts and responses

STEP 4: DEVELOP A PARTNER STRATEGY

I've developed partner strategy plans for almost every type of consumer industry and many business-to-business categories. The biggest mistake I see clients make in partner planning is that they are complacent. Most companies merely react to partner offers that come their way, rather than being more strategic by identifying who they want to partner with and creating a negotiation plan for acquiring those partners. The second biggest mistake is that companies don't set clear partner pricing and negotiation strategies. Without these strategies, companies typically don't adequately leverage opportunities or negotiate the highest return possible. The third biggest mistake is that companies don't have clear partner evaluation rules. Without evaluation rules, companies start the analysis process from scratch each time an offer is made, or worse, they spin their wheels starting negotiations on partnerships they later realize aren't strategically beneficial.

To help you better plan your partnership strategy, I've provided a list of the most important steps in developing a partner strategy, and on the following pages I explain these steps.

- Identify the objectives of your partner strategy
- Review various partnership models and develop a strategy
- Develop a partner selection strategy that ensures partners are a good strategic fit
- Identify potential partners that will enhance your partner strategy
- Develop a partnership pricing strategy
- Develop a partner revenue forecast for all revenue-generating initiatives
- Develop a partner negotiation strategy

Identify the Objectives of Your Partner Strategy

There are many viable objectives you could establish for your partnership strategy. But ultimately, your partnership objectives should tie to your business and e-loyalty objectives. To adequately cover every conceivable objective, and give my advice for implementing each, would fill another book. So I have merely listed some common partnership objectives below to stimulate ideas for creating partnership objectives that best support your website and e-loyalty strategy.

- ▦ *Bring more value to your customers.* If your customers want it and you can't provide it, find a partner who can. Example: partner with other websites that excel in the types of content or product that your customers want.
- ▦ *Reduce expenses.* If providing a benefit is too costly, then find a partner who wants to provide the benefit or share your expenses in return for access to your customers. Example: AOL has deep direct marketing pockets, so share your next direct mailing piece with AOL in order to share direct mail expenses.
- ▦ *Provide access to specific customer segments.* If a partner already has a relationship with a specific segment, use their relationship to introduce your product or to start your own relationship. Example: partner with websites that target seniors (such as ThirdAge.com) to reach a senior audience for your website.
- ▦ *Provide credibility.* If a partner's branded content or product can add credibility to your own, use that partner's brand wisely to increase the credibility of your own brand. Example: familiar brands like Johnson and Johnson for baby-oriented credibility, or The Gap for instant "coolness" credibility with teens, or IBM for technology.
- ▦ *Keep the relationship alive between infrequent purchases.* If a partner provides the interim products and services between your customers' purchases of your infrequently purchased product, partner with these companies so you can continue the relationship between purchases. Example: Between PC purchases, partner with or lease the product rights to software and accessories that PC owners frequently buy between PC purchases.
- ▦ *Start the relationship before your competitors do.* Find a partner who

specializes in the life stage just before your product life cycle, and use that partnership to initiate your own customer relationships sooner. Example: eToys bought BabyCenter.com to start the relationship sooner.

▒ *Engender trust for your e-commerce process.* Use partners to make customers more at ease with buying from your online store. Example: e-trust.com and the Better Business Bureau are the most common partners that endorse sites, but there are many websites that are earning widespread e-commerce credibility that others can trade on.

▒ *Provide affiliate marketing revenues.* Find partners who will pay you commissions or acquisition revenues. Example: the largest affiliate marketer is Amazon.com, but most websites have some sort of affiliate program.

Review Various Partnership Models and Develop a Strategy

Many different partnership strategies exist to help you improve the value of your Web offering and to defray expenses. Not all of these partnership models will be appropriate for your e-loyalty program, but I encourage you to review the many types of partnership before assuming that the current e-rage is right for you just because it works for some high-visibility sites. And keep in mind that when a website finds a partnership strategy that really brings value, it isn't likely to tell the rest of the world, especially its competitors, just how successful it is. In many instances, smaller websites are capable of building much more strategic partnerships using boutique partnership models because they can integrate the partnership into all aspects of their website without the approval of multiple layers of management and competing divisions. So if you manage a smaller e-business, be confident in the knowledge that you can probably be more creative in your partnership strategy and seize short-term opportunities more quickly. Here is a list of partnership models you should consider, regardless of your size.

▒ Business partnerships
▒ Affiliate marketing partnerships

- Advertising partnerships
- Web page/section sponsorships
- Research partnerships
- Distribution partnerships
- Content partnerships
- Permission marketing partnerships
- Reward provider partnerships
- Point program partnerships
- Partnerships with personalities that can help position your website
- Certification partnerships that bring credibility to your site
- Syndication partnerships

Develop a Partner Selection Strategy That Ensures Partners Are a Good Strategic Fit

Think of your partner selection strategy as a series of filters that evaluate partners based on partnership objectives and business rules you've identified to measure the value of a partnership. Having this evaluation model on hand when partners "come-a-calling" will enable you to evaluate partner opportunities more quickly so that you spend less time discerning a potential partner's value and more time negotiating your best deal. Likewise, it will make the process of identifying potential partners that you want to pursue a much quicker task that yields better strategic direction.

Every website will have its own rules for evaluating potential partners. The following list is not meant in any way to be complete, merely suggestive.

- Partner has complimentary marketing goals
- Partner has similar target customer segments
- Partner has synergistic customer segments (e.g., partner sells diapers, you sell training pants)
- Partner's products are valued by your customers
- Partner's products don't compete with your products
- Partner must be an admired expert in it's field
- Partner must be one of the top-selling brands in its industry

▦ Partner's brand must be as strong as yours
▦ Partner's reputation must provide a halo effect
▦ Partner must have deep pockets
▦ Partner must have a permission marketing vehicle you can use
▦ Partner has an e-loyalty experience they will share
▦ Partner must provide a specific distribution channel
▦ Partner must provide an immediate online capability (auctions, chat, point program, etc.)
▦ Partner must be willing to sign a two-year agreement
▦ Partner will offer exclusivity, or be willing to accept the terms of your exclusivity
▦ Partner is not working with your competitors

Identify Potential Partners That Will Enhance Your Partner Strategy
Once your partner evaluation model is developed, you'll be ready to develop a list of potential partners to consider. And this alone is a very important point: don't wait for partners to make you offers, be aggressive in acquiring partners. The best partner candidates will be hotly pursued, and you do not want to be left with second best. An aggressive partnership plan also requires a senior executive that not only has the business experience to understand all the terms of a relationship but also can be trusted with the authority to act in the best interest of the company. Your potential partners won't be impressed with your "wet-behind-the-ears" graduate student whose eagerness is driven by commission more than the desire to create a win-win relationship.

Identifying partners is a research process that is both an art and a science. The science aspect includes scouring company indices online and offline, combing related articles for news of outstanding companies in a given field, networking for recommendations and even some sleuthing to identify e-businesses not yet launched. The art of identifying partners is seeing the given potential of even the smallest website, the synergistic relationships possible from two seemingly unrelated e-businesses, the magnitude of one small idea or the various win-win outcomes of a strategic marriage. Developing smart partnership strategies that your competitors will find difficult to match and that your customers will perceive as enormous value comes with experience. This once again proves the need for a senior executive to orchestrate this important business function. Because the art and science of identifying potential partners is more involved than many other implementation processes, I'm not able to provide a list of generic identification tools that would be helpful to the majority of readers of this book. This is truly a process where customization to your business is imperative.

Develop a Partnership Pricing Strategy

There are many ways to charge or pay for partnership opportunities: flat fees, scaled fees, commissions, percentage of revenues or profits and so on. Selecting the most profitable fee structure isn't always possible; it frequently is dependent on a partner's business model, measurement capabilities, ability to pay at given intervals or industry norms. Because this subject is so expansive, I can't cover it completely here. However, I do want to address quickly the importance of establishing a pricing strategy that will enable you to optimize all of your partnership initiatives. A pricing strategy isn't as much about setting exact prices as it is about creating price supports, and developing a set of guidelines that determines the price you offer and ultimately negotiate. Here are three broad pricing strategies, which I offer merely as examples. There are, of course, many other effective pricing strategies.

- ▣ *Cafeteria Program:* offering a wide variety of partner marketing opportunities which are presented as single purchase opportunities. Companies can buy one or all of the items on the "menu" (e.g., section sponsorships, syndication rights, featured speaker, etc.). The drawback to this program is that the relationship is rarely integral to the monetary transaction because the partners merely come to buy and have few expectations of more strategic exchanges.
- ▣ *Exclusivity Program:* developing only a few strategic partnerships that are offered as an exclusive in return for a premium fee. These could be Web site feature/section exclusives, industry exclusives or

target-audience exclusives (e.g., exclusive right to target set demographics using personalized Web techniques). The relationship is bound by stringent rules that do not always lead to win-win outcomes for the Web site or the customers. Though the partnership frequently supports the highest price, it frequently limits you in the many other strategic opportunities in the marketplace.

▦ *Tiered Program:* selling various relationships in a good, better, best scenario whereby benefits increase with each tier or level of commitment. Additional benefits are offered with each consecutive tier. Companies essentially select the depth of relationship they want based on budget resources and the degree of interest in the site's target audience.

I am a proponent of tiered partnership strategies because they most effectively leverage your partnership strategy. To illustrate how a tiered partnership strategy works, I have included a partnership tiering strategy below. This partnership strategy would be appropriate for a content site that recommended vendors to its visitors.

I. Partnership Level 1: Advertiser
   A. Benefits Offered
      1. Receive banner space that is contextual
      2. Receive banner space that is targeted to individual
   B. Price
      1. Pay per click or click through based on location of ad and on database technique used (e.g., standard ad fee for contextual, higher fee for targeting individuals)

II. Partnership Level 2: Affiliate Relationship
   A. Benefits Offered
      1. Discount on advertising opportunities in Level 1
      2. List company in financial vendor referral lists (e.g., insurance info page has referrals to insurance companies at the bottom)

B. Price
  1. Pay per lead (using click through or registration) or a percentage of purchase (first purchase normally carries a higher percentage than subsequent purchases)

III. Partnership Level 3: Full Partner Relationship
  A. Benefits Offered
    1. Limited free advertising as in Level 1
    2. Benefits of Level 2 with priority placement
    3. Cobranding of a financial tool (e.g., insurance calculator, loan calculator, etc.) and logo appears on tool
    4. Permission marketing—included in four e-newsletters per year
  B. Price
    1. Flat fee, negotiated on the basis of the partner's value

IV. Partnership Level 4: Sponsor Relationship
  A. Benefits Offered
    1. Limited free advertising as in Level 1
    2. Benefits of Level 2 with priority placement and bolded type
    3. Benefits of Level 3
    4. Sponsorship of one specific area on website—type of area determines fee
      a. Sponsorship of home page area
      b. Sponsorship of a communication vehicle like an email advisory service
      c. Sponsorship of content section (e.g., loans, investments, banking, etc.)
      d. Sponsorship of a micro site: (e.g., home loans, mutual funds, CD rates)
      e. Sponsorship of an application or tool (e.g., loan payment calculator)
    5. Permission marketing
      a. Included in 4 e-newsletters per year

          b. Exclusive rights to sponsor specific reminder email services (e.g., investment, insurance, savings reminder emails)

      6. Optional add-on opportunities (available only with a Level 3 or Level 4 relationship)

          a. Cowrite an article with company name and URL link inserted in article

          b. Advertisement at bottom of e-newsletter

          c. Advertisement at bottom of reminder emails

  B. Price

    1. Fee is dependent on area or feature of website sponsored

Develop a Partner Revenue Forecast for All Revenue-Generating Initiatives

Once your pricing strategy is in place and you have developed a list of potential partners ranked by desirability and availability, it shouldn't be too difficult to estimate the potential revenues from establishing partnerships. Typically, this forecast is projected in accordance with the development of new partnership opportunities on the website, so the forecast will likely follow the website implementation schedule. Where partnership opportunities are fully implemented, the phasing of revenue streams will be driven by the sheer quantity of time required to identify and negotiate fees. Last, this partner revenue forecast should be based on receipt of funds, not the date that the funds were negotiated.

Partner revenue forecasting models can be complex. On the e-loyalty website you will find a partnership model that can be adjusted to reflect many different variables. You can see it at www.e-loyalty.com.

Develop a Partner Negotiation Strategy

Your plan for partner negotiation strategies should include the following.

■ *Prioritizing potential partners.* This should be loosely based on your partner evaluation model. Depending on how many evaluation criteria a potential partner can meet, a negotiation priority would be assigned. In this way the negotiation priority for partners that meet 100 percent of your evaluation model criteria would be ranked significantly higher than a potential partner meeting only 50 percent of the desired criteria.

▨ *Directions for negotiating prices.* Pricing is covered in the section above, but note that your negotiation strategy should provide your partner sales reps with specific rules for setting floors and ceilings on prices.

▨ *Rules of engagement.* This includes operational specifics on approval authority, allowed expenditures, disclosure of information and so on.

▨ *The relevant sales messages for each partner.* Much like the importance of positioning statements for customer programs, partnership offers also need positioning statements. Potential partners will immediately need to see the value proposed.

▨ A *partnership sales presentation.* This presentation will be used to attract partners and to persuade partners of the value of your offer. It may have several sections that are generic, but most topics should be tailored to the potential partner.

STEP 5: DETERMINE RESOURCES REQUIRED, BEST SOURCES AND ASSOCIATED COSTS

To complete your e-loyalty ROI model (Step 7) and your implementation timetable (Step 9), you'll need to determine the resources required to implement your e-loyalty program or features, the likely source of these resources and the probable costs. Start by developing a table of operational support required. Then list beside each item a ranking of the preferred sources for attaining that support, and in the third column, the associated cost for each source. Here's an example for two implementation resources.

Implementation Resource Required ▓	Preferred Source(s) ▓	Estimated Cost ▓
Partner marketing manager	Internal staff	1 man year $100,000–$125,000
Live chat application	Talk City TheGlobe.com	$100,000 $75,000

Here is a list of potential categories of implementation requirements you'll need to review for your resource identification process.

- Database design, hosting and maintenance
- Web design
- Web applications
- Human resource requirements (internal and outsourced)
- Creative and promotional agency support
- Consulting support
- Project management and fielding of research
- Partnership fees paid
- Advertising/marketing projects
- Outgoing and incoming customer communications
- Customer service support
- Legal advice
- Administrative support

Locating companies to provide applications, programming and consulting for your implementation needs can be tough because the landscape of providers keeps growing and changing. It's hard to keep up with which companies are new, which have been acquired and which have been ranked as one of the best in each of the various e-loyalty provider areas. That's why I have provided a list of resources on the website that supports this book. There you'll find Web applications, customer relationship management (CRM) software development companies, personalization tools, a database design specialist, customer support vendors, email management tools and more. And if you're looking for outsourcing resources, you'll find a list of outsource vendors on the site as well. I'd like to list the companies here, but by keeping the list on the website, I'll be able to keep it a bit more up to date. Find a list of resources to address your implementation issues at www.e-loyalty.com.

STEP 6: FINALIZE THE PROGRAM FORECASTS AND BUDGET

Forecasting Participation and Liabilities

Forecasting participation is one of the more difficult models that most Web marketers need to complete. The difficulty lies in forecasting customer behaviors for a Web offering you've never provided before, or no one has provided; therefore, there is no historical data on which to base the forecast. Finding data for similar customer behaviors and developing assumptions that allow you to apply the data to your own marketing rules, and even extrapolate the data to match the size of your customer database, is both an art and a science. But mostly it's experience. Though participation can be a difficult forecast to accurately complete, it is the most important projection you'll need for forecasting all other revenues and expenses. Therefore, if you don't have the skills to tackle this yourself, this would be an important area to outsource to professionals.

You may need only a liability forecast if you are offering some type of reward or benefit that is incremental to spending or participation. Your general expenses for your e-loyalty initiatives should be included in the expense section of your budget and ROI calculation. For point programs, this liability forecast is a critical step prior to moving forward in the implementation process. Many point programs and reward programs have been killed after the liability forecast projected much higher expenses that the company ever imagined. This is why strategies for minimizing liability should be included in the forecast process. For example, you might develop strategies for minimizing point liability through point breakage tactics such as point expiration and through tactics that increase the perceived value of rewards, thereby lowering the overall reward costs. For more information on point valuation, point liability forecasts and tactics for lowering reward costs visit the companion website for this book at www.e-loyalty.com.

Developing a Program Budget

Once your partner strategy, member participation, communications plan and operational costs have been identified, you'll have the information needed to create a program budget. Though it can be time consuming, I encourage you to build this budget from the ground up, with specific fixed and variable costs. This type of budget detail should closely resemble a direct marketing budget that develops a cost per communication piece for various customer participation levels that allows marketers to scale their budget to match various customer participation rates. Use the same direct marketing rigor to track the revenue associated with each e-loyalty initiative. From these expenses and attributed revenues, you can measure the profitability of each e-loyalty tactic and fund only those that generate incremental revenue or help meet critical business objectives. Demanding this type of detail in your budget now will make future adjustments based on various participation rates easier and make completing an ROI on your program or on facets of your program much more accurate.

STEP 7: ADOPT AN EXTENDED ROI TO JUSTIFY AND DEFEND YOUR BUDGET

If you're going to be a successful e-loyalty marketer, you'll have to prove it with numbers because e-loyalty is more akin to direct marketing, where

198 ◼ Ellen Reid Smith

ROI measures have been a proof point for years, than it is to general Web marketing tactics. More important, if you are to secure a sizable slice of the corporate budget pie needed to implement e-loyalty, quantitative proof of your positive return on equity will be imperative.

Stated simply, the return on investment (ROI) includes standard math: *(incremental revenues + savings from program) − program expenses = ROI.* Like any marketing program, your e-loyalty program or features should have a positive ROI. However, developing the revenues and expenses for an ROI on e-loyalty isn't a traditional business computation and can be more complicated. Some of the revenues and expenses aren't readily available. But I want to challenge you to apply some "new math" to the ROI process by including in your ROI calculation the value of enabling your e-business to achieve fundamental marketing advantages or business opportunities that wouldn't have been possible without your e-loyalty initiative. Therefore, to develop a complete picture of the value of your e-loyalty program requires an "extended ROI" calculation. Now I'll walk you through the basic steps of developing an extended ROI.

Start the ROI Model by Calculating Incremental Revenues
The first step is to earmark all incremental revenue generated by your e-loyalty program. That would include revenue from all types of transaction that are directly attributable to your e-loyalty initiatives. If you're launching a membership program, you'll need to know the "before" and "after" average transaction rates for these customers. Or you can track the average transactions for members versus nonmembers with the same characteristics. Here are the revenue areas that you'll need to include in this incremental revenue section of your extended ROI.

Incremental revenue generated by incremental transactions

- ◼ Increase in revenue from additional pages viewed with ad-generating banners

▩ Increase in revenue from higher click-through rates

▩ Increase in revenue from additional vender referral fees

Incremental revenue from incremental purchases

▩ Revenue from repurchases

▩ Revenue from interim purchases of items related to your product line sold through your e-loyalty program (possibly partner or third-party products you merchandise and sell)

▩ Revenue from stimulating multipurchases

▩ Revenue from cross-selling initiatives

▩ Revenue from upgrade or up-selling activities

Incremental revenue from database-related marketing

▩ Incremental revenue from increased response rates to targeted offers

▩ Value of higher margins on direct sale of aging and discontinued merchandise

▩ Revenue from increased click throughs generated by personalized advertising

Incremental profits attributable to customer referrals

▩ Revenue from new members gained through viral marketing or member-get-member programs

▩ Revenue from customer gift-giving promotions

▩ Revenue from advertising on pages forwarded to friends by customers

Incremental revenue from partner marketing

▩ Revenue from partnership and sponsorship fees

▩ Revenue from permission marketing participation fees

▦ Revenue from the sale of incremental advertising placements

▦ Revenue from sales commissions from affinity marketing

▦ Value from the sale of content/syndication rights to partners

▦ Revenue from the sale of your products by partners

Calculate the Savings Generated by e-Loyalty Initiatives

This second step is frequently left out of most marketing ROI calculations, but it is very important to e-loyalty initiatives because much of the value of e-loyalty is in the associated marketing and operational efficiencies it generates. The savings generated by e-loyalty should be treated as a "credit" on your e-loyalty balance sheet, and added to incremental revenues as part of the extended ROI calculation: (revenue + savings) − expenses = ROI. The following list gives some of the savings I've seen e-loyalty programs generate, but there are many, many more areas where e-loyalty can make your website more efficient. So I challenge you to build your own list and send it to me on the companion website to this book, www.e-loyalty.com.

1. Reduced acquisition costs (both retained and referred customers)

2. Advertising savings

▦ Savings from reduced expenses using direct versus mass marketing

▦ Postage savings from email versus snail mail

▦ Savings from creating customer evangelists using customer-get-customer marketing programs rather than using expensive mass advertising

▦ Decreased expenses on clearance sales advertising

3. Service center savings

▦ Savings from letting customers help themselves or customers helping other customers

▦ Saving by routing service calls from phone to Internet

4. Database and research savings

- ▓ Value of not having to buy customer names/data
- ▓ Research expenses reduced through the use of online customer panels

Reduced need for acquisition spending

5. Savings from using member-get-member programs instead of acquisition advertising and promotions

6. Inventory liquidation savings when members-only sales were used (could also be calculated as the incremental revenue difference from the price increase for selling to customers versus liquidators)

Calculate Incremental Program Expenses

In this incremental expenses portion of your extended ROI you'll want to limit expenses to those that are clearly incremental. For example, if you already have an advertising staff that supports your general e-business, it is typically not necessary to expense this staff against your e-loyalty project unless an additional head count were needed to support the e-loyalty advertising project management process. Evaluating each expense by asking "Would this expense be in my budget if it weren't for my e-loyalty initiatives?" is a quick way to identify expenses that are likely to be incremental. Of course, websites that integrate e-loyalty into every process of the e-business may have a more difficult time extricating the incremental expenses from the overall business expenses. While I advocate this degree of integration, it makes developing an ROI specifically for e-loyalty initiatives very difficult. The upside of this problem is that e-businesses that completely integrate e-loyalty into their business probably don't need an e-loyalty ROI at all since their overall business ROI reflects customer loyalty effectiveness. Here are the types of expenses you need to consider in calculating incremental expenses.

- Web page development
- Incremental database programming
- Incremental Web applications or support engines
- Incremental cost to host and maintain Web pages devoted solely to e-loyalty
- Incremental staff required
- Incremental partner marketing
- Incremental service, benefits and rewards solely generated by e-loyalty initiatives

And here is a list of expenses that should not be included in e-loyalty expenses.

- General Web advertising that uses the e-loyalty program as its acquisition message (your business would have done some form of acquisition advertising without the e-loyalty program)
- Partner marketing expenses that are actually business development expenses (this is true when your e-business would have sought a relationship with partners even without a formal e-loyalty partner program)
- Customer communications that would be sent without a program (simply making communications the responsibility of e-loyalty managers doesn't make them an incremental e-loyalty expense)

An Alternative ROI Methodology: ROI per Customer Retained

Once you have completed a detailed and itemized ROI for your program and are confident of its accuracy, you may want to simplify the process by calculating an ROI per customer retained (total ROI figure divided by the number of retained customers). This method may also be used for estimating an ROI when data for calculating incremental revenues and expenses is too difficult to attain or where there is very little data, as is the case with infrequently purchased products like cars and homes that have long product life cycles.

The ROI per customer methodology requires developing a quantifiable figure that represents the average value of a retained customer. Calculating this average requires the same revenue and expense identification I've detailed in the previous ROI steps, including the extended ROI concepts of savings. The total is then divided by the number of retained customers to derive the average ROI. Using the ROI per customers method will require you to take a firm stand over the ownership of the retained customer and the associated incremental value. You'll need to emphatically take credit for every retained customer participating in your program. If you don't have a formalized program, you'll have to assume a reasonable percentage of your generic customer base.

While averages are easier to work with, I would recommend you bite the bullet and do the extra analysis required to determine the value of each type of retained customer. For example, retaining a high-value customer will generate higher profits than retaining a low-value customer. I've briefly outlined how you would modify the extended ROI calculation to better capture the ROI per customer.

- ▦ Identify the difference in revenues for customers in each customer lifetime value index (see Step 2, in "Identifying the Customers You Want to Be Loyal" in "The Seven Steps to Designing an e-Loyalty Strategy" to review the calculations for establishing customer lifetime values and lifetime value indices).
- ▦ Subtract the average expense per customer from the average incremental revenue per customer in each index to establish a profit value for one retained customer in each CLV index. (Note: if expenses vary greatly by customer value segment, you may need to develop a more specific expense-per-customer figure for each lifetime value segment.)
- ▦ Determine the incremental increase in number of retained customers over average retention rates.
- ▦ Multiply the number of incrementally retained customers by the exact or average CLV index value to generate a more accurate ROI for your e-loyalty initiatives.

The Value of Meeting Business Objectives

The last step involves identifying business value resulting from your e-loyalty program that can be hard to quantify, such as the value of meeting business objectives. Sometimes simply quantifying the business values outlined in this step of your extended ROI calculation will provide the fodder your executive staff needs to justify e-loyalty spending. The values in this step of your extended ROI are more persuasive because they track larger, more strategic leaps in profitability and business growth. Like all meaningful valuations, these calculations may take a bit more effort because the values are typically spread over several different business processes, or may effect the entire business growth plan. But even if you merely identify these values and broadly estimate the associated values, your management team will start to gain a clearer picture of the value of your e-loyalty initiatives. Again, the list that follows is intended only to be illustrative, since the list of business objectives attained through e-loyalty on your website will be different and more specific.

1. The value of attaining increased customer data

    ▦ Savings from not having to purchase customer data through other sources
    ▦ The value of the ability to customize/personalize content/sales recommendations
    ▦ The value of an increased customer knowledge to make each business decision
    ▦ The value of the ability to use data mining to forecast trends

2. The value of being able to initiate one-to-one marketing strategies

    ▦ The savings and incremental revenue attributable to your ability to build products that loyal customers want (e.g., less manufacturing/inventory waste and increased sales revenue)
    ▦ The value of more efficient marketing tactics because you know

which customers respond to which kind of marketing offers, promotions or sales

3. The value of a more intelligent customer dialogue

▦ The value of improved customer readership of your communications because your e-loyalty program made your communications more valuable to customers by tailoring messages to individual needs
▦ The value of more frequent and productive feedback from customers, which can be used to improve product features, quality and marketing

4. The value of greater organizational effectiveness
5. The ability to launch new products faster
6. Efficiencies from centralizing customer communications
7. Increased business growth from moving from a product-focused business to a customer-focused business
8. The value of better research

▦ The ability to quickly contact customers for research projects for more timely research results
▦ The value of having more customers participate in research requests because their relationship with your website makes them want to participate

9. The value of stimulating incremental increases in key business measurements

▦ Increased time on site per visit
▦ Increased frequency of visits
▦ Higher satisfaction rates
▦ Lower customer churn rates

■ Lower ratio of browsers to buyers (i.e., getting more browsers to buy)

Step 8: Develop a Plan for Measuring Success

The major components for developing a plan for measuring success are:

■ Identifying the measures of success for e-loyalty
■ Developing a plan for measuring program metrics
■ Identifying the technology or measurement systems required to implement these measures
■ Determining database and software requirements for calculating, saving and analyzing success metrics
■ Developing a plan for easily reading, analyzing and distributing these measurements so that they can be used to improve e-loyalty initiatives

Bullet points two through five above are squarely dependent on the measures you identify in the first bulleted item. The software, financial calculations and analytical processes will depend upon your business model and technical operations. So generically describing these last four bullet points would not benefit most readers. Therefore I will concentrate on the most important step—identifying the measurements of e-loyalty success—the one step most likely to trip up marketers.

Measure Success Using a Compilation of Measurements

I see too many presentations at seminars where a loyalty marketer stands up and tries to demonstrate the success of his or her loyalty program based upon the incremental increases they have seen in their customer satisfaction measures. Well, I have news for all these misguided marketers: *satisfied* customers defect companies everyday, but *loyal* customers are much less likely to jump ship after them. So while satisfaction is a valuable weather vane, it won't measure the temperature of customer loyalty.

There are several measurements more effective than satisfaction to measure e-loyalty. I have listed the following three most common techniques.

Financial Measures. First, I'll cover the loyalty measures your finance officer will love most. In these methods, loyalty is measured by tracking customer behaviors that indicate they value your website and its offerings.

- Return visit or repurchase
- Return more often or buy more (share-of-time/wallet)
- Recommend to others (advocacy)

These are the quantitative proof points that your customers are loyal. However, in an Internet world where a business year is completed in months, loyalty can also move fast and appear to be more short term. Therefore, these customer behavior measures are sometimes not as effective as we would like at measuring the depth of customer loyalty. For loyalty commitment, we need to look at how well we are providing value to the customer.

Value Measures. Nope, you're not having a big book-reader deja vu. I am repeating myself because we have now come full circle in the loyalty cycle. Value is the key both to discovering loyalty and to measuring it. I covered this same theory of loyalty based on value in the section on identifying loyalty drivers (see "What Generates e-Loyalty?" in part I). The same theory that says loyalty is driven by value drivers—product offering, product quality, brand image and price—can be applied to measuring loyalty. To understand how deep the loyalty is among frequent buyers, you need to determine how well you are delivering on your customers' most important value attributes. Keep in mind that this measure of value isn't necessarily a product's real value, but its perceived value in all four categories of value. For example, many buyers think that there is value in a $10,000 Rolex watch, but the real value driver at work here is image, not quality, price or service. Here is a list of ways you can measure the value you provide using the four loyalty drivers of value.

Measure attitudes on content/product quality

▩ Belief in accuracy of content
▩ Belief in quality of products and services

Measure attitudes on website service

▩ Belief that the website has great service, even if they haven't needed to use it
▩ Reduced service calls
▩ Reduced complaints

Measure perception of price

▩ Perceived value of price as compared to other alternatives
▩ Perceived cost of defecting to competition (what customer must give up)

Measure image of product and company

▩ Belief that your website/product is the best
▩ Belief that your company will do what's right and take care of customers
▩ Belief that your website or product will take them into the future (continuously upgraded content, cutting-edge product features or upgradability)

Participation Measures. Finally, I present you with the cheaters' guide to measuring loyalty. It won't give you the most accurate picture of loyalty, but it is fairly fast and will probably make investors who have short-term vision very happy. This snapshot of e-loyalty success is based on the premise that participation equals loyalty, and for this reason, some content or community websites might find that these measurements come fairly close to a true loyalty measure.

You can measure program participation by analyzing:

▩ Registration rates (indicates interest and trust)
▩ Churn rates (measures increasing/decreasing customer base)
▩ Growth in visitors to website (indicates that others see value in the site's concept)
▩ Percentage of customers participating in program offerings (indicates interest)
▩ Growth in pages viewed per visitor (indicates growth in interest)
▩ Response rates to online surveys (can indicate customers care)
▩ Response rates to direct marketing offers (indicates email readership)
▩ Percentage of customers participating in referral programs (indicates trust)

STEP 9: DEVELOP A VIABLE TIMELINE WITH IMPLEMENTATION LEADERS

There are a dozen or so project management software packages on the market that can help you develop an e-loyalty project timeline and implementation process that include all the relevant tasks required and that are dependent on each other for launch. But these project management tools are only as good as the input you give them. In the list of implementation tasks that follows, I didn't include all the obvious implementation steps you should have in your timeline, but instead I focused on keys to making this timeline viable.

▩ Be sure to include checkpoints and milestones with the ramifications of not meeting these milestones clearly noted on the project management charts
▩ Don't just identify tasks; also clearly identify responsibilities. And don't loosely give responsibility to a department, but to an individual—individuals are much less likely to shirk responsibilities than departments.
▩ If you are going to launch a pilot program or test market program,

integrate these preparations into the launch plan for the overall program so that no one will be tempted to "re-create the wheel" or generate other inefficiencies.

▓ Ensure the timeline is aggressive, but viable. This is a tricky one. I personally like to lean on the side of severely aggressive for my first draft of the timeline, because human nature causes workers to challenge immediately the team's ability to meet the schedule. Case in point: when was the last time someone on one of your teams volunteered to implement their tasks in less time than was required? Starting with a very aggressive timeline gives you negotiating room and makes others feel good when they believe they have won the negotiation for more time. However, there is a fine line between being so aggressive that everyone thinks you are an unrealistic project manager and not being aggressive enough.

▓ The plan needs to include all the tasks required for integrating e-loyalty initiatives into the rest of the website marketing and operational calendars. So including major milestones for business groups that impact your launch is advised.

▓ Don't let your ability to launch drive your date for launch. You should start with a marketing or strategic business calendar and ask, "If we could launch this program anytime, when would we do it?" Granted there is merit to a first-strike advantage, but launching a program when there is too much "noise" in the marketplace from holidays, national events, weekly work schedules and so on, can subvert any first-strike advantage. You want to launch at the most advantageous time so that the initial results are good.

▓ Never underestimate the time your lawyers will take to rake you over the coals. Build in plenty of time for a legal review *prior* to starting your implementation plan, time to rework major program concepts after your lawyers change their minds and time for them to copyedit all your program communications. I love lawyers for keeping me out of court, but there are days when you want to wring their necks.

The Four Biggest Challenges in Implementing an e-Loyalty Program

mplementing an e-loyalty program in a corporation that hasn't ever focused on loyalty initiatives or measures will probably be one of the hardest things you've ever done. Now I know all the website founders out there would disagree with me because launching a website can be pretty darn challenging. But the key difference in launching your own e-loyalty–focused website is that you make the decisions and you settle the arguments—you're in charge. For marketers in large organizations, implementing an e-loyalty program is similar to running a political campaign in the backyard of your political opponent—your job is to influence the workers while your peers mark your every move in an effort to shoot you down. You can minimize the internal warfare if you spend more time keeping everyone happy all of the time, but this results in an implementation timeline that is so long that your business objectives will change before you launch—and I've seen half-implemented programs get killed under these circumstances more than once. Gutsy marketers can sometimes teach us a thing or two about implementing in the midst of political warfare. Gutsy marketers implement so fast that most people don't even know what hit them until the program is up and the resulting measurements make everyone happy with their newfound revenues. Then this gutsy marketer has to leave because no one will ever forgive him for all the success he caused.

The difficulties I've seen in implementing e-loyalty programs are no exaggeration. As I said before, I've been on the inside and on the outside of dozens of e-loyalty projects and have *never* seen an e-loyalty project have all the players on board all the time. And this is why two of the four challenges identified in this section address the political battles every e-loyalty marketer faces. The other two challenges I cover involve keeping focused on the e-loyalty principle of customer lifetime value and getting the money to fund e-loyalty initiatives. There are many challenges—my list originally had nine—but when you synthesize all the issues, it really boils down to these four challenges:

Challenge #1: Integrating e-Loyalty and Adopting It as a
    Business Goal
Challenge #2: Gaining Consensus and Garnering Support
Challenge #3: Maintaining a Customer Lifetime Value Focus
Challenge #4: Appropriating the Funding and Resources Required

CHALLENGE #1: INTEGRATING E-LOYALTY AND ADOPTING IT AS A BUSINESS GOAL

For companies still using a product-focused business model rather than a customer-focused one, integrating e-loyalty will be extremely difficult, if not impossible. Because e-loyalty requires many of the same internal organizational and operation requirements as customer relationship management (CRM) and one-to-one marketing, most of the integration warnings espoused in a dozen or more books covering these two disciplines are also applicable to e-loyalty. The following are the important advisor points on CRM changes.

- Your website will be the catalyst for change because it forces a customer-centric approach to businesses.
- Your website will force business operations to work in perfect harmony, which is usually a far cry from the political battleground between groups like product development and manufacturing or marketing and sales.
- You'll need CEO support to resolve disparate and often feuding factions within a company that don't see eye to eye.
- The website will require all offline and online processes to be linked, especially in the areas where customer contact is concerned.

One area that many companies don't immediately connect e-loyalty to is the employee evaluation system. For example, while I was a vice president in IBM's Consumer Division, one of the larger factors in determining the division's profit sharing was the measurement of customer satisfaction. IBM took a biannual (sometimes only annual) reading of customer satisfaction as one of the fundamental measurements of business success. We all hoped to God that the survey wasn't conducted near any service incidents or bad press; otherwise, a temporary fluctuation in customer satisfaction levels could tank our profit sharing. It also meant that no one was willing to risk treating our best customers best, for fear that the survey might include too many low-value, less-satisfied customers. As I state many times in this book, satisfied customers defect every day. Basing a business unit's success on customer satisfaction rather than loyalty as measured in repurchase and retention rates doesn't accurately represent success at all. At best, it represents short-term customer attitudes. Measuring success on satisfaction also goes against the proven theory of increasing loyalty by excelling at customer service resolution. It's often more effective and profitable to aim for an excellent customer service resolution process than spending exorbitant resources on achieving a 100 percent defect-free product or radically reduced service center calls. The goal of lowering customer complaints to zero in the PC business is particularly unrealistic because the majority of hardware problems are actually user problems. Being a glutton for punishment, I raised the flag that the measurement really should be changed to customer loyalty (repurchase, upgrade, cross purchase, etc.) or simple customer retention rates if the measure really was to be a gauge of that year's hard work. Management agreed that satisfaction as a measurement had its weaknesses, but wouldn't change the measurement because it might affect profit sharing. Management was spending resources on an e-loyalty initiative, and giving it lots of lip service, but wasn't willing to change employee measurements to reward the achievement of that objective; consequently, the customer retention efforts didn't make the headway they could have. All the focus was on satisfying all customers equally; therefore, it couldn't excel at fulfilling the needs of the best customers. Now I don't mean to pick on IBM, because they certainly do many things well, and needless to say, most of IBM's competitors haven't made the significant strides in implementing a customer loyalty strategy that IBM has, but it illustrates my point: to encourage employees to go against the current and achieve an e-loyalty focus, you have to ensure that employee rewards are consistent with your e-loyalty strategy.

CHALLENGE #2: GAINING CONSENSUS AND GARNERING SUPPORT

Be prepared for the battle to gain consensus because everyone has his or her own idea of what e-loyalty should be, and some people will hate yours. It's inevitable. You'll think you have the perfect plan, it has management's endorsement, and no sooner than you settle into the implementation the alternative plans will start coming out of the woodwork. I don't want to sound like I'm not in favor of soliciting ideas to improve a plan. All viable ideas that follow e-loyalty principles should be considered. But at some point you have to stop considering new ideas and gain consensus around the best idea. You have to move forward and get traction. More important, you can't keep second-guessing your strategy every step of the way. You need to maintain the course by sticking with your strategy until you have measurable results that prove otherwise, even if this means turning down potentially profitable side strategies that don't support the main strategy.

Running a business really shouldn't be based on democracy, but the amount of campaigning required to get buy-in on the fundamental business changes required to implement e-loyalty will lead you to think the democratic process is alive and well in corporate America. So as unpalatable as glad handing, deal making and strong arming are, you'll have to garner support up and down the management chain and you'll have to do it more than once. Just when you think you have full buy-in and you start to focus on implementation rather than politics, a cry will go up to encourage others to disavow support of e-loyalty initiatives. This hap-

pened so often at IBM that I had an employee who's job was "chief evangelist." The reason constant evangelistic measures are needed is twofold:
(1) turnover in employees creates a constant need for selling the strategy
and eliciting support; and (2) the force of the undertow trying to prevent
employees from following the strategy can lead them to frequently lose
their perseverance—or even their good judgment. You'll need a plan to
gain and regain support over and over again until the e-loyalty program is
no longer thought of as a "program" at all, but rather as the accepted way
of doing business. Here are some suggestions for selling your strategy and
garnering support.

Selling Senior Management on the Idea

Before you waste one breath on selling an e-loyalty strategy, your management must buy into the following principles of e-loyalty.

- It is more cost-effective to retain customers than to acquire them.
- Loyal customers are more profitable.
- All customers are not equal.
- Recognize and reward according to lifetime value.
- Communications must be two way and personalized.
- Loyalty exists when there is an opportunity cost for defecting.
- Short-term loyalty can be bought, long-term loyalty must be earned.

With these principles as a common starting ground, gaining consensus
and support of an e-loyalty strategy is much easier.

I like to start off e-loyalty presentations with what I call "the big scare
tactic": the competition is going to eat us for lunch if we don't do this program. To prove that my scare tactic has substance, I review current competitive e-loyalty initiatives, analyze case studies from other industries in
which companies that failed to adopt customer retention strategies died a
slow death and detail the potential impact on our company if the competition were to adopt a strong e-loyalty strategy. No exaggeration of the
truth is required because the Internet makes competition more prevalent
and enemies more nimble. Managers realize they either have to get on

board or spend the rest of their careers wondering why they doubted themselves. I probably use this scare tactic because of the military influence early in my career and because Sun-tsu's *The Art of War* is one of my favorite books. He advises:

> Throw the troops into a position from which there is no escape and even when faced with death they will not flee. For if prepared to die, what can they not achieve? Then officers and men together put forth their utmost efforts. In a desperate situation they fear nothing; when there is no way out they stand firm. Deep in a hostile land they are bound together, and there, where there is no alternative, they will engage the enemy in hand to hand combat. Thus, such troops need no encouragement to be vigilant. Without extorting their support the general obtains it; without inviting their affection he gains it; without demanding their trust he wins it. (Samuel B. Griffith translation, 1963)

Nothing seems to rally the resolve of executives, the cooperation of managers and the passion of workers quite like a single clearly identified enemy and the threat of losing.

Once I have management's attention, I prove why my e-loyalty initiatives will take on the competitive threats we face *and* have plenty of extra benefits, such as:

- Minimizing comparison shopping
- Improving lead quality
- Gaining control of customer information
- Reducing expenses by focusing resources on the right customers
- Increasing the efficiency of promotions, cross-sell, up-sell and other marketing initiatives
- Providing a mechanism for attracting sponsorship fees

Selling Peers on "What's in It for Them"
In larger companies, each department wants its team to be successful. Sometimes this departmental success comes at the expense of the greater good of the company. It's not healthy, but it is prevalent, usually due to the greater focus on departmental performance and not total corporate performance. So one of the most effective ways to garner support from your various internal groups is to explain carefully what's in it for them. The sales department or sales channel will initially think your e-loyalty initiative is another time-consuming, ineffective promotion—that's what most sales professionals think marketers do best and sometimes they're right. So you'll need to state explicitly how the program will sell more product, and how they can use it to generate additional commissions. Since the advertising department is evaluated on brand awareness and customer trial or acquisition, you'll need to explain how your e-loyalty program is an effective customer acquisition tool that is going to make attracting customers to the brand easier. Management will want to know how it effects bottom-line profitability, so you'll need to ensure they understand your e-loyalty ROI measurements and the incremental profits tracked by this ROI. And last, shareholders will want you to show how it provides corporate growth, either through a larger customer base or incremental transactions. Regardless of what internal group you are trying to persuade, the key is to identify how they measure success, then focus on how the e-loyalty strategy can improve that measure. Ideally you'll want to work with them to develop ways they can use the program to increase their critical success measurements.

Selling Employees on a Possibly Difficult Management Transition
When management is fully committed to e-loyalty, a clear strategy and a specific implementation plan, I recommend selling employees on the idea by hosting several all-employee seminars that begin with covering the concepts of e-loyalty and the advantages of such a strategy. I have frequently been brought into a company to conduct this program launch seminar, but it really works best when the senior managers are involved in

both the teaching and the delivery of the new strategy. Employees need to see an unwavering degree of buy-in from senior management because you are asking them to turn their world upside down in order to achieve this unfamiliar business objective. This kind of radical change butts heads with what I see as the number one managerial challenge: most employees don't like change. So you better sell employees on this concept, and sell it well if you're going to be successful.

Once employees have a clear understanding of the concepts, senior management can then present the specific e-loyalty plan to be implemented. If at any time employees don't think there is a clear mandate and a viable plan, then political undercurrents will slow the process by trying to undermine it every step of the way. I speak from experience, having been on the inside and on the outside of many corporations that were plagued with political animals trying to destroy a sound business strategy. In most cases it was the younger staff members who worked like hell to implement a program their CEO decreed as the corporate goal, while their own managers fought and undermined much of their subordinates' work. This is why gaining consensus and garnering support is critical to a successful e-loyalty implementation.

CHALLENGE #3: MAINTAINING A CUSTOMER LIFETIME VALUE FOCUS

This is what you'll hear time and time again when you try to implement an e-loyalty strategy that treats best customers best: "But it's not fair." Hold fast and strong because life's not fair and your most valuable customers earned the differentiated products, service, pricing and other benefits you provide them. Customer service centers are probably the biggest proponents of treating all customers the same. For years they've been judged on an indiscriminate measure of satisfaction from high-value and low-value customers alike. The concept that we don't want to service very low-value customers because it's not profitable can curl their toes. In these situations, I find that profitability numbers are very convincing.

Usually, customer service managers are focused on quality of calls, abandonment rates, first call resolution rates and other measures of total satisfaction. But when you show these managers that some products don't have the margin to support live customer service, whereas other products do, they seem to understand the value of earning a profit. Change the belief that treating best customers best is a matter of discrimination into a more accurate view that best customers earn enhanced services. Most of us have been trained to apply the golden rule to all customers—and in the rare instances where you have unlimited resources to offer all customers the best, this is possible. But since most companies don't have unlimited resources and you'll want to save the best benefits for your best customers, you need to take the time to bring employees on board. This is critical if employees are to be leaders in helping to identify techniques for treating best customers best, and funding those techniques by identifying ways to reduce the cost of unenhanced service.

A second department within your company that you will find difficult to keep focused on a MVC strategy is business development. They will bring business alliance and acquisition opportunities to you with a disregard for its effect on MVCs. It will be your job to evaluate each new business opportunity by determining if it supports your focus on MVCs by enhancing the experience of this group.

Finance managers focused on quarter-to-quarter results are also likely to oppose your customer lifetime view when spending doesn't generate associated revenues in the same fiscal quarter. That's because a lifetime view of a customer's value suggests you don't focus merely on past or current profitability, but on future and potential profitability, so spending now on customers who won't become high-value customers in the next few quarters will seem like a poor ROI. It may be even harder for you to justify expending resources on low-value customers who will never have a high lifetime value, but who will serve as advocates for your product and influence the sales of many other customers. Without a measurable, direct correlation between these advocates and other customer revenues, finance may question your spending. Again, education is everything. If you define the future value of customers and develop clear strategies for measuring the success of your investments in future values, finance will be more likely to adopt your plan—at least until your first round of tangible proof.

I've saved the most difficult challenge for last: an advertising department that sees its budget rerouted to e-loyalty while your company changes the focus from acquisition to retention. When your advertising director sees your plan to minimize acquisition costs in favor of higher spending on best customer retention efforts, she will start pushing the pins in her voodoo dolls. Nothing smarts for an advertiser more than having her budget taken way by some e-loyalty guru who can track and prove an ROI on targeted incremental spending promotions and customer retention efforts. But using effective e-loyalty tactics to encourage customers to recruit other customers (viral marketing) has never held much glamour for traditional advertisers. Nor has the seemingly dull palette of a black-and-white email. The creativity and resources that have been spent on indiscriminate marketing now need to be focused on attracting MVCs. This means running acquisition programs on a much smaller scale that targets individual high-value user groups. It means killing the feel good psyche brand ads and replacing them with messages that drive home the benefits most important to high-value customers. It isn't always possible to bring this advertising foe around to assist you and your team. However, getting an outside expert to educate your advertising director on the future of increased direct marketing initiatives and less mass advertising can be a first step. The second step would be to find a way to make working on your team an excellent opportunity for her to learn the direct marketing trends that will enhance her own resume.

To keep employees focused, I like to paraphrase an Abraham Lincoln quote: you can meet all the needs of some of the people all of the time, and some of the needs of all the people all of time, but you can't meet all the needs of all of the people all of the time—that is, if you're going to make a profit. The goal is to identify which customers will be most valuable if you not only meet all of their needs, but exceed those needs by providing more than expected and by anticipating future needs. Trying to be everything to everyone will make you merely average, so convincing your management that not all customers are equal and shouldn't be treated equally is a very important step in both designing and implementing your e-loyalty strategy.

CHALLENGE #4: APPROPRIATING THE FUNDING AND RESOURCES REQUIRED

So you need an e-loyalty program, but your budget can't support it . . . that never stopped me! I've always thought of e-loyalty programs as cash cows: if properly nurtured, your e-loyalty program will pay for itself. The key is to prove your e-loyalty initiatives drive incremental revenues and create independent revenue streams.

In Step 7 of my implementation guide ("Adopt an Extended ROI to Justify and Defend Your Budget"), I cover in detail the process of computing an ROI for your program. So I won't repeat that process here. But this is the right place to point out why calculating an ROI and using it as a measurement is so important: it justifies your budget and your success. Therefore, to appropriate the funding required, you will need analytical proof that your e-loyalty initiatives generate incremental revenue in excess of the cost of implementing the program. No problem! But before you begin waiving your ROI calculation banner and claiming your share of revenue, be sure you have put the following processes in place.

■ Measurement processes that track incremental revenue generated by your e-loyalty efforts
■ A process for identifying and earmarking all incremental sales revenue generated by your e-loyalty program as your e-loyalty revenues (sometimes this works best when you can operate your e-loyalty program as an independent cost/revenue center)
■ Your own process for tracking committed partner revenues generated from your e-loyalty initiatives because the payment and

accounting of these revenue streams will be too delayed to support
your current initiatives
▨ Take a firm stand that you own this retained customer value.

My experience is that most businesses are so inept at tracking and asso-
ciating incremental revenues with individual marketing investments that
not only will they be thrilled you have some type of quantitative proof
that their marketing strategy is working, but few will be able to poke holes
in your ROI calculation. Most of your colleagues either haven't learned
to calculate marketing ROIs, haven't set up the measurements required
or simply haven't taken the time to calculate ROI. You'll be a hero, and
you'll have quantitative proof that you earned your slice of the corporate
budget pie.

But to be effective at using the ROI calculations to justify your budget,
you'd better have some pretty impressive independent revenue streams
from partners. Not only is it one of the easiest ways to quickly increase
your ROI, it is also irrefutably attributable to your e-loyalty efforts. And as
I point out in my extended ROI calculation in Step 6 of my implementation guide, these partners will also produce many "less quantifiable" benefits and profitable opportunities that you may not have access to
otherwise. So creating revenue opportunities and attracting partners who
want to take advantage of these opportunities will need to be a major
focus of your efforts. Here are some suggestions for improving your ability
to generate stand-alone revenues.

Build partnership and sponsorship opportunities into your website
design

▨ Develop navigational levels to your content that can be easily
sponsored (e.g., computers for small, medium and large enter-
prises)
▨ Categorize topics so they can be stand-alone subjects, each with
a separate sponsor (e.g., instead of creating a large category such

as "investing," create categories such as saving for college, planning for retirement, creating wealth, etc.)

▦ Let partners build or sponsor your interactive applications (e.g., your mortgage payment calculator, annual return estimating tool and your compound interest tool can all be sponsored by a partner)

▦ Create lifestyle areas both to target your content and to create sponsorship opportunities for companies wanting to target a specific life stage or lifestyle (e.g., health content for teens, pregnant women, seniors, etc.)

Actively attract partners with deep pockets

▦ Offer unique communication opportunities

▦ Develop the ability to increase response rates by using your target communication capabilities

▦ Demonstrate that you have built a relationship that inspires your customers to want to read your communications (i.e., you can increase readership and response rates)

▦ Develop a section of your website devoted to selling potential partners on the advantages of partnering with your website

Seek out partners to lower expenses

▦ Attract partners with complimentary marketing goals to share your communication and advertising expenses

▦ Find partners to provide rewards at a reduced cost in return for marketing exposure

▦ Conduct joint research projects with partners to reduce research expenses

Optimize partnerships by identifying and leveraging customer synergies

Sell permission marketing opportunities

The biggest key in maximizing revenue through partner relationships is to create as many partner marketing opportunities as possible and to treat your partners like they are just that: partners in your business. If you can gain a reputation for being not only a profitable partner but also a very strategically beneficial partner, much like women.com has done, then word will get around this small Web world, and your actions will speak louder than words.

PART

Critical Website Design Factors and Some Great Examples

The Basics of Website Usability

n previous sections of this book, I've outlined detailed strategies for building e-loyalty programs and developing customer contact strategies to keep your customers coming back. All of this advice has been given on the assumption that your website is worth coming back to at all. Before even the best e-loyalty program will be effective at retaining customers, you have to meet the basics of Web usability—easy navigation, two to three clicks to any solution, fast page loads, effective search engines, a quick shopping checkout process, server reliability, ability to handle peak load times and so on. Before you fly past my comment and assume your site is user friendly, consider this: several magazine reviews of websites in the first quarter of 2000 identified the percentage of websites where customers can actually find what they are looking for to be less than 40 percent. That means that more than half the readers of this book shouldn't assume they are ready to implement a great e-loyalty strategy until they remedy their usability programs. The simple fact is that many websites focus on the bells and whistles before nailing down basic customer satisfaction.

I began this book with a discussion on what drives loyalty and outlined why loyalty can't be measured as satisfaction. But here is where satisfaction plays a very important role in engendering e-loyalty: you can't expect to have a successful e-loyalty strategy without covering the basics of user satisfaction first. If magazines are filled with articles about sites that don't pass basic customer usability standards and these same magazines provide great advice and instructions for achieving the minimum customer satisfaction level required for success, why are 60 percent of all sites still unnavigable or unsatisfactory to users? The three biggest reasons are: first, the "call to action" is unclear, second, the navigation is not designed around solving customer problems and third, the site doesn't deliver customer service basics.

GET THE "CALL TO ACTION" RIGHT

Have you ever been to websites that look more like a magazine than a store, with only occasional links to merchandise here and there? Or have you visited the site of a well-known brand, only to find the website is all about building their brand so your only route to shopping is the small cart in the far upper-right-hand corner of the page? This problem results from the e-marketer not delineating its goals and objectives and designing to meet them (Step 1 of my seven steps to an e-loyalty strategy). With the objectives clear the appropriate call to action should also be clear.

In its simplest form, success on the Internet is measured in terms of visitors who complete your "call to action." Your call to action should be the item that drives your business model. For e-commerce sites the call to action would be a purchase, for advertiser-supported sites it would be to click throughs to pages where high-dollar advertisements are located, for auction sites it would be bids or postings—you get the idea. Success is turning visitors into customers. This is referred to as your "conversion rate." On e-commerce sites the conversion measure is also called the "browse-to-buy ratio," and on member sites it might be the "browse-to-join ratio." Regardless of what your business model is, you should have a conversion rate that measures this as a success factor. To raise conversion rates, e-business managers have two choices: they can spend huge ad budgets to increase the number of visitors to the site or they can spend money on Web design to improve the conversion rate itself. Increasing the effectiveness of your site is by far the most effective way to improve conversions because it is normally the least expensive proposition and it is a long-term strategy that will generate exponential gains as traffic increases. I've provided an example below of the two choices for increasing conversion rates.

EXAMPLE: METHODS FOR INCREASING CONVERSION RATES

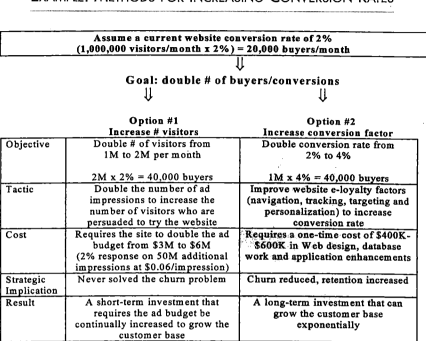

	Assume a current website conversion rate of 2% (1,000,000 visitors/month x 2%) = 20,000 buyers/month	
	⇩ Goal: double # of buyers/conversions ⇩ ⇩	
	Option #1 Increase # visitors	**Option #2 Increase conversion factor**
Objective	Double # of visitors from 1M to 2M per month 2M x 2% = 40,000 buyers	Double conversion rate from 2% to 4% 1M x 4% = 40,000 buyers
Tactic	Double the number of ad impressions to increase the number of visitors who are persuaded to try the website	Improve website e-loyalty factors (navigation, tracking, targeting and personalization) to increase conversion rate
Cost	Requires the site to double the ad budget from $3M to $6M (2% response on 50M additional impressions at $0.06/impression)	Requires a one-time cost of $400K-$600K in Web design, database work and application enhancements
Strategic Implication	Never solved the churn problem	Churn reduced, retention increased
Result	A short-term investment that requires the ad budget be continually increased to grow the customer base	A long-term investment that can grow the customer base exponentially

Doubling an advertising budget to double conversions can be a very expensive proposition, but sites try to solve their acquisition problem in this very way. The argument for doubling an advertisement budget looks particularly foolish when the cost of redesigning the website to double the conversion rate from 2 percent to 4 percent requires half the expenditure of an expanded ad campaign. Considering that most sites have single-digit conversion rates, increasing conversion rates can have a huge impact for a lot less money. This focus on improving conversion rates rather than advertising isn't new to bricks-and-mortar retailers. Although traditional retailers have significant advertising expenditures, they spend equally large portions of their marketing budgets on merchandising, store layouts and endcap displays that pull you into their shopping labyrinth. In traditional retail, it's all about conversion, and even when they've converted you into a buyer, they hit you again with impulse items in the checkout lane. Many mothers know the success of in-store calls to action as they make a beeline for the one checkout lane that is sans candy. But for the most part, e-tailers seem to overlook the importance of perfecting a virtual store navigation that will drive customers deeper into the site, peak their interest in products and ultimately improve conversion rates. Your call to action is the biggest first step in driving conversion rates, so if your home page isn't explicit about what you want customers to do, then you need to take a look at the first critical design criteria in the next section of this book, titled "Make Your First Impression Count."

YOUR NAVIGATION SHOULD SOLVE PROBLEMS

Customers come to the Web to solve problems. Even the guy who goes to the Web to buy bath soap has a problem: he's out of bath soap. Customers come to the Web for solutions. I realize the "solutions" word has been horribly overused, but think back to its true meaning, before it was bastardized by technology advertisers. When a customer comes to your website for bath soap, he doesn't begin the process by thinking "Gosh, I wonder what the manufacturer of my bath soap thinks about its customers." Nor does he start the process by wanting to talk to others about how they use bath soap. Sure, these questions might be relevant at some point in a customer's "relationship" with his bath soap manufacturer, but the bottom line is that he wants to solve his problem first: to buy a replacement product. So the primary navigation should be to solve this problem. Only after the basic problem has been solved—that is, you've taken him to a page with bath soap selections—is it logical to start your secondary objectives of building brand loyalty and ultimately having an intelligent dialogue. Conversely, on a website for your local electric utility, you don't go to the home page to replenish electricity. For this product category, you probably do want to know something about how your electricity is made, how it's priced or a bit about the environmental attitude of the utility company. A very different solution is needed for non-e-commerce websites—addressing the most common solutions sought by visitors will be the key. Solution-based navigation is vitally important in achieving usability and ultimately loyalty; that's why I've included it as one of the critical design criteria on the following pages.

DELIVERING THE BASICS OF CUSTOMER SERVICE

Ellen Neuborne, a writer for *Business Week*, stabbed the customer service conundrum right through the heart with an article titled "It's the Service, Stupid." After the first great e-tailing Christmas in 1999, loyalty to e-commerce sites began dropping. It wasn't the Christmas experiences that drove this drop; it was driven by e-tailers who began diverting monies from service into advertising. E-commerce satisfaction rates were down because service on the Web was actually getting worse, not better. Ms. Neuborne added another interesting point: that service at bricks-and-mortar stores has been declining steadily over the past several years as well. So why is it that e-tailers aren't taking advantage of an area where traditional retailers are particularly vulnerable? It's a shopping feature that could be used to win over bricks-and-mortar customers. If e-tailers would focus on service they could turn occasional buyers into loyal customers because traditional retailers have left the door wide open. I'm not convinced that service alone will win over customers, but Ms. Neuborne is absolutely right in identifying service as a major cornerstone of e-loyalty. It's a cornerstone because service is fundamental to website usability. It's the minimum standard that must first be met before a sophisticated e-loyalty program can differentiate a website from other websites.

Just what level of customer service is the minimum standard depends on your product and industry. Customers expect a higher level of customer service when purchasing high-dollar items as opposed to low-dollar items. And when investments are the product, you can bet customers will demand a much higher interaction with customer service reps and want these reps available more hours of the day than, say, the customer service department for bath soap. So the type, the frequency and the quality of customer service depends on the product, the industry and the level of service provided by your competition. That's why one of the ten most important Web design concepts is buying as much customer service as you can afford. How much is enough? The only way to know is to talk to your customers. I wouldn't purport to know what level of service is right for your site until I had visited with a sample of your most valuable customers because much like all other design principles, developing service levels for your "average" customer will do just that: produce average results at the expense of high-value customers.

The Ten Most Important Web Design Concepts to Master for e-Loyalty

irst, I want to make it clear that I am not a graphic design artist. So if you're expecting graphic design standards, you probably have the wrong expectations of this section of the book. What I mean by e-loyalty design concepts are the basic strategies you need to use in developing design guidelines for your Web developers to ensure that all Web design stimulates customer retention. Your e-loyalty design standards should be completed long before the masters of digital art even begin to create your website. These standards are the strategy behind your website design and cover the navigation strategy, the basic usability and the degree of interactivity. In the days of traditional advertising, this might have been called "the creative brief," but only if it included the strategy behind the prescribed design. An e-loyalty design guide is a bit more substantial than a creative brief and has a longer shelf life, but should be used in a similar fashion in that it drives every navigation design decision and is used to evaluate every completed page. Website producers should use e-loyalty standards to guide all new or revised pages to ensure the customer retention strategy is integrated throughout the site.

With total website integration as the ultimate goal of an e-loyalty strategy, limiting a list to the ten most important e-loyalty design standards is next to impossible. I'm not ashamed to say that I had trouble limiting my advice to the list below. I started the process with at least one hundred or more important design points and, quite frankly, it was hell to keep taking important points off the list. So I cheated a bit and incorporated many important points under each of my ten most important design concept recommendations. Hopefully this shorter list will be more digestible and ultimately more actionable. When you're ready for additional design criteria, visit my website at www.e-loyalty.com, where other website designers and strategists have offered what they think are the most important design criteria.

Every top ten list begs to be challenged, both for the audacity of limiting advice to ten points and for thinking ten critical points can be prioritized. Even though my top ten list is not prioritized—points are listed in order of steps you take to build a relationship—I'm sure by posting a top ten list I have invited my own slew of arrows. So I want to cover myself here, and caution readers against relying on this short list as their only e-loyalty guidelines. To cover all of the important Web design concepts would require listing every major design component of a website, and my advice is that you do just that: integrate each of these e-loyalty design factors into every component of your website and use this list to test each component of your Web design. After all, integrating e-loyalty into all areas of your website should be a your ultimate design goal.

So here they are, the ten most important Web design concepts to master for e-loyalty. On the following pages I'll cover the concepts and give examples of websites that have mastered each. Since there will always be new online masters of each of the top ten critical design factors, I invite you to log onto www.e-loyalty.com and submit your own suggestions of websites that have mastered the following critical design factors, or you can play it safe and simply read what others deem to be the best. Hopefully I'll hear from readers who used this advice to become masters of e-loyalty themselves.

CRITICAL WEBSITE DESIGN FACTOR #1
MAKE YOUR FIRST IMPRESSION COUNT

Quick Tips

▨ Make the value proposition clear
▨ Ensure that your best customers see themselves in your site
▨ Make the call to action clear
▨ Recognize new visitors and offer a website tour
▨ Ensure fast page loads
▨ Exceed expectations on the first transaction

"Make your first impression count!" my mother always said. I could tell her I had a meeting with the president of the United States and her first question would be, "What are you going to wear?" Although my traditional mother with her "Southern" sensibilities may have taken this to the extreme, she was on the right track. When it comes to first impressions, the Web is no different than your first meeting with the president of the United States. You have only seconds to get this very busy person's attention and create a desire in him to stop the receiving line and have a dialogue with you. Will it depend on what you wear, or the design of your website? You bet! "Dressing" your site for a teen visitor will require an entirely different online look than "dressing" for a new mother looking for advice on bathing a newborn. And if your site is appropriately dressed and you get your first crack at that long-awaited dialogue, you better ensure it's intelligent. This means getting your visitor to the content they're expecting as quickly as possible, and presenting it in a tone and format that is perceived as "intelligent" by the visitor. You can imagine that the writing style for a new mother would not be perceived as "intelligent" by the teen visitor—how many teens think adults are intelligent, anyway? You'd be much better off letting teens talk to teens if you're looking for intelligence as defined by this rebellious subculture.

One of the questions I'm always asked is "How long do I have to make my first impressions count?" In 1998, I kept hearing people use the thirty-second rule of design. The rule held that you have thirty seconds to engage a visitor on your website: ten seconds to tell him what your site is about, ten seconds to decide if you have what he is looking for and ten seconds to connect him to what he is looking for. Today, it's the fifteen-second rule, and that's if you're lucky. I shouldn't have to remind you — but I will — that slow page loads will eat into your fifteen seconds so badly that you'll lose your golden opportunity before it begins. So if you are going to use high-intensity graphics on the home page, give users of slower modems an option to bypass the download.

But in terms of page load times, how fast is fast enough? Vincent Flanders, author of *Web Pages That Suck*, has some great advice for determining just how fast your page loads need to be. You can find his advice on his website of the same genre, www.WebSitesThatsuck.com. On his website, Vincent outlines two very simple guidelines for evaluating whether your Web page is too big, and therefore making your load time too long.

1. As you click the URL, start holding your breath. If the page is still loading when you have to gasp for air, the page is too big. Michael Willis and his fellow scuba divers and other folks who are able to hold their breath for long periods can't use this method.

2. As you parachute out of an airplane holding a wireless laptop, click the URL. When the page finishes loading, open your chute. If you crash into the earth before the page loads, the page is too big. Have your next-of-kin tell the Web designer to optimize the page further.

On a more serious note, Vincent has some practical advice for measuring page size to minimize load times. His advice is to "do what the big boys and girls do." To determine what was generally acceptable to the mass population of Web users, Vincent examined the page sizes and load times for the top ten and bottom ten of the top one hundred Web sites according to Media Metrix's August 1999 rankings. Based on this analysis, he determined that the target page size should be between 34.4K (average for the top ten) and 47.8K (average for all sites), but that it certainly would be acceptable to create a page size between 47.8K and 61.3K (average for the bottom ten sites). This is sound advice, and will make your internal arguments over page load times more objective and therefore less of a creative battle.

Even if the time allotment on the thirty-second rule is outdated, I still believe in the concept behind this rule. While sophisticated surfers may evaluate a site much faster than in thirty seconds, particularly if they've linked from another site that is holding their attention, the three priorities of the rule are still valid. In the first five seconds, visitors must "see themselves" in your site. The design must feel like a place that is inviting or intriguing. This can be particularly difficult if you have an extensive product line that targets a wide range of customer segments. In this case, you would want to navigate visitors to a "subhome page" that matches their problem set, age group or other defining characteristic as soon as possible.

Massive content sites like women.com, ESPN or IBM have to help visitors quickly cut through the thousands of pages to get to an area of the site that addresses their problems or interests as soon as possible. Women.com segments by women's life stages (students, mothers, working women, etc.). ESPN navigates you to the sport of your choice, and IBM talks to you based first on the size of your business and then on your technology needs. Once these sites lead you to the correct subhome page, they tailor content and style to match the visitor's interests. In other words, they try to bring intelligence into the dialogue as soon as possible by immediately navigating customers to an area where the website speaks their language. Once on the subhome page, they can clearly present a targeted "call to action" that solves the visitor's problem or matches his or her objective. For sites with a diverse customer base, one call to action on the home page usually doesn't "fit all."

Because Fidelity Investments has products that serve multiple audiences (customers in different life stages or income levels) it needs an initial call to action that fits all customer types, with links to subsequent, more targeted calls to action. Fidelity.com has a great solution to starting with one call to action: "We help you invest responsibly." That short sentence says it all. It differentiates the site as a teaching and investing site, it tells you they care about their customers and it creates a brand that is perceived as superior. And these messages are relevant for all customer types looking for safety in investing. The easy links to products and solutions complete the call to action. While it's a radically different message, Ameritrade also has a singularly potent call to action. Its home page only has four points to absorb: a big $8 commission sign, a log-in for customers, a new account button and a link to more information. Ameritrade is about cheap trade prices and the site wants you to open an account. The message is made strong and clear with one big dollar figure and only three actions you can take based on that message.

If customers are going to give websites only fifteen seconds for their first impression, why do websites continue to cram more and more on the home page? It certainly doesn't make their chances of meeting the new fifteen-second rule any better. I think this home page clutter is the result of the "two-click rule" taking precedent over the "fifteen-second rule." The two-click rule mandates that customers should be able to get from the home page to the product or article they are looking for in two or three clicks. While quick navigation is important, there's a thin line between faster navigation and too much to navigate on the home page. Since I've always been known as a rule breaker, it shouldn't be surprising that my advice is never to mindlessly apply either rule. Customers will forgive three clicks over two clicks to get to a product if they've maneuvered flawlessly through the process. You have to weigh "more clicks" against losing visitors who abandon your site because the navigation was too abbreviated to decipher or the navigational options per page were too deep to wade through.

Developing a home page that both achieves a great first impression and appeals to loyal, experienced customers can be difficult. Using a splash page that appears only for new customers (a cookie indicates a previous visit) and offers a newcomer tour is a great way to keep new customer sales pitches from overtaking your home page. Sure you need a logical navigation that even a newcomer can decipher, and you need some new visitor links for customers like my husband who hates to read the directions. But overall your home page should be about retaining customers. The home page should talk to them like loyal customers so they *will* become loyal customers. No website does this better than The Motley Fool (see my example at the end of this section).

The last point in making your first impression count is about exceeding expectations. Great service companies like Marriott Hotels, Virgin Airlines and Disney have lived by this standard since their inceptions. The rule is just as valid for online companies. If you have customers register for your newsletter, sending an immediate return email saying thank-you for your subscription is empty when you can exceed expectations by including the selected newsletter in the email just as quickly (this is a real pet peeve of mine). If you finally persuade a bricks-and-mortar customer to try your online site, exceed expectations by offering something special not found in his local store (special prices, new products, better service, etc.). When a new customer surfs your site, use a pop-up window to welcome him and ask if you can be of help. If a customer orders a gift certificate for a friend, send a small thank-you gift certificate to the customer to reward his recommendation to a friend. If you are shipping, get the package there faster than expected by upgrading the mode of shipping. I could go on and on, but you get the idea: in your customer's first transaction with your website, it is extremely important to exceed expectations in whatever way you can.

GREAT EXAMPLES: MOTLEY FOOL, LANDS' END AND PLANETRX

Fool.com. I could use The Motley Fool for almost every design factor in my top ten list, which is why they appear frequently in this list and throughout this book. The feature these self-professed "fools" use that I think epitomizes how to make your first impression count is the welcome splash screen and newcomer tools on MotleyFool.com. On its "New Visitor Information" link, they announce that they offer "financial advice you can actually understand," and back that up with six training segments for new investors. There's also a tour, and search help. Even the visitor registration continues building on the great first impression. From it's welcoming message, "Hello Stranger!" to its call to action, "Become a Fool," the profile request lightheartedly asks for user information and for "other foolishness" that includes where you heard about the site, your investing experience and other information.

Lands' End. I heard a marketer for Lands' End talk about her design philosophy, which is based on customer research to determine if their website exceeds expectations. What a novelty Lands' End is: they don't test for usability, they test to see if they exceeded usability. When they found that merely listing the clothing category sections (women's, men's and children's) on the vertical navigation bar wasn't meeting savvy buyers' needs, they lengthened the list to include breakouts of each clothing section. For Lands' End, their new website visitors weren't new customers, they were loyal customers who chose to buy on the Web. So exceeding these loyal customers' expectations required a different strategy than one aimed at new customers.

PlanetRx. In 2000, many first time buyers at PlanetRx were pleasantly surprised to find their orders arrive by priority shipping at no extra charge. I know *I* was surprised. But it makes lots of sense. If you're going to reward a customer with upgraded shipping, why not do it on the first order so that you exceed expectations and tie the gratification as closely as possible to the order? I also got a gift with my first order: a set of body washes that was so elaborate I thought they mistakenly included the item. Upon checking my order sheet, it noted the body wash set was a gift. The whole experience exceeded my expectations and made me feel a little less silly about ordering drugstore items by mail. I'm a loyal customer who hasn't even tried other drugstore sites because it would be hard to exceed the expectation set by my first order with PlanetRx. Do I expect every order to arrive the next day? No, but I'll always remember the first order. And guess what, that's what I tell others about. What a great retention and advocacy technique!

CRITICAL WEBSITE DESIGN FACTOR #2
MAKE IT SIMPLE TO SOLVE PROBLEMS

Quick Tips

- ▦ Base navigation on solving customer problems
- ▦ Provide a customer-centered organizational architecture
- ▦ Make page navigation tools consistent
- ▦ Embrace the two-click rule whenever possible
- ▦ Eliminate clutter
- ▦ Make sure your search engines are effective
- ▦ As customers master the Web, ensure that your site matches their increased sophistication
- ▦ Make finding products easy and buying them quick and efficient

Start by asking yourself, "What are the main problems our customers are trying to solve when they come to our website?" I doubt their problem is that "they need to buy clothes." Their problem is more likely that they don't have the right clothing to wear for the upcoming prom, board meeting or triathalon. You're solving clothing event problems—not selling pants, shirts and jackets à la carte. And even if your customer did come to your website for an à la carte shirt, you want them to leave with an outfit: a clothing solution to a problem they may not have remembered they had. Now you might argue that lots of people go to the Web with the objective just to "shop"; that is, to browse just for fun with the possibility of buying something not too far away. Most websites make unstructured browsing so unproductive that I hesitate to believe there is much of this behavior taking place. I'm more inclined to believe that all those customers "browsing" your site for fun are actually looking in vain for a solution. Even teenage girls, the ultimate "browsers," are looking to solve a problem. Either they want to look older, or slimmer or just more like everyone else. The problem they want to solve is to "fit in." Therefore, they want to solve the problem of learning "what is in style."

As a consultant, I travel too much, so I buy clothing based on its ability to resist wrinkling. Eighty percent of my closet could be wadded up on the floor, rehung and ready to wear in twenty-four hours. That's the problem I need solved: I need clothes that won't wrinkle. TravelSmith.com is the only website I know of that solely addresses and solves my problem by presenting clothes that don't wrinkle. Other sites could get a much bigger share of my wallet if they would create a solution path that caters to those of us who travel regularly.

Gosh, I make it sound simple, but there are hundreds of websites that don't seem to think so. There are usually two reasons companies think solution navigation is difficult: their website is a study in "design by committee," or their product-focused website is a mirror of their mismanaged organization, which can't seem to get customer focused. I could show you site after site that present so many navigation options on the home page that finding a solution becomes a chore for the customer. They irrationally think that if Yahoo.com is so successful with fifty links off their home page, they will be, too. After all, it doesn't cost any more to add ten additional links from the home page. The problem is that it costs them dearly in usability and ultimately loyalty. Customers don't know what they're supposed to do. Bombarded with options, they leave.

But the worst culprits of bad navigation are companies that continue to force an organizational product focus into a medium that begs for a customer focus. You know which websites I mean—their home pages list product categories rather than user paths or solutions. Product-focused organizations can be seen in many technology hardware manufacturer websites that list servers, PCs, notebooks, printers and accessories as navigational choices. For these manufacturers, bundling products at retail is their bread and butter, but it is almost impossible to bundle products on their websites. You also see a product focus in many automobile manufacturer sites that still list autos by sub-brands rather than car styles. Why don't they show us which cars would be best for a family or which car would best solve my husband's midlife crisis? We all know these are solutions that customers desire, so why not help customers solve their problems? And you know, selling more automobiles would be a great side benefit to satisfied visitors.

GREAT EXAMPLES: FRAGRANCENET, MYLIFEPATH AND CLINIQUE

FragranceNet.com. Some have criticized this site by noting that its design looks like it was developed in a high school girl's bedroom. It's simplistic, but hey, it's unbelievably simple to navigate. It quickly solves problems through both an intuitive navigation and unbelievably fast page loads made possible by that high school girl design. But because it understands high schoolers, it also assumes visitors can't spell. That's why the wrong ending "fragrance.net," the wrong spelling "fragrence.com" and even the wrong spelling and ending "fraNgrance.net" all lead you to the same great site. Smart, huh? The same "smarts" are applied to searching for products. I began a search not knowing the name of a perfume I had tried in a store. I remembered it had something to do with celestial. I searched on celestial, on moon and on stars and was pleasantly surprised that each entry located the perfume, Stars and Moons. Last, I don't want to miss mentioning the fact that Fragrancenet.com has award-winning customer service — a great fundamental upon which it is building a loyal following.

MyLifePath.com. Compare this site to other leading health information sites and you will quickly see the difference in a solution site. It first tailors solutions to you by segmenting the site by gender and age, then lists problems to be solved for each family-member category. The goal, which is to solve problems by letting consumers search on their symptoms, more closely mimics the approach consumers have toward their health. Compare this to other leading health sites that merely list diseases as a means of navigation (usually the most profitable diseases) or take the Yahoo! navigational approach to medicine by overwhelming you with medical concerns. Navigation strategies focused on diseases compound the problems of Western medicine, which rewards labeling diseases over curing them, and it is an approach more and more health-conscious individuals are moving away from. Sure there's a time for navigating by disease, and MyLifePath offers that choice too. But taking a total body approach that lets consumers help themselves makes more sense for a long-term Web relationship and therefore makes a great e-loyalty navigational strategy. MyLifePath makes it clear that you don't have to have a disease to visit, merely a health problem that needs solving. Whether it's learning about getting you through sleepless nights of baby teething or chemotherapy, it's about the whole life cycle, not just one disease. And for that reason, its navigation engenders long-term customer loyalty.

Clinique.com. Few websites have as clean a navigation as Clinique. The Clinique site is about selling product by finding your makeup solution. Clinique.com's simplicity makes both its design appealing and its navigational strategy excellent. The navigation solves basic problems: "what's new?" (for existing customers) and "which products are right for you?" (for new customers). And last spring, they helped solve seasonal problems in their offers titled "Clinique's prom guide" and "Clinique's Mother's Day gift center." Clinique was one of the first cosmetics lines to have a "diagnosis" approach to skin care, and it has developed interactive tools that keep it a leader in this personalized approach. The interactive tools help perfect the product solution. If the diagnosis doesn't solve your problem, there's easy email to its consultants on most pages. Lastly, Clinique keeps its navigation standardized across the site—offering it at the top and the bottom of pages. The navigation offers four different ways to navigate the site. So whether you're a new or a loyal customer, Clinique.com will meet your shopping preferences.

CRITICAL WEBSITE DESIGN FACTOR #3
DESIGN FOR YOUR BEST CUSTOMERS

Quick Tips

■ Design your site for your most valuable customers (MVCs), not your average customers
■ Ensure your most valuable customers see themselves in your website
■ Make MVCs feel valued and privileged
■ Organize navigation and product offerings based on what MVCs value most
■ Master a "voice" that appeals to your MVCs

I've spent a whole chapter addressing this subject of designing your site for your best customers instead of your average customers. So I won't repeat that advice here. However, I do want to remind you that designing your website for your MVC doesn't mean that you design solely for your MVC to the exclusion of your other customers. Designing for your MVC means offering a clear path for solving the problems most likely to be plaguing your MVC. So if your best customer is female, but you sell to males, too, make the path for each clear, to ensure there is a customized experience for women. Making designs generic so they will appeal to both men and women will result in a site that doesn't intrinsically appeal to either sex. The same goes for finding the right voice. If your best customers are teens and relate best to humor, don't hold back on teen comedy throughout your general website. However, if you have a profitable adult customer, or adults want to learn more about the site that their teen is frequenting, you might want to make a path for adults that spares them the teen laughs. Not only will teen humor be less amusing for adults, it's not the voice they want to hear.

There is creative expertise in talking to your best customers so they feel valued and so the benefits you offer them as MVCs appear as privileges. For example, you don't need to sell loyal customers on your products; they know them. Thanking them for their continued loyalty becomes a much more important message. You have to know when to quit selling and start thanking. Even when providing new information, the content you provide to loyal customers who are very familiar with your products will differ from that of new customers. Talking to loyal customers as if they have a beginner's level of knowledge is insulting and demonstrates that you don't know the extent of their loyalty. To be honest, few advertising or Web agencies really get this conversation right, so it will be up to you to ensure the voice in your communications is right for each level of customer familiarity. The best way to approach the difference between old customers and new customers is to think of them as friends who know you so well they can almost finish your sentences. For example, if you remind your best friend that your children are named Jamin and Julie, she will give you a funny look or will firmly announce "duh!" If you continue to remind her of your children's names each time you meet, your best friend will stop thinking of herself as a best friend, and instead as an acquaintance. It's no different with loyal customers. You need to talk to them in fewer words, with fewer basic descriptions and more in-depth coverage of features or issues. They will value the fact that you assume a basic level of knowledge and have matched their growing sophistication with your products or services. If you're afraid they won't understand, provide links to basic product descriptions.

GREAT EXAMPLES: HIFI AND HERHIFI
THIRDAGE AND MOTLEYFOOL

Hifi.com and HerHifi.com. For a brilliant example of designing for one
gender that's more valuable than the other customer, check out
Hifi.com and HerHifi.com. Hifi.com knows that men are commonly
the more valuable customer, but there is definitely a female customer
segment that will spend big dollars with a site that understands they
might buy stereos for different reasons than men. These two sites clearly
demonstrate that this company knows the importance of designing
for its best customer: stronger graphics (blocks for men/swirls for
women), deeper color palette (strong green for men/pastel greens for
women), more direct language (experienced tone for men/helpful
tone for women) and more direct navigation (product-oriented for
men/solution-solving for women). By creating two sites, it met the
needs of both groups without being condescending to women. It's
likely the website's female audience could become a much higher
value segment using a site design that caters to their needs rather than a
man's approach. Gosh, this sounds like I'm stereotyping and sexist, but
if gender didn't make a difference for websites, why would we have popular sites like women.com and iVillage that cater exclusively to
women? Even with all the flack some websites might receive, we're
going to see more and more dual websites that cater to different users,
whether it be based on gender, race, experience levels, geographic location or other differences.

ThirdAge.com. Including this website might puzzle you at first. You probably think it has already designed the site for its most valuable audience: seniors. So where's the great design technique? It's simple, too
simple to even notice. ThirdAge has designed for its MVCs by designing around the most profitable sponsors. Since computers, pets,
health, money and travel are profitable sponsor/advertiser categories,

ThirdAge developed its content areas around these topics. Building around profits not only provides ThirdAge with more profitable sponsor and advertising opportunities, it also attracts and retains visitors who are interested in these subjects—a self-fulfilling prophecy of sorts. It's a simple but profitable philosophy. And one more thing I applaud ThirdAge for: it lets seniors talk about what seniors want to talk about—sex. While others think sex is a taboo subject for seniors, ThirdAge finds it a retention topic, so it features sex-related topics prominently on the home page. It approaches sex in a mature fashion that's not available on other websites. Since the site's most frequent visitors want sex content, it gives them sex content. Whether it's sex, pet news, PC information or financial guidance, ThirdAge successfully gives its MVCs what they want most because that's how it recruited them to begin with.

Fool.com. I'll say it again, this website by The Motley Fool is my all-time favorite example for how to build e-loyalty. The Fools excel in almost every category. But designing for their best customers is something they do differently. While most financial websites are constantly in the acquisition mode by designing home pages that appeal to new customers, the Fool.com home page is designed for existing customers, and possibly even frequent customers since you need to know the Fool's "lingo" to get through some of the section titles. The site's voice is humor and familiarity. It jokes with customers as if they are old friends and insiders. For new customers, there is a splash page that appears if you don't have a cookie from the site. This onetime splash page, which appears on your first visit, provides a site tour and insight into the Fool's lingo and philosophy. For loyal customers, the site has the sound of an old and trusted friend. For those customers who are somewhere in between new and loyal, the site makes it aspirational to become an insider, to join the ranks of the "fools." Brilliant in an unassuming way, like almost every aspect of this site. Fool.com is simply one of the best.

CRITICAL WEBSITE DESIGN FACTOR #4
CREATE VALUE AND ENGENDER TRUST

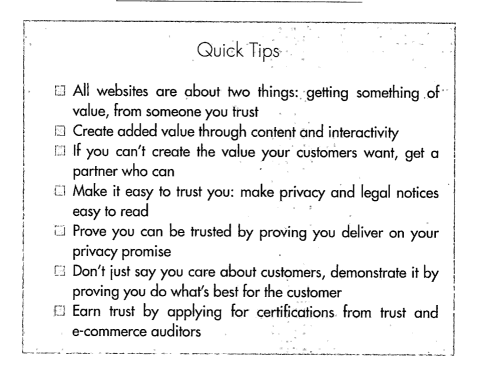

Quick Tips

☐ All websites are about two things: getting something of value, from someone you trust
☐ Create added value through content and interactivity
☐ If you can't create the value your customers want, get a partner who can
☐ Make it easy to trust you: make privacy and legal notices easy to read
☐ Prove you can be trusted by proving you deliver on your privacy promise
☐ Don't just say you care about customers, demonstrate it by proving you do what's best for the customer
☐ Earn trust by applying for certifications from trust and e-commerce auditors

Creating value is so closely tied to relevance that the two should go hand in hand. If your content is relevant, it's valuable. If your coupons are relevant to your customer's next purchase, they are more valuable. If your games are considered fun by your target audience, they will be valuable. If your partners are relevant to your target audience, then they will help you create value. Even a point program with a very "rich" redemption rate will not be of value if the award chart doesn't contain items of value. Too often I see value applied only to discounts, coupons and sales, when there are many other things your customers find valuable. You'll need to talk to them to determine how they define value. If you can't create the value your most valuable customers want, find a partner who can.

There are lots of ways to engender trust, but first you need to cover the basics of stating your privacy policy and rules for customer engagement. Much of earning trust is based on setting expectations and consistently meeting those expectations. Even websites whose business model is *not* about providing privacy (e.g., they provide some type of value in return for the right to sell names to advertisers) can earn customer trust if they establish what the nonprivacy policy is and honor the rules around this policy. The main exception to this is when you try to excuse yourself from all blame. On a major financial site, I clicked on the link to get stock quotes and was faced with a screen that wanted my acknowledgment of a screen that said, "You are accessing information provided by third parties. Company XYZ does not guarantee the accuracy, completeness or timeliness of the information presented." You can be sure I found another provider of stock quotes. I trusted the financial site less because it was willing to provide partner information that it could not endorse. This type of warning is on lots of stock quotes, but the total "disowning" of responsibility was a real trust prohibitor.

I like a website that wears its trust on the home page. Fidelity.com expresses its trust as its brand positioning that on the Web becomes the home page call to action: "We help you invest responsibly." Another website that proudly exhibits its trust factor is the website A-OK.com, a transaction-processing company. A-OK understands that trust is the core of its product, so its very first screen carries this effective trust-building message: "A-OK is an agent of trust. As such, A-OK will never sell or pass on an individual's financial or personal information without that individual's expressed permission. Ever." The firm close with "ever" really emphasizes the site's commitment to earning trust.

Building trust starts with the home page, but should be incorporated throughout the website. AmericanExpress.com does a great job of telling customers why they should trust the company with personal information by stating what it will do and will not do with each piece of information provided, right beneath each entry blank. By being up front about its intentions and not requiring customers to click through to a privacy policy (although a link to the full privacy policy is also embedded in the forms), it engenders trust by being forthright.

GREAT EXAMPLES: EBAY, PURINA AND MSN GAMEZONE

eBay.com. This is the master of online trust. I would go so far as to proclaim that the feature that holds its e-loyalty strategy together is trust. eBay uses a feature called SafeHarbor™ to group the comprehensive safety resources and customer protection services that generate trust in its site and its buyers and sellers. SafeHarbor features outstanding examples of site rules, privacy and user courtesy. But even more important are the seller-feedback databases, escrow accounts, insurance and verified sellers program. All this adds up to the most trustworthy auction site on the Web, one that has successfully held its leadership role against new competitors.

Purina.com. Before it revamped its website in early 2000, Purina used its sponsorship and involvement in top dog shows like the Westminster dog show to develop trust in its brand. The site objective appeared to be about engendering trust through the respect dog experts gave Purina. The new site tries to gain trust through empathy for dogs. Purina needs to gain respect in the dog world given that its competition continually tries to belittle grocery store brands as a source of strength. It was, and I feel still is, important for Purina to prove that its products make champions. This trust was effectively carried into its original website, which featured the world-acclaimed dog show and the various champions who were fed Purina products. While the new website still features champions raised on Purina, it no longer tries to earn trust through association. The new site design has traded in its highbrow trust for probably one of the goofiest features I've seen on the Web: pet horoscopes. It will be interesting to see how effective the new site becomes.

GameZone.com. To earn the trust of gamers, The GameZone offers what appears to be a very objective review of games. In addition to its own review of games, The GameZone features reviews by affiliates and sometimes even reviews from competitor sites. It creates value and trust by not just reviewing a game (all sites have this) but by aggregating all game reviews so visitors can make more informed decisions. This feature has an added benefit in that it overcomes one of the barriers to purchase: ability to compare. The GameZone gains the trust of visitors by demonstrating that it can be trusted to be objective in game reviews and in all its advice.

CRITICAL WEBSITE DESIGN FACTOR #5
INCLUDE FEATURES THAT START AND CONTINUE A DIALOGUE

Quick Tips

- ☐ Implement features and interactive tools that require future dialogue
- ☐ Tell your customers what to expect from each dialogue tool you offer
- ☐ Reward customers for starting the dialogue by offering rewards for profiling
- ☐ Respond to customers as quickly as possible to keep the dialogue going
- ☐ Personalize as much as you can afford to in order to create an intelligent dialogue
- ☐ Ensure that the dialogue progresses at the customer's pace

---

In part 2 of this book, I outline how you can persuade your customers to want a relationship. Well, this design factor is the companion to that strategy. In order to persuade customers to communicate and have a relationship, you need to provide tools to make starting the dialogue easy. These tools could include reminder services, new product sale notices, email newsletters, contests with notices that include contest answers and winners, wish lists with availability notices or a membership program that includes multiple opportunities for dialogue. Regardless of the tool selected, you need to tell customers what they can expect from the dialogue, which can be contained with your privacy and permission marketing statements, but probably should be reiterated at time of sign-up.

Once you have the dialogue started, you need to deliver as quickly as possible. At a minimum, you'll need to verify sign-up in an auto-reply email. But don't send an "empty" welcome email. Make the first dialogue memorable by providing something of value—an interesting fact, a reprinted copy of your most popular newsletter or a discount coupon of some type. I think the unexpected reward is particularly valuable, but I don't agree with promoting the sign-up by offering a reward unless the reward is more of what your site offers. If you offer content, give content. If you offer discounts, give a discount. I don't believe in unrelated promotions such as points in a major point program unless it's part of your ongoing customer experience, because the unrelated nature of the reward attracts nontargeted customers. You have to be careful with sign-up incentives. Bribing customers to start a dialogue they don't want to have will do nothing more than clutter your database. On the other hand, rewarding them with what the program offers as its core content is an excellent acquisition tool because customers value the content. Garden.com is a great example of this type of discipline. Garden.com's registered user base is probably smaller than you'd expect, but the list is highly valuable and active. If your website offers points for each article read or for each dollar spent, then offering points for sign-ups is entirely appropriate and offers a great opportunity to get a program currency balance started.

You need to ensure that the dialogue exchange progresses at the customer's pace. I like communication options. For example, offer customers a daily, weekly or biweekly communication program. As customers become familiar with the weekly program, remind them of the daily program and make it easy to change their communication preferences. Just like human relationships, we typically want to take it slow until we're sure that we are going to like this relationship. If you ease into the relationship and respect customers during the "dating" stage, they will be more likely to say "yes" when you're ready to ask for an "engagement" commitment.

GREAT EXAMPLES: YAHOO!, AMERICAN AIRLINES/ TRAVELOCITY AND AMAZON

Yahoo.com. This site probably has more dialogue starters than any site I know of. Between birthday reminders, stock alerts, all types of newsletters, chat topics and more, Yahoo! initiates and keeps the dialogue flowing between its server and millions of users every week.

AA.com/Travelocity.com. Both of these websites have mastered the ongoing intelligent dialogue. American Airlines was one of the first companies in any industry to send weekly email alerts that customers couldn't wait to receive. The weekly AASpecials featured bargains not available anywhere else. Travelocity.com, a subsidiary of American Airlines, now has fare minders that alert customers when a fare drops to a designated level or when a flight has been altered. Its new service, which pages customers regarding changed flight plans and offers to amend travel plans, will continue to make the company a leader in intelligent dialogues.

Amazon.com. This site is probably the king of dialogue and Oprah is the queen communicator on the site (she now appears on other sites, including her own Oxygen network, but her book club was made famous on Amazon). Many people have reported that one of the things that makes Oprah so successful is that she doesn't "act"; she's just as genuine on her television show as she is in real life. Her book club reflects this honesty and is a shining example of making digital relationships more human. She talks to her club members like they were members of her personal book circle, and the club responds to readers in a human way. The language, the pace and the style of communication all mimic a small, personal book circle and your personal relationship with its founder.

CRITICAL WEBSITE DESIGN FACTOR #6:
SEIZE EVERY OPPORTUNITY TO BUILD COMMUNITY

Quick Tips

☐ Include links to your communities throughout your site
☐ Create controversial content that generates discussion among visitors
☐ Use partners to enhance community
☐ Enhance the value in community participation by using moderators
☐ Make participation anonymous
☐ Use emails to drive participation in communities
☐ Create an inviting meeting place, not a stale bulletin board
☐ Make it easy to interact with the site and other visitors
☐ Give meaning to the community exchange with moderated discussions
☐ Localize the experience geographically when possible

GREAT EXAMPLES: SIEBEL SYSTEMS' SALES, WOMEN,
ETRADE, SMARTGIRL AND TALKCITY

Sales.com. Siebel Systems was too good at building community—so good, they spun off the site into a stand-alone business. Sales.com is a website where sales reps of all types go to make their days more productive, to gather information and to share leads with other sales reps. The site was and still is a huge success and a textbook model for building community. The site started as Siebel's relationship-building tool and turned into a self-standing community of its own that sells memberships to a premium community experience. The site itself is a community in that members drive much of the content. It has every tool a perfect business community should have: personalized pages, newsletters, chat rooms, bulletin boards, resource rooms, shared job postings, virtual meeting rooms, travel alerts, networking opportunities, reminder services and more. It has become the daily meeting place for sales reps who want to better manage their sales and their careers. It is unequivocally the best community I've seen in the business world.

e*Trade.com. This site is a great balance of community and e-commerce. The site is definitely about trading, but the community features bring it more depth and even a little fun. e*Trade's "The Hub" offers predictable community techniques that aren't predictable at all. Bulletin boards are segmented into ongoing boards that center around investors' life stages, investing topics and market areas, but it keeps other boards more timely by having daily stock chat topics and daily news topics. There are also live events that give members the perception of privileged "access" to financial movers and shakers. Last, but not least, e*Trade has developed its own type of fun that can compete with the likes of The Motley Fool. e*Trade has raised investment game play to an art. It has an ongoing investment game to see who can make the most with $100,000 of virtual money, but its seasonal games tied to events like basketball's March Madness is the stuff great publicity is made of. e*Trade demonstrates great balance, which is absent in many sites, as in the case where you keep wishing those pesky "buy here" buttons would get out of the way of the content. e*Trade does a great job at keeping trading its focus.

Women.com. This site is a leader in community building. While the conversation topics on this site have been the target of some overly intellectual critique, the fact is that women.com members love the interaction, build community fast and trust women.com to keep bringing them closer together. One of the simple but effective techniques women.com uses is "What Do You Think?" links from articles that lead to short surveys. A few days later, the site posts notices about "Here's What You Said" and the survey results along with some comments are shared with the community. Here's an example I recently saw on women.com. The article was titled "Women.com visitors share their favorite singles spots." At the end of the article it provided the opportunity to "send this page to a friend" or connect to the related bulletin board to see what others' suggestions were for best places to meet singles. A funny point, though. There are quite a few men who have figured out that women.com is a great place to meet women and this particular bulletin board had several men soliciting ideas on where to meet women based on where women like to look. People love to know how their opinions stack up against others, and women.com provides many opportunities for women to share and compare.

Smartgirl.com. SmartGirl is a website for girls, by girls. It is the ultimate in community in that its members not only drive the content, they write a good part of it. And good writing is rewarded by being an entry requirement for submissions to SmartGirl—a sort of rite of passage to becoming a "smartgirl." Sure, other chat sites have members contribute content, but on SmartGirls.com the content carries a more permanent feel because the posting of articles is made to look like a girl's own Web page. The site also has many opportunities to participate in chats and contests and other interactive community events, but creating content is what builds the uniqueness behind this site and is what ultimately attracts the target audience: "smartgirls."

TalkCity.com. I have TalkCity on my list because it does a great job of moderating chat. I have always thought chat for the sake of chat didn't really provide much value. The value comes in the form of skilled moderators with expert knowledge. One of the reasons TalkCity has such robust chat participation is its MyPoints program rewards participation. This would not be the right approach for most chat rooms, but since TalkCity's business model is really about research, versus merely hosting chat, stimulating participation with points is a smart idea and works well.

CRITICAL WEBSITE DESIGN FACTOR #7: DELIVER ALL PARTS OF THE SALES CYCLE OR SUBJECT COVERED

Quick Tips

- Provide more than just the information on your products
- Create an expert knowledge base in your field
- Provide comparison points for shopping
- Make it easy to buy as well as return goods
- Sell auxiliary or peripheral items that complete the experience/product
- Extend the relationship by enhancing the ownership experience

To be loyal to an e-commerce site or special topic content site, the customer needs to be able to fulfill the full range of activities and transactions as well as find all associated information. If you're a bird-watcher, you don't want to go to a store that sells only bird feed. You want to see new bird feeders, buy books on identifying birds, have an expert advise you on your bird feeder issues and ultimately be able to share a tale or two about birds you recently saw. To do this would require delivering on all parts of the sales cycle of bird feeders. This is an important point in building deeper and more lasting relationships. You have to provide the full cycle so your customers don't go elsewhere to fulfill the missing link in your sales cycle, and be scooped up by the competition. It's the same with business-to-business sales cycles. No where is it more obvious than in the technology hardware arena. Technology manufacturers are finding that their customers not only want one-stop shopping for the full sales cycle around hardware (e.g., information, installation, software, service, training and consulting) but that the business is more profitable when it provides the higher-margin services that were once considered outside the hardware sale. Sure it took Lou Gerstner, CEO of IBM, six years to offer a full basket of products and services, but it's far easier in other industries to license products, hire experts and even partner to offer a full sales cycle.

Customer research keeps finding that one of the main reasons customers abandon shopping carts is because they can't compare products. But it's not just about price comparison. Whether comparing specifications on a printer, the style and color of two sweaters or the delivery schedules on raw materials, customers need to compare so they feel as though they are making the most informed decision possible. This goes double for women, who as a group tend to value comparison shopping even more than men. Why not make side-by-side product comparisons available on your site using a split-screen or pop-up box approach? And if your site is all about low prices, use comparison pricing or price guarantees to build your price leadership position at the same time you close more sales because customers can compare prices.

Never underestimate the post-sale part of the sales cycle. Too often the relationship stops with the close of a sale, particularly with infrequently purchased items. A post-product dialogue with your customers can be an opportunity for reinforcing the purchase and enhancing the experience by providing information on how customers can get more value out of your products and services. For example, even if your site revolves around content like health issues, maintaining a relationship after the illness has been cured is important for keeping your site top of mind for future illnesses. To reach healthy people, keep the dialogue open with wellness advice and nutrition information. Maintaining a dialogue that enhances the product will also keep the communication channels open so you will know when it's appropriate to start selling the repurchase. But the post-sale content must be valuable and must also be genuine. Customers easily see through thinly veiled newsletters that operate on the objective of collecting customer data rather than providing high-value content.

GREAT EXAMPLES: DAIMLERCHRYSLER, ROLLERBLADE AND TRAVELSMITH

Jeep.com. Jeep is the only auto website that devotes more space to post purchase than new purchase. Jeep understands that Jeep buyers are focused
on the post-purchase experience. I don't mean service issues or gas
mileage (although service is delivered on the site), but rather the way
their vehicles make them feel after the purchase, when they join in the
Jeep owner events. The site focuses on Jeep news, jamborees, Camp Jeep,
concept cars and other Jeep content. On the home page, all parts of the
sales cycle are covered, but six of the nine links are about post-purchase
experience. And there is a "World of Jeep" page that takes customers further into the Jeep legacy than most automakers even remember. Jeep
knows that their vehicle is about post-purchase thrill and the other Jeep
owners with whom they are immediately associated. Sure, you could
argue that luxury cars are about the owner image of prestige, but the Jeep
site takes it one step further by making its offline events like Jeep Jamboree and Camp Jeep into virtual events that all owners can feel a part of.
Most people would probably say Saturn does a better job of building post-
purchase community and product enhancement, but go to the Saturn
home page and you'll see it is definitely about selling, selling, selling.

Rollerblade.com. This site does a great job of getting me right into a pair
of rollerblades, feeling the wind in my hair, telling me exactly what
the next steps are in the adventure and in product upgrades. It also
demonstrates that it's a great post-sale source for blade repair advice
and best skating paths. But just when I'm committed to buying, it
drops the most important part of the sales cycle. It doesn't offer online
sales, something we could forgive if the channel conflict was too
rough, but the dealer locator offers only four locations in the United
States, three of which are in California. I have to call an 800 number
to get more dealers, but given the website dealer list, my expectations
aren't good. The site doesn't engender any type of loyalty or retention
because it can't deliver on the most important part of the sales process.

TravelSmith.com. This site sells travel clothes, but it also covers a wide range of information about being best prepared for any type of traveling. Better yet, it matches clothes, luggage, equipment and travel tips based on the type of traveling you're going to do. The site covers every angle around travel clothes by helping you with climate forecasts, clothing customs, destination tips, minimizing a travel wardrobe, packing and even your reentry through immigration. It also offers travel gadgets, luggage, books and other items that enhance a trip or make travel more bearable for frequent business trips. If that's not enough, it compares its products, one against the other, for various packing, itinerary and climate conditions. The site understands that serious travelers want a one-stop shop for advice and clothes they can trust to travel well. And the sales cycle ends with an unconditional guarantee to refund any purchase if the clothes did not meet your expectations on the trip—no questions asked. With the exception of actually buying airfare and hotels (which a good partner could provide), this site is truly the full service travel planner for visitors who have a trip for which they want the best possible experience.

CRITICAL WEBSITE DESIGN FACTOR #8
PROVIDE THE BEST SERVICE YOU CAN AFFORD

Quick Tips

- ▨ Make service easily accessible
- ▨ Anticipate customer problems or needs
- ▨ Provide the tools so customers can help themselves
- ▨ Offer service 24/7 and live whenever possible
- ▨ Where appropriate, offer personal service representatives
- ▨ Make return policies easy to use

Customer service used to revolve around the call center, but it is no longer the epicenter of customer service, at least not for e-businesses. E-customers have high expectations for choice of contact media, timeliness and quality of help that are only getting higher as the Web makes customers expect customization, demand speed and reserve loyalty for only those sites which provide content and service in the format they prefer or that best serves them. Customers' growing power is changing the rules and the standards for customers' service. Sites that earn customer loyalty will have to help customers via their chosen medium, at their pace, and when its most convenient for them. The traditional focus and customer service measurements on minimum time with customers must be expanded to incorporate how satisfied a customer was with the total delivery of the service.

And just to make things more complicated, customers will also want one customer service contact for all issues with your company. That means if a customer wants to email you at your website about a bricks-and-mortar transaction, you will be able to help him or her, and vice versa for online purchase complaints aimed at bricks-and-mortar store managers. The customer sees one company with multiple outlets, but he will expect them to act as one.

Given enough profit margin, all sites would offer customers the best service available, and in a perfect world there would be live links to customer service from every website. We might get there in the near future, but until then, you'll need to offer the best service you can afford. However, in very competitive situations, like online toy sales, your best had better meet the market standards or you won't last long. So offering the best service you can afford assumes you at least offer service that is equal to or better than your competition. Offering the best service you can afford is frequently a trade-off between quality and quantity of customers served, or between timeliness and medium used. In order to offer the type of quality service your MVCs demand, you may have to limit how many customers receive premium services in order to manage your service expenses. This is where providing less costly online tools that allow customers to help themselves will make a significant difference. Customers have come to expect that immediate response times to service inquiries is unlikely with many companies or unlikely due to a low price. This expectation of slow service actually inspires customers to help themselves by tackling easier problems using friendly and fast online diagnostic and service tools. Making self-help tools easy to locate and use will encourage this behavior. However, if timeliness is required to retain your best customers, you may have to discontinue some traditional phone service for low-value customers in favor of faster email service that requires fewer service reps. Email service can take advantage of prewritten service responses to save time and can even make it possible to manage two live customers simultaneously.

While I think it is entirely appropriate to provide service that is commensurate with the value of a customer (in terms of profit or advocacy), it is important that you are clear as to your policies for providing various levels of service. Customers must understand that the differentiated service levels are based on fair practices. I always fall back on the airlines for the best examples of treating best customers best. In no other industry are the various levels of service more obvious to customers than in an airline terminal. The airlines' best customers, gold and platinum customers, go through shorter lines, get earlier sign-ups for upgrades, board earlier and receive other seemingly coincidental benefits like free liquor when the attendants have limited change, and hotel vouchers when planes don't connect. Infrequent customers tolerate this discrimination because they know that frequent travelers have earned their privileges and because the airline ensures that the nonfrequent travelers get a satisfactory level of service. The point is that your frequent or MVCs must earn the service privileges through an objective process that is made public and that your service for all other customers must be satisfactory. Otherwise, disparities in service will impact customer satisfaction at all levels. As is the case with many techniques for treating best customers best, these programs work best when they have formal names and standards for membership. Through this formalized process, there is no mistaking the intentions and the requirements, and the program can be used as an incentive to which customers can aspire.

GREAT EXAMPLES: THE GAP, FIDELITY AND TOYSRUS

Gap.com. The Gap online gets a gold star for anticipating when customers need help. For example, the bottom of its women's jeans page carries a message that reads, "Need help finding the right pair?" When the new window pops up, it's not about shoes or all the other items the Gap sells, it's solely about finding the best-fitting jeans. Your first goal is to find the right size, but the Gap knows it's not just about size, so it simultaneously offers to help you "find the right fit," "find the right wash" and even lets you "compare fits." This anticipation of customer needs makes this website's service stand out.

Fidelity.com. Fidelity doesn't provide its highest level of service on the Web to all its customers, because to do so would be unprofitable. But it does provide as much service as is reasonable given a customer's value. I'm sure if Fidelity's management wasn't as stringent on investment returns, it might cut into investor returns and provide every customer with a personal planner. But Fidelity knows that personal attention costs more money. So Fidelity's service programs are based upon the amount of money a customer has invested with Fidelity. Its premium customers get preferred services. It doesn't advertise this disparity in service levels, in fact, its regular service is called "gold" service. But if you are a high-value customer, you can be sure you'll be made aware of the many additional services you can take advantage of from Fidelity.

Toysrus.com Toys 'R' Us has responsive 24/7 service and helps customers by both email and phone. However, where it really stands out in the service category is in bridging the gap between e-commerce and bricks-and-mortar sales, as a means of defending its market share against e-tailing newcomers like e-Toys. Toys 'R' Us allows customers to return e-purchases at local stores. Likewise, the online customer service department can tell you whether its retail stores carry an item that the website is out of or doesn't carry. The customer can choose his or her preferred method of resolving problems.

CRITICAL WEBSITE DESIGN FACTOR #9
MAKE IT EASY TO RECOMMEND YOUR SITE

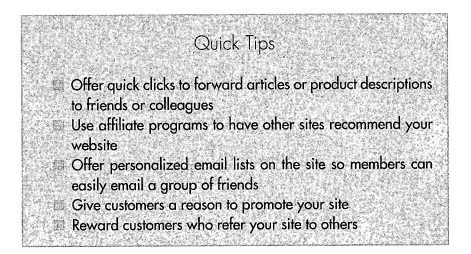

Quick Tips

- Offer quick clicks to forward articles or product descriptions to friends or colleagues
- Use affiliate programs to have other sites recommend your website
- Offer personalized email lists on the site so members can easily email a group of friends
- Give customers a reason to promote your site
- Reward customers who refer your site to others

This design factor is easy to describe and easy to understand: add tools to your site that make it easy for visitors to recommend your site to others. So why do so many sites miss this opportunity? It's as simple as posting an email link to every article that says, "Email this to a friend." Or you can get more creative on clothing sites and let visitors forward "dream closets" with the clothes they want for Christmas, or buttons that let visitors forward a particular item to friends with their choice of queries: "Would this look good on me?" "Do you think it's cute?" "Would chicks dig this?" or the all-time favorite, "Does this make my butt look big?" Make referring your site easy and fun, and it's more likely to be referred.

One of the areas many websites overlook is the importance of gift certificates to their website. Sending a gift certificate is the ultimate referral, so why not thank every gift certificate purchase with a reward? One obvious reward is to send a token gift or a dollars-off coupon to a gift purchaser. But you could also reward the buyer by making the gift certificate of greater value by shipping it within a gift itself. Victoria's Secret shipped gift certificates in elaborate fabric-covered boxes one year. Toy companies could send gift certificates in a small candy-filled container for a little immediate gratification. I've often wondered why cosmetics companies don't give away their tote bags and samples with every gift certificate instead of limiting trial samples to customers who have already tried the product. Use your imagination; come up with a clever idea for delivering your gift certificates, and make them of greater value to your buyers and your new customers.

Many sites ask registering visitors to tell them who recommended the site to them. Do these sites then send thank-you rewards? I doubt it, but I would hope so. If the reward was valuable enough, you can be sure the site would be actively recommended in the future. The other way to reward referrals is with affiliate programs. Affiliate programs are formalized programs that pay websites for all the links from their site to the referred site. The payments can be a fixed rate per click through, but more frequently they are a percentage of the referred visitors' first purchases and often a percentage of a preset number of future purchase transactions.

GREAT EXAMPLES: CLICKZ, UPROAR, CBS SPORTSLINE AND ASKME/TRIPOD

ClickZ.com. This online marketing magazine (e-zine) was probably one of the first sites to make sending articles to a friend easy. At the bottom or top of every article is a link to email the article to a friend. One tip to increase usage of these automatic emails is to ensure that you won't use the email address of any recipient.

Uproar.com. Game sites have lots of creative ways to have their customers recommend their sites, since many games require multiple players. Letting players send invitations to private game rooms or private tournaments can be a very effective way to use existing customers to recruit new customers. Uproar also optimizes player-get-player programs by using an affiliate program that lets affiliates put the game "Trivia Blitz" on their own site while Uproar pays for the players. Uproar has various versions of the game to make it more relevant (classic, sports, entertainment, etc.). The member-get-member tactic is very successful because the game is targeted and because it's so easy to load onto a website.

Sportsline.com. This sports site is big on rewards, and if you pay attention, you'll notice that many of its promotions, prizes and contests feature awards that require group play, to be enjoyed. Pizza parties are big, as are trips for you and your buddies to a game. The strategic finesse here is that to enjoy your prize, you have to become an evangelist for the site. And who better to recruit new visitors than a happy winner? But CBS Sportsline could go one step further. I've always thought it could launch a successful visitor-get-visitor program by capitalizing on the way we all love to razz our friends when our favorite team beats theirs. Why not provide funny animated greetings sent by email from the site that contain the final score and a poetic jab that really gives it to your archrival team?

Askme.com/Tripod.com. These sites have raised community evangelism to an art form. Customers are given the tools and hosting mechanism for building their own personal Web site and placing it within a directory of topics on the site. Through this process, customers develop approximately 90 percent of the content on the hosting site. The host site rewards customer websites based on how much traffic is driven to their personal websites (essentially sharing a portion of ad revenues with the customers). These sites rely on customers both to create content and to

drive traffic to the site. They only step customers don't help with is selling advertising, and these sites will probably have mastered that by the
time this book hits the shelves.

CRITICAL WEBSITE DESIGN FACTOR #10
CREATE AN OPPORTUNITY COST FOR DEFECTION

Quick Tips

- Offer personalization that gets smarter with use
- Offer points and unique rewards
- Use access to make the experience unique
- Deliver on a value point better than all your competitors
- Create best-customer exclusives like service, free shipping,
  advance notices, etc.

If you've ever heard me give a seminar on e-loyalty, you've heard me
mention this last critical design factor over and over again. Creating an
opportunity cost may be easy to understand, but it's hard to implement
well. The difficulty lies not only in the ability to create a compelling reason to return, but also in creating a program that your competition can't
easily match. I discussed the strategy behind creating an opportunity cost
in Step 5 of the section titled Seven Steps to Designing an e-Loyalty Strategy, so I won't repeat the strategic aspects in this section. However, I do
want to cover several examples because this concept can be implemented
so many different ways that getting creative with a basic benefit can be
the basis for a great opportunity cost concept.

GREAT EXAMPLES: EBAY, CBS SPORTSLINE, SIEBEL SYSTEMS SALES AND AMAZON

eBay.com. I have to list eBay's SafeHarbor™ again as a great example, but this time, it earns its honors because it is one of the most unusual types of opportunity cost on the Web, and one of the most effective to boot. The website uses a feature called the Feedback Forum to create an opportunity cost for sellers who defect to other auction sites. On Feedback Forum customers post their experiences with the seller and, in turn, sellers use this feedback to demand higher prices or just more frequent bidding as "proven" or "trusted" sellers. If a seller decides to defect to another auction site, he or she will have to start from scratch in building feedback, and that could cost some higher bids. Sure the Feedback Forum stimulates buyers, too, since more will bid if they trust the sellers, but the real value comes in retaining sellers—for without sellers, eBay would have no buyers. With auction applications popping up on lots of sites, it provides eBay with a very effective mechanism for creating an opportunity cost for defecting to other auction sites.

Sportsline.com. Sportsline has successfully implemented a point program that creates an opportunity cost for defection that its competition is having trouble competing with. One of the most important techniques behind its program is the use of awards that cost little or nothing to acquire, but which have huge perceived values for sports fans. The awards let members chat online with a sports celebrity, keep an autographed ball, attend an interview with an MVP, ask their favorite pro athlete a question and participate in many other unique online experiences. As you can see, the value is enormous to the right fan, but for Sportsline.com the award is merely a fuller use of its press privileges, which permits access to sports stars. These unique awards are also smart because the clout necessary to attract sports stars to participate in these award experiences is difficult for most competitors other than ESPN to match. But ESPN will likely drag its feet before matching the program, because ESPN has always prided itself on being unique in the sports scene. Copying these very unique awards would be too obvious a move, one ESPN would avoid unless no other alternatives seem available.

Sales.com. The reason behind Siebel's online community success with sales reps is also the reason why visitors don't want to defect. Sales.com's major customer feature is a sales lead management tool that creates a powerful opportunity cost. Once the sales rep enters his lead information and calendar, the tools make tracking leads a breeze, and offer company briefings to prepare reps for sales calls. Not only is this one of the best tools in the business and free for entry-level management resources, but the fact that sales reps enter data that cannot be automatically downloaded into a different software or website makes the opportunity cost for defection very high.

Amazon.com. Amazon has spent a lot of money and toiled long hours to deserve the opportunity cost it creates with its personalized programs that recommend books for readers, music for musicians and toys for children of various ages. Because its powerful recommendation system uses collaborative filtering to make suggestions better and better with use, customers see the feature as an opportunity cost for defecting. They like the recommendations they get (particularly for CDs) and don't want to start all over again from scratch, building a database on a competitor's site.

PART

Final Thoughts

The e-Loyalty Process Shouldn't Be Overwhelming

At this point, I have covered so many e-loyalty requirements, tips and critical success requirements that you may be second-guessing your ability to really tackle this e-loyalty animal by yourself. But it really isn't as complicated as it seems. What I've laid out in this book are guidelines to building a number of different kinds of e-loyalty strategies, but to be really effective at engendering loyalty you need to pick one major e-loyalty strategy and limit the number of relationship-building tools you implement. Your ability to focus on one killer brand-defining e-loyalty program strategy is what will make your site successful—not a myriad of average or "me too" customer programs. But regardless of which e-loyalty strategy you select, you'll still want to tackle the development process using the seven steps to creating an e-loyalty strategy that I've listed here and which are discussed in part 2.

Step 1: Clearly Establish Your Goals and Objectives
Step 2: Identify the Customers You Want to be Loyal
Step 3: Develop Your Website Around an Intelligent Dialogue
Step 4: Design Your Website for Your Most Valuable Customers, Not Your Average Customers
Step 5: Formalize an E-loyality Program for Your Most Valuable Customers
Step 6: Persuade Your Customers to Want a Relationship.
Step 7: Constantly Improve E-loyalty by Listening and Measuring

But even the greatest e-loyalty strategy won't make you the next Bill Gates without a well-crafted implementation plan, directed by conscientious team players. The implementation guidelines I presented in part 3 will be your template for making a successful implementation a reality. The implementation steps that follow should be your focus.

Step 1: Develop and Test e-Loyalty Concepts to Finalize Your
    e-Loyalty Strategy
Step 2: Develop an Initial Business Case to Test the Details of Your
    Program Concept
Step 3: Create a Customer Contact Plan
Step 4: Develop a Partner Strategy
Step 5: Determine Resources Required, Best Sources and Associated
    Costs
Step 6: Finalize the Program Forecasts and Budget
Step 7: Adopt an Extended ROI to Justify and Defend Your Budget
Step 8: Develop a Plan for Measuring Success
Step 9: Develop a Viable Timeline with Implementation Leaders

In most dot com start-ups, there isn't much time for politicking and infighting because everything moves so fast. So your challenges will likely be limited to not enough time or money. Those of you in larger companies have some of these same challenges, but layered on top are the challenges of internal bureaucracy. Regardless of company size, you'll benefit from getting a "heads up" on the biggest challenges you'll face. My suggestions for tackling these challenges are outlined in part 3.

Challenge #1: Integrating e-Loyalty and Adopting It as a Business
    Goal
Challenge #2: Gaining Consensus and Garnering Support
Challenge #3: Maintaining a Customer Lifetime Value Focus
Challenge #4: Appropriating the Funding and Resources Required

And I never want to forget the Web designers, because without creative talent and technological strength most e-loyalty programs would fall flat on their faces. Web design is truly the "art" of e-loyalty. In creating a "look and feel" that engenders the e-loyalty you're striving for, I encourage you to remember the following Web design factors detailed in part 4.

Design Factor #1: Make Your First Impression Count
Design Factor #2: Make It Simple to Solve Problems
Design Factor #3: Design for Your Best Customers
Design Factor #4: Create Value and Engender Trust
Design Factor #5: Include Features That Start and Continue a Dialogue
Design Factor #6: Seize Every Opportunity to Build Community
Design Factor #7: Deliver All Parts of the Sales Cycle or Subject Covered
Design Factor #8: Provide the Best Service You Can Afford
Design Factor #9: Make It Easy to Recommend Your Site
Design Factor #10: Create an Opportunity Cost for Defection

Resources to Get You Started

There are so many great sources of ideas for creating or enhancing your e-loyalty program that I wanted to list some of them here. These are websites that I use to find new ideas, keep up with the latest software developments and monitor laws that have ramifications for all our e-loyalty programs and relationship-building practices. I recommend the following websites, but to get the most current list you'll need to log onto the website for this book at www.e-loyalty.com.

www.1to1.com
www.1to1web.com
www.accelerating1to1.com
www.business2.com
www.businessweek.com
www.channelseven.com
www.clickz.com

www.cluetrain.com
www.connectingonline.com
www.crm-forum.com
www.cyberatlas.com
www.cyberdialogue.com
www.directmarketing-online.com
www.dbmarketing.com
www.emarketer.com
www.esomar.nl/codes_and_guidelines.html
www.forkinthehead.com
www.forrester.com
www.ftc.gov/bcp/conline/pubs/buspubs/coppa.htm
www.iconocast.com
www.idg.com
www.inc.com
www.infoweek.com
www.internet.com
www.internetnews.com
www.internetweek.com
www.jup.com
www.marketingtips.com
www.marketingwise.com
www.microscope.com
www.netmarketing.com
www.netb2b.com
www.olaf.net
www.personalization.com
www.relationshipmarketing.com
www.redherring.com
www.relationshipmktg.com
www.rmstrategies.com
www.salon.com
www.senate.gov/~murkowski/commercialemail/

www.techweb.com
www.thestandard.com
www.truste.org
www.upside.com
www.useit.com
www.webreview.com
www.wired.com
www.zdnet.com

The e-Loyalty Website as a Resource

ecause the lead time required for publishing a book through the offline publishing industry still requires almost a full year, some of the advice and resources in this book will become dated. That's why I've created a companion website for this book at www.e-loyalty.com. At this website you will find updated information on vendors who can help implement your e-loyalty program and modeling tools to help build program forecasts and budgets. You'll also find articles by other e-loyalty experts that will help stimulate your creative planning process and provide invaluable tips for enhancing your e-loyalty efforts. There are even submissions by readers like you who came up with an idea that others can learn from. And if you want to hear more of my advice on e-loyalty, you can sign up for my monthly newsletter. Or if you want some one-on-one advice, you can contact me through the website as well.

So keep your investment in this book growing by logging on to www.e-loyalty.com and hopefully we'll stimulate each other's minds with an intelligent dialogue or two.

See you on the Web!

The Future of e-Loyalty

P redicting the future of e-loyalty is not that difficult if you keep in mind that human relationships and online customer relationships are pretty consistent in their development, needs and expectations. There's a life cycle to the relationship-building process, and the Web is merely expediting this process for hundreds of websites. So, in thinking about the future, think in terms of how your own expectations of relationships have changed over the years. As elementary school kids, we didn't know we weren't all the same, but by junior high school we floated from social group to social group trying to discover our friends and eventually ourselves. As aggressive businessmen and women, we worked to build relationships that helped us succeed. And finally, now that we are comfortable with who we are and what we've accomplished, we merely look for relationships that mirror who we are and that make us feel comfortable. It isn't that big of a stretch to apply this unsophisticated relationship development process to the Web. The Web will go through various changes as its users' Internet sophistication increases and their available time diminishes. Ultimately, we will trust online transactions more, rely on them more and ease into a lifestyle that is driven by our Internet interactions. Website features, business models and customer loyalty programs will all change to accommodate users' changing needs and expectations.

Given this theory that Web relationships mimic human relationships, the future for websites that want to build e-loyalty with sophisticated users will require them to focus on microrelationships that offer visitors finely tuned images of themselves. This means that just about the time you've perfected e-loyalty for your general site, you'll be needing to granularize that strategy to mirror each of your target customer groups. It could mean microwebsites or minisites within your current website. But consumers and businesses alike are going to demand that websites have *exactly* what they are looking for, not a variation on it. It's the beauty of Web technology, eventually coming back to haunt us. Because to perfect these microsites will not only require more and more personalization technology and more and more staff, it will also mean that you must have customer experts to guide each of your microsites. Future loyalty strategy documents will be divided into segments such as e-loyalty for women or e-loyalty for Latino women or even e-loyalty for young professional Latino women.

A more demanding customer who wants everything personalized will also be more loyal to sites that use formats and mediums that match his lifestyle and personal technology. So be prepared to communicate with your customers via mail, email, instant message, page and abbreviated website views that can be accommodated by the many different handheld electronic devices that will infiltrate our daily lives.

So, for the last time in this book, I'll refer you to the supporting website, www.e-loyalty.com, because this new frontier of e-loyalty specialties will be explored there and you won't want to be left behind.

Index